Optimization and
Variation Reduction
in Quality

Other McGraw-Hill Quality Control Books of Interest

Optimization and Variation Reduction in Quality

Wayne A. Taylor

Sponsored by the American Society for Quality Control

McGraw-Hill, Inc.
New York   St. Louis   San Francisco   Auckland   Bogotá
Caracas   Lisbon   London   Madrid   Mexico   Milan
Montreal   New Delhi   Paris   San Juan   São Paulo
Singapore   Sydney   Tokyo   Toronto

Library of Congress Cataloging-in-Publication Data

Taylor, Wayne A.
    Optimization and variation reduction in quality / Wayne A. Taylor
; sponsored by the American Society for Quality Control.
    p.   cm.
    ISBN 0-07-063255-3
    1. Quality control-Statistical methods.   2. Taguchi methods
(Quality control)   3. Process control—Statistical methods.
I. American Society for Quality Control.   II. Title.
TS156.T39 1991
658.5′62′015195—dc20   91-8121
                                                               CIP

1 2 3 4 5 6 7 8 9 0   DOC/DOC   9 7 6 5 4 3 2 1

ISBN 0-07-063255-3

*The sponsoring editor for this book was Gail Nalven, the editing
supervisor was Kimberly A. Goff, and the production supervisor was
Donald Schmidt. This book was set in Century Schoolbook. It was
composed by McGraw-Hill's Professional Publishing composition unit.*

Printed and bound by R. R. Donnelley & Sons.

To Ann, Diana, and Lisa

Contents

Preface

Optimization and variation reduction have received much attention in recent years. The journals and magazines are full of articles on statistical process control (SPC). SPC has proven to be an extremely effective practice of reducing manufacturing variation. Several leading US companies have made SPC a requirement for their suppliers. Hundreds of training programs and software packages are available to help one implement SPC. But while gains are made, it does not take long to realize that much of the variation has been built into the product, through product design, process development, and material selection. To finish the job one must go up front and address variation during product design.

More recently Taguchi's methods (TM) have made experimental design popular and advanced its application. TM provides effective practices for both optimization and variation reduction and allows one to address these issues during design. But a cloud of controversy surrounds TM with many competing practices being proposed. Further, neither SPC nor TM provide the full set of tools required.

While SPC and TM provide many practices for optimization and variation reduction, a wealth of other lesser known methods also exist. Other practices include Multi-Vari charts, analysis of means, component swapping, and variation transmission studies, to name a few.

State-of-the-art technology has, and continues, to advance rapidly. However, it is not the purpose of this book to help advance state-of-the-art technology. Instead, this book advances the practice of methods for optimization and variation reduction. This practice lags considerably behind technology.

To this end, this book draws on the teachings of a wide variety of experts. A partial list includes:

- Walter Shewhart: statistical process control
- W. Edwards Deming: statistical process control
- Genichi Taguchi: Taguchi methods
- George Box: experimental design
- Dorian Shainin: components swapping

This book is written for the practitioner, both engineers and scientists, involved in product design, process development, and manufacturing. It simplifies optimization and variation reduction by identifying the basic principles and strategies. It integrates the different practices into a single system, covering product concept to manufacturing. This book covers all the different situations practitioners will encounter. It is practical; selecting the simplest approach, avoiding inefficient and ineffective methods, and avoiding unnecessary complications. Because the objective is to improve the practice of methods for optimization and variation reduction, step-by-step procedures are given for many practices. The goal is to provide everything the practitioner needs. Unfortunately, the book falls short of this objective in the area of experimental design. However, in this area references and recommendations are given.

The application of the practices presented in this book result in dramatic improvements in product quality, product cost, and time to market.

Wayne A. Taylor

Optimization and
Variation Reduction
in Quality

Principles
and Strategies

Chapter

1

The Nature of
Optimization and
Variation Reduction

1.1 Objective of Book

The goal of any manufacturer should be to simultaneously

- Improve quality
- Reduce costs
- Shorten development times

The methodologies for optimizing product and process performance and for reducing variation are essential to achieving this goal. Optimizing performance improves quality. It results in more fuel-efficient cars, stronger garbage bags, lower levels of harmful emissions, and more reliable spacecraft. Reducing variation further improves quality. It results in fewer defectives and fewer substandard units.

By improving quality, the methods for optimization and variation reduction reduce costs. They do so by reducing waste in the form of scrap, rework, and costly inspections. Optimization can also be used to reduce costs and increase output directly. Line speed may be increased. Material may be saved. Energy usage may be reduced. Variation reduction, done correctly, can also reduce costs. The trick is to make the product robust to variations of the materials and manufacturing process and to tighten up on only the critical tolerances and only to the degree required. Tolerances on noncritical tolerances can be relaxed to achieve cost reductions.

Efficient methods of optimization and variation reduction can shorten development time. They reduce the amount of experimentation necessary to achieve the desired results. However, even more important, their proper use early in the design cycle will prevent problems early on. This reduces the number of problems and delays that develop later on which typically delay market entry.

The methods of optimization and variation reduction covered in this book have been used to

- *Design better electronic circuits.* Using these methods, electronic circuits are commonly designed that are less sensitive to variation in their components. This allows the use of lower-grade components, dramatically reducing costs. This also makes the circuits less sensitive to usage conditions such as temperature and humidity. Finally, this makes the product more reliable. Since the circuit is less sensitive to component variation, deterioration in the components will result in a more gradual deterioration of performance.

- *Maximize seal strength.* These methods were used to achieve a breakthrough in the sonic sealing of medically safe materials. This breakthrough made possible a new line of products. Traditional methods had failed after 9 months of effort. The breakthrough was accomplished in a matter of weeks using the methods of this book. Use of these methods up front could have shortened the development time by 6 to 9 months. Subsequent efforts have improved the process substantially below 50 defects per million. This is remarkable performance for a product that came very close to being canceled.

- *Reduce fill variation.* These methods were used to cut the variation in a filling operation to one-tenth of its former level with little capital investment. This reduction in fill variation significantly improved the quality of the product, resulting in an expanded market. Unfortunately, the division producing this product had already spent many millions of dollars developing a new process based on the belief that the current process was not capable of achieving this level of performance. These development costs put this division in the red for several years running, resulting in the division being sold and many of the employees losing their jobs. All this was completely unnecessary.

These are just three of the many examples given in this book.

The objective of this book is to make the reader proficient in the strategies and tools for optimizing product and process performance and for reducing variation. The material covered in this book is essential to any engineer or scientist involved in product development, process development, or process improvement. In addition, management should have a clear understanding of the principles and strategies covered in Part 1.

Statistical process control (SPC) and Taguchi methods (TM) are two important approaches to optimization and variation reduction that have received special notoriety in recent years. Associated with these two approaches are many tools including control charts, capability studies, parameter design, tolerance design, and the Taguchi loss function. These approaches are thoroughly explained in this book. However, these tools represent just some of the many tools available. This book integrates these two popular approaches with many lesser known tools into an extremely efficient and effective approach to optimization and variation reduction. The tools have been selected and organized under three guiding principles:

- *Best demonstrated practice.* If alternate approaches are available, only the most effective is included. Outdated approaches are not included simply for completeness.

- *Simplicity.* If a simpler method exists that can achieve 90 percent of the results, the simpler method is the one selected. The goal is to get the reader up and running as quickly as possible. However, references to the more advanced methods are given along with guidance on when they should be used.

- *Completeness.* Methods are given to handle all tasks required to effectively accomplish optimization and variation reduction.

This book provides a full chest of tools capable of handling most problems. But just knowing how to use the tools is not enough, any more than knowing how to use a hammer, a saw, and other tools gives one the ability to build a house. Also necessary is an understanding of certain principles along with strategies for applying these tools in different sequences to achieve the desired results. Part 1 covers the principles and strategies for optimization and variation reduction. Special attention is given to understanding variation. False myths and lack of understanding of variation hamper many variation reduction projects. Parts 2 through 4 then cover the tools necessary for implementing these strategies.

After reading this book, the reader should be better able to design products, develop processes, and further improve processes so as to improve performance and quality, reduce costs, and shorten development times.

W. Edwards Deming says, "Optimization means cooperation." Optimization and variation reduction requires the cooperation of everyone involved with the product including product designers, process developers, manufacturing, purchasing, marketing, and of course management. An important part of accomplishing optimization and variation reduction is the simultaneous development of the product and process.

Along with the principles and strategies, Part 1 lays out the responsibilities of each party.

1.2   Five Categories of Problems

There is a wide variety of different types of optimization and variation reduction problems. These problems include maximizing battery life, minimizing harmful emissions, designing a pump that can be accurately adjusted, designing a copier that is robust to paper weight and humidity, maximizing output, and developing accurate diagnostic tests to name a few. However, despite the variety of problems, all optimization and variation reduction problems fit into five broad categories:

1. Larger the better
2. Smaller the better
3. Target value
4. Target function
5. Uniform around the average

The following sections explain these five categories.

Before turning to these sections, the bell-shaped curve needs introduction. The bell-shaped curve, shown in Fig. 1.1, is a smoothed-out histogram. The center of the curve represents the average. The width of the curve represents the variation. The wider the curve, the more variation present. Histograms and the bell-shaped curve are covered in detail in Chap. 5.

Larger the better

The first category of optimization and variation reduction problem is *larger the better* (Fig. 1.2). In this type of problem the overriding con-

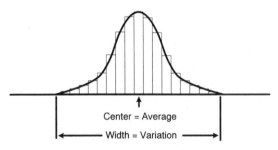

Center = Average

Width = Variation

Figure 1.1   A bell-shaped curve.

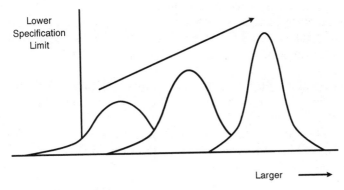

Figure 1.2   Larger the better.

cern is getting some characteristic as high as possible. There are, however, generally constraints that must be observed. Examples of this category include maximizing battery life, horsepower of engine, process yield, and output.

For the larger the better case, only a lower specification limit is appropriate. Low values must be guarded against. But there is no limit on how high they might be. In fact, higher values are preferred. The ideal value is infinity. To get as many of the values as high as possible requires concentrating primarily on driving the average higher. However, the variation cannot be ignored. No matter how high an average is obtained, excessive variation can still cause some units to fall below the lower specification limit.

Smaller the better

The second category of optimization and variation reduction problem is *smaller the better* (Fig. 1.3). This category is the opposite of the first

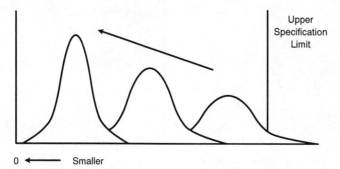

Figure 1.3   Smaller the better.

category. The overriding concern now becomes one of getting some characteristic as close to zero as possible. Once again there are general constraints that must be observed. Examples of this category include minimizing harmful emissions, processing time, battery usage, and vibration.

For the smaller the better case, only an upper specification limit is appropriate. High values must be guarded against. But there is no limit on how small they might be. The ideal value is zero. To get as many of the values as low as possible requires concentrating on both reducing the average and on reducing the variation around this average.

The larger the better and smaller the better cases are closely related. Taking the reciprocal (1/x key on a calculator) of a larger the better characteristic results in a smaller the better characteristic.

Target value

The third category of optimization and variation reduction problem is characterized by the existence of an ideal value called the *target value* (Fig. 1.4). Every unit should be as close to this target value as possible. One example is the force required to open a potato chip bag. Too high of an opening force makes the bag too difficult to open. Too low of an opening force may result in the bag accidentally opening in transit. The ideal value is the one that reaches the best compromise between these two requirements.

For the target value case, both upper and lower specification limits are required. Both excessively high and excessively low values must be guarded against. The only acceptable values are those near target. To get as many values as close to target as possible requires getting the average as close to the target as possible and minimizing the variation around this target.

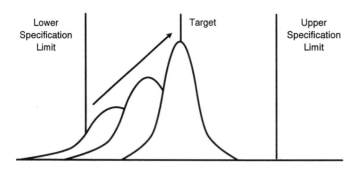

Figure 1.4   The closer to target value the better.

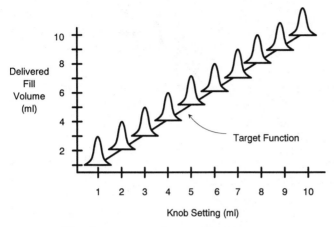

Figure 1.5   The closer to target function the better.

Target function

The fourth type of optimization and variation reduction problem, *target function,* is typical of complex hardware. In this situation there are certain controls which are adjustable by the user. For example, on a filling machine the user, in this case the operator, has a knob for adjusting the fill volume. There is not an ideal fill volume. The desired fill volume depends upon the knob setting. There is, however, an ideal relationship between this knob setting and actual fills, namely the actual fills should all be as close to the knob setting as possible. Figure 1.5 shows this ideal relationship. For any knob setting, the average fill volume should be equal to the knob setting. Further, there should be minimum variation around this average. This ideal relationship is called the target function. The target function gives the ideal target value for all possible settings of the user-adjustable controls.

There are a number of ways the product can deviate from the target function. Some of these are shown in Fig. 1.6. Figure 1.6*a* has a bias. The average fill volume is 1 ml higher than the knob setting. Figure 1.6*b* has the wrong slope. A change in the knob setting of 1 ml results in only a ⅝-ml increase in the average fill volume. Figure 1.6*c* The third shows an unwanted curvature, and Fig. 1.6*d* shows excessive variation. Both bias and wrong slope are generally easily fixed through calibration and changing the gearing. The other two problems are more difficult to fix.

A second example is a car. The accelerator, brake pedal, and steering wheel are all examples of user controls. Figure 1.7 shows a desirable relationship between the steering wheel and angle of turn. This

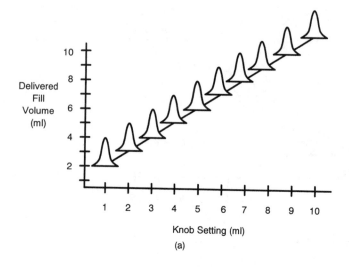

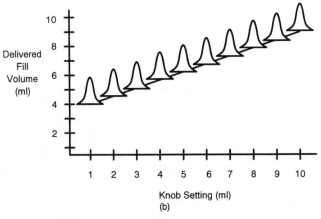

Figure 1.6   (*a*) Bias; (*b*) wrong slope.

figure illustrates that not all target functions are straight lines. In fact there is a wide variety of possible target functions. Another example is that of a push button. One particular push button is supposed to close a circuit when pushed with a force of 6 lb or greater. The ideal target function is shown in Fig. 1.8.

Uniform around the average

The last type of optimization and variation reduction problem is *uniform around the average*. In this situation, there is a wide range of acceptable averages. However, there is a very tight requirement on the

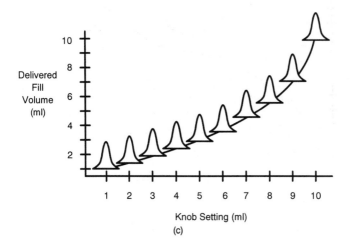

Knob Setting (ml)

(c)

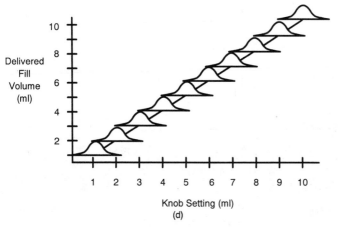

Knob Setting (ml)

(d)

Figure 1.6 (*Continued*) (*c*) unwanted curvature; (*d*) excessive variation.

variation around this average. This results in the best lot being the one with the smallest variation regardless of the average. The ideal value is the lot average. Every unit should be as close to this average as possible. (See Fig. 1.9.)

This situation occurs with diagnostic test kits. The customer receives a kit of 100 vials coated with enzymes for performing an assay. Also included in the kit are reference standards. The assay equipment is calibrated using the reference standards and several of the vials. Then the rest of the vials are used to assay patient samples. There is wide latitude in the amount of active enzyme coated on the vials from kit to kit. The calibration procedure adjusts for differing amounts.

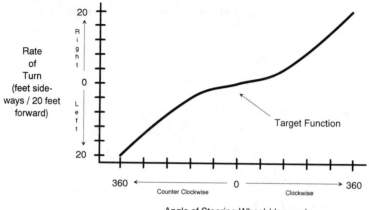

Figure 1.7   Target function for steering wheel.

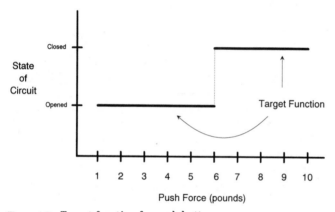

Figure 1.8   Target function for push button.

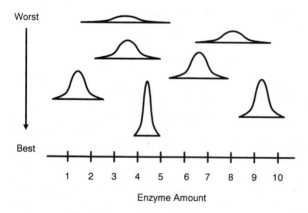

Figure 1.9   The closer to average the better.

However, within a kit, it is very important that the variation in the amount of active enzyme be very small. This variation determines the accuracy of the assay. In this situation, there is neither an upper nor lower specification limit for individual units of the product. However, there is generally an upper specification limit on the variation (or equivalently the coefficient of variation). There may also be much wider limits set on the average.

For the uniform around the average case, reducing the variation is of primary importance. However, there may be advantages to having a consistent average. Imagine in the example above if it were possible to produce all kits with the same average. This may allow less frequent calibrations and may simplify the assemblage of kits.

Commonalities

It is useful to distinguish among these five categories of optimization and variation reduction problems in that they will require slight variations in the strategies and methods later on. But despite their differences, there are important commonalities. Common to these categories is an ideal value and the desire to get as many units as possible as close as possible to this ideal. This requires getting the average as close to this ideal as possible. It further requires minimizing the variation around the average. This leads to the following two definitions:

Optimization of the Average: To achieve the most desirable average.

Variation Reduction: To reduce the variation around this average.

Both objectives are important. No matter how well the average is optimized, excessive variation can result in poor quality. Similarly, no matter how much the variation is reduced, a poor average can result in poor quality.

The word *optimization* used by itself will refer jointly to the optimization of the average and to variation reduction. The goal of optimization is that every unit perform at its ideal value.

There is an old joke about statisticians: A statistician is one, who having his head in the freezer and feet in the oven, will tell you that on the average the temperature is just fine. This may sound ridiculous, yet designers fall into this trap every day. Optimizing the average while ignoring the variation is the same thing. On the average the product is good. However, in actuality, much of the product may be outside of specifications. The extremes are just as important as the average. Whenever one hears the word optimize, it should be understood to mean that every unit of product is to perform as close to optimal as possible. This requires optimizing the average and reducing the variation.

These two objectives are inherently linked. As we will see, parameters affecting the average may also affect the variation, while parameters affecting the variation will always have some effect on the average. As a result the two objectives must be accomplished simultaneously. As will be seen throughout this book, those tools traditionally thought of as optimization tools, like response surfaces, are also invaluable aids in reducing variation. Further, those tools traditionally thought of as variation reduction tools like control charts can provide valuable information for optimization of the average.

1.3   Three Sources of Variation

Variation is readily apparent in the plant. This is the result of such things as variation in materials, fluctuations in key process parameters, differing processing conditions, and operator variation, and will be referred to as manufacturing variation. This is the first source of variation.

Not all the variation the customer will observe can be readily observed in the plant. First, customers use the product under a variety of different environments and in differing manners. For example, a copier that works well in the lab using the recommended paper and in a controlled environment, may frustrate the customer who is trying to make transparencies or who is using the copier in a high-humidity environment. The second source of variation is the variation in product performance that results from differences in the manner and conditions under which it is used. Further, over time, the product performance may change further. The copier that works fine when first purchased, may quickly deteriorate. The third source of variation is that variation in product performance that results from deterioration over time. The total variation is the combined variation from all three sources.

Total variation = manufacturing variation

+ usage variation + variation due to deterioration

Both usage variation and variation due to product deterioration are just as important as manufacturing variation in the customer's eyes. All three cause the product to deviate from the ideal and can cause the product to fail. When reducing variation, these last two sources of variation should not be overlooked.

Manufacturing variation

Manufacturing variation is the variation that is most readily visible within the plant. It is the variation in product performance resulting from such things as fluctuations in the process parameters and materials, wearing and changes in tooling, and changes in the methods, operators, and manufacturing environment. Formally, manufacturing variation will be defined as the variation up to the time the product is delivered to the customer. Thus manufacturing variation will include variation resulting from storage and transportation of the product.

Statistical process control (SPC) and other efforts by the plant to reduce variation address only this source of variation. When reducing manufacturing variation there are two objectives:

1. Achieving a stable process
2. Achieving a capable process

An *unstable process* is one characterized by change (Fig. 1.10). Each time a set of samples is selected and a histogram drawn, the average has shifted. The variation may also change. The process is unpredictable and difficult to control. At any time an emergency might arise. Much time is spent dealing with the many emergencies. Sampling inspection is required to sort good lots from bad lots.

A *stable process* (Fig. 1.11) on the other hand is one characterized by a lack of change. Hour after hour looks the same. It is not that all variation has been eliminated. But the variation that remains consistently falls within certain well defined limits. The process is predictable and much easier to control. Taking a process that is unstable and making it stable reduces variation. A stable process, however, is not necessarily a good process. It is consistent. But, to be a good process, the variation that remains must safely fit between the specification limits.

A *capable process* is a stable process whose remaining variation fits

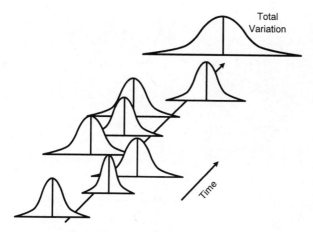

Figure 1.10 Unstable process.

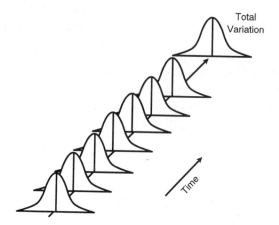

Figure 1.11   Stable process.

safely between the specification limits (see Fig. 1.12). It consistently produces quality product, hour after hour, day after day. If the process is stable, but the remaining variation does not safely fit between the specification limits, the process is said to be not capable. A consistent percentage of units are defective. To sort the good from the bad 100 percent inspection is required. The capability of the process depends upon the average as well as the variation around this average. Therefore, achieving a capable process requires both optimization of the average and variation reduction.

SPC is used by many plants to help achieve stable and capable processes. Important tools of SPC include the control charts and capabil-

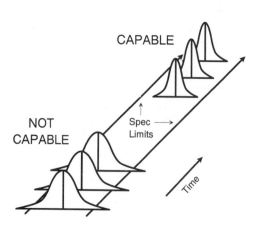

Figure 1.12   Process capability.

ity studies. These are invaluable for assessing the stability and capability of the process and for helping to make a process stable. In this book other complementary tools will be explored that can help accelerate the process of achieving a stable process, improve the capability of a process, and help achieve both objectives during product and process design. The ideal situation is to design the product and process so that at start-up the process is stable and is capable of producing the product.

Manufacturing variation can always be reduced by tightening up controls of the manufacturing parameters. This, however, increases costs. A more cost-efficient approach is to design the product and process to be *robust* (less sensitive) to the fluctuations in the process and materials. This second approach, robustness, should always be tried first. If, however, it becomes necessary to tighten up control of the manufacturing parameters, it is important to tighten up only on the critical parameters and then only to the degree necessary. Anything else is overcontrol and unnecessarily drives up costs.

Variation due to manner and conditions of usage

Reducing manufacturing variation is not enough. One must also reduce variations in product performance due to the manner and conditions under which the product is used. A copying machine might perform well in the lab using vendor-supplied paper. However, when used with other sources of paper the performance might be significantly worse. When used with transparency film, the copier might soften the film causing jams. The copy quality might also deteriorate even with the vendor paper when used in a tropical (high humidity) environment.

Usage variation can be measured in the plant by testing the product while simulating actual usage conditions. However, usage variation is outside the control of manufacturing. SPC and variation reduction programs in the plant can do nothing to reduce usage variation. Usage variation (Fig. 1.13) must be addressed during the design process. Since it is impossible to tighten up on the usage variation, the product must be designed to be robust to this variation.

Variation due to product deterioration

Manufacturing variation and usage variation still do not account for all the variation in product performance that the customer will experience. These two sources only account for the variation the customer

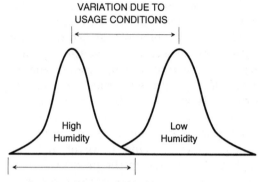

Figure 1.13   Usage variation.

will see when first using the product. These are of primary importance for disposable products that are used only once. However, many products are used over and over. For repeated-use products, once the product reaches the customer, it will start to deteriorate and wear, adding even more variation into the performance of the product. Plastics become more brittle, springs lose their elasticity, and bearings gradually wear down. The customer is not just interested in how well the product works when first received. More important is how well the product functions over its total useful life.

Figure 1.14 shows how *variation due to deterioration* combines

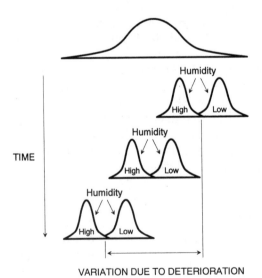

Figure 1.14   Total variation.

with usage variation and manufacturing variation to give the total variation in product usage that the customer will experience. Failing to take into account variation due to deterioration may lead to some poor designs from the customer's viewpoint. Take two automobile designs. The first design, with clean filters, new plugs, and perfectly tuned, averaged 42 mi/gal during initial testing. However under normal usage conditions it averages only 20 mi/gal. The second design averages between 25 to 30 mi/gal depending on how well the car is tuned and on the conditions of the plugs and filter. During initial testing it averaged 29 mi/gal. This second design is clearly the better design from the customer's point of view. However, during initial testing, the first design appeared to outperform the second one.

Like usage variation, variation due to deterioration is outside the control of manufacturing. However, it is possible to measure it in the plant. Measuring variation due to deterioration requires special testing to simulate aging of the product. Reducing variation due to deterioration requires selection of higher-grade materials, tightening design specifications, and designing the product to be robust to the deterioration.

When optimizing the average and reducing variation, it is important to consider all three sources of variation. Otherwise suboptimal product can result.

1.4   The Goal

The goal of optimization and variation reduction is perfect product. This requires designing product, developing the processes, and improving these processes so that *every unit of product performs exactly as required, every time, for all manners and conditions of use.*

Exactly as required means that all product should be as close as possible to the ideal value. This requires optimization of the average. It also requires minimizing the variation around this average. *Every time* and *for all manners and conditions of use* signify that all three sources of variation must be reduced, not just manufacturing variation.

The goal of optimization and variation reduction is to take the current total variation (Fig. 1.15), reduce the manufacturing variation (Fig. 1.16), reduce the usage variation (Fig. 1.17), reduce the variation due to deterioration (Fig. 1.18), and center the average on target (Fig. 1.19).

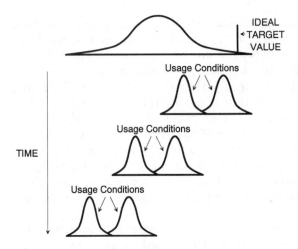

Figure 1.15   Current total variation.

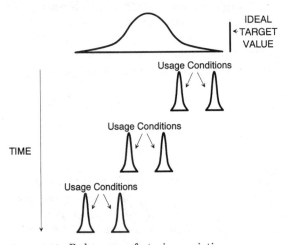

Figure 1.16   Reduce manufacturing variation.

1.5   The Importance of Reducing Variation

Why is reducing variation important? Two answers are generally given:

1. Reducing variation decreases the number of defects thereby improving quality

2. Reducing variation results in wider operating windows making the process easier to control

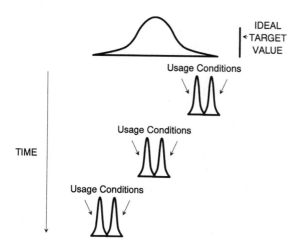

Figure 1.17 Reduce usage variation.

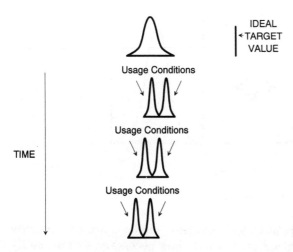

Figure 1.18 Reduce deterioration.

Both of these answers are correct. Figure 1.20 shows how reducing variation decreases the number of defects. This raises the issue of whether there is any benefit to further reductions once the variation has been reduced to the point that it fits within the specification limits. The answer is "yes." Further reductions in variation result in wider operating windows. Figure 1.21 shows how this happens. These wider windows make the process easier to control. Further, shifts of the process are less likely to result in defects. Problems can frequently be detected and eliminated without a defect ever being made.

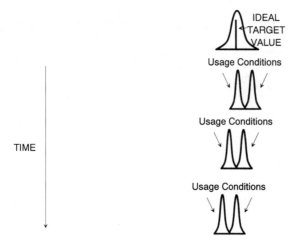

TIME

Figure 1.19   The goal.

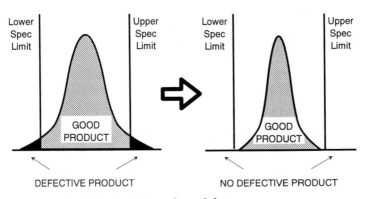

Figure 1.20   Reducing variation reduces defects.

However, the benefits of wider operating windows are not the only benefits of reducing variation beyond that necessary to minimally meet the specifications. Further reduction of variation can also benefit the customer. The fallacy of specification limits is that they lead to the perception that all units within the specification limits are equally good, and all units outside the specification limits are equally bad. Figure 1.22 shows the loss of releasing a unit under this belief. If the unit is within the specification limits, there is no loss. If the unit is outside the specification limits, the loss is the cost of replacing the unit, say $10. This will be referred to as the *all or nothing* loss function (Fig. 1.22).

The all or nothing loss function may be appropriate for certain situations. It does not, however, fit the vast majority of situations. Most

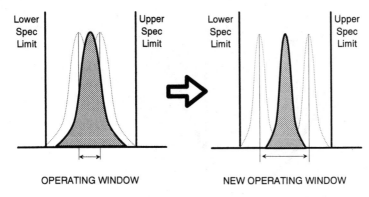

OPERATING WINDOW   NEW OPERATING WINDOW

Figure 1.21 Reducing variation widens operating windows.

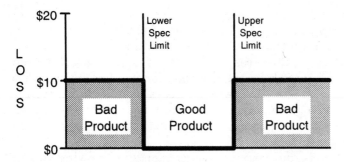

Figure 1.22 The all or nothing loss function.

of the time there is an ideal value that is best for the majority of the customers. The further one deviates from this ideal, the less excited the customers are about the product and the more dissatisfied they become. Some customers are more demanding than others. The further one deviates from the ideal value, the larger the number of customers who will complain. This situation is better described by the *Taguchi loss function* shown in Fig. 1.23.

The Taguchi loss function has been shown to apply to a large variety of products including the color density of televisions* and the response time of transmissions. Some individuals are not satisfied with even the best televisions currently available. As the color density worsens more and more people complain. Finally, the color density becomes so bad that even those with severe eyesight problems notice the problem. Further, as the color densities worsen, consumers take more

---

*L. P. Sullivan, "Reducing Variability: A New Approach to Quality," *Quality Progress,* July 1984.

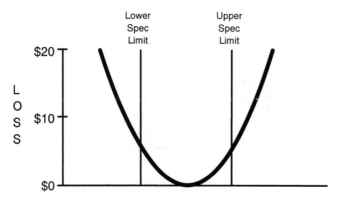

Figure 1.23   The Taguchi loss function.

severe actions, from complaining to themselves, bringing it in for repair, to refusing to buy it. The Taguchi loss function certainly better fits this situation than the all or nothing loss function.

With transmissions, if the response time is too short, a jerking sensation results. If it is too long, the transmission will feel sluggish. The best transmission is one that switches gears as quickly as possible short of producing a jerking sensation. Again, more and more customers will complain louder and louder the further the transmission deviates from this ideal.

The bottom line is that you may feel comfortable knowing you are producing everything to specifications. After all, isn't *zero defects* the goal? But your competitor may sneak up on you in identifying the customer's ideal value and reducing the variation to better satisfy these customers. You may be dismayed by your dwindling customer base and fail to understand why. After all, you are producing everything to specification. This scenario and its many variations have been repeated dozens of times resulting in plant closures and product lines being lost. The fallacy is in thinking the goal is zero defects. The real goal is an absolutely perfect product, with every unit at the ideal.

This still leaves one question unanswered. If specification limits are misleading when it comes to making product, why are they needed if they are needed at all? Specification limits do in fact serve a useful purpose. They indicate what to do with units of product once it has been made. Figure 1.24 shows how specification limits should be established using the Taguchi loss function. These limits are the intersections between the Taguchi loss function representing the loss due to releasing the unit and the second line representing the loss due to discarding the unit. Between the specification limits, the best decision is to release the unit. Outside the specification limits, the best deci-

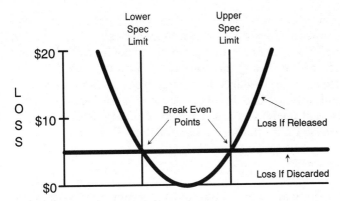

Figure 1.24   Setting specification limits.

sion is to discard the unit. The specification limits indicate what to do with the product once it is produced. But, just because it is best to release a unit that is barely within the specification limits, does not mean that one wants to produce such a unit. Production's objective must be to produce every unit as close as possible to the ideal. This requires optimizing the average and reducing the variation.

So far there are three reasons for reducing variation:

1. Reducing variation decreases the number of defects, thereby improving quality and reducing scrap, rework, and so forth

2. Reducing variation results in wider operating windows making the process easier to control

3. Reducing variation causes more units to be closer to the ideal value resulting in more satisfied customers

But one reason is still missing. This is perhaps the most important reason of all. Reducing variation makes new products possible. This in turn can spur the development of new products. Most new product ideas never make it to market. Most are shelved early on because of the infeasibility of making such a product. Reducing variation increases manufacturing capability. This in turn provides the technology required to produce many of these new products. Fewer ideas are shelved.

The effect that reducing variation has on new product development is real. In 1987 three Japanese companies topped General Electric in the number of US patents received: Canon, Hitachi, and Toshiba.* General Electric had held the number one spot for 25 years. One

---

*"Eyes on the Prize," *Time Magazine*, March 21, 1988.

might argue that most of the Japanese patents are for minor improvements and that many of the US patents are for more significant items. If so, what about VCRs, compact disks, floppy disks, and Walkmans? These are but a few of the many innovations of the Japanese. Further, the Japanese are ahead in research into such areas as high-resolution TV and superconductivity. The Japanese are no longer copycats. They are the technological leaders in many areas. This is partially the result of their increased manufacturing capability.

1.6   Benefits

The methods of optimization and variation reduction improve quality, reduce costs, and shorten development time. (See Fig. 1.25.)

Quality improves because of

1. Fewer defects.

2. Better product performance as a result of more product being closer to the ideal.

3. Broader product applicability as a result of the product being more robust to variations in the manner and conditions under which it is used.

4. Improved reliability due to reducing the effect of product deterioration and wear.

Costs are reduced because

1. Whenever quality improves, waste in the form of scrap, rework, costly inspections, and so on, are reduced, decreasing costs and improving productivity.

2. Manufacturing processes are easier to control when they become more stable and have wider operating windows.

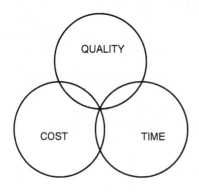

Figure 1.25 Benefits.

3. Less expensive manufacturing processes may be used by making the product robust to the process.

4. Less expensive materials can be used by making the product robust to material variations.

5. Overcontrol is reduced. Whenever possible, the product and process are made robust instead of tightening control. When required, control is tightened on only the critical parameters and then only to the degree necessary.

Total development time, the time from conception to market, is shortened because

1. More time is invested in initial product design in order to prevent problems downstream. Start-ups proceed more smoothly with fewer delays and higher initial quality.

2. The methods provided allow for efficient research. In one extreme case, 9 months using traditional methods failed to identify a solution to a particular manufacturing problem. The product was delayed to market. The methods presented in this book solved this problem in just weeks.

3. The methods provided allow prediction of performance under actual manufacturing conditions and actual conditions of use which may be broader than study conditions. This reduces the number of unanticipated problems that develop at start-up causing delays.

In addition, the methods of optimization and variation reduction can help spur new product development through increased manufacturing capability.

The methods of optimization and variation reduction presented in this book offer a clear competitive advantage to any company that adopts them. Their impact has been repeatedly demonstrated in both Japan and many leading US companies. However, competitive advantage is just a temporary thing. The time is rapidly approaching when the effective use of methods for optimization and variation reduction will be a prerequisite for staying in business. In some industries, including the electronic and automotive industries, this is already the case.

1.7 Summary

Objective of book

The methodologies for product and process optimization and variation reduction are an essential element of any program to improve quality, reduce costs, and shorten development time. The objective of this book is to provide readers with principles, strategies, and tools that will improve their performance when designing products, developing new processes, and improving existing processes.

Statistical process control (SPC) and Taguchi methods (TM) are important approaches to optimization and variation reduction. They are not, however, complete. They need to be combined with other important principles and tools. Optimization and variation reduction requires the cooperation of everyone involved with the product, including product designers, process developers, manufacturing, quality, purchasing, materials engineers, and of course management.

Five categories of problems

There are five categories of optimization and variation reduction problems:

1. Larger the better
2. Smaller the better
3. Target value
4. Target function
5. Uniform around the average

These categories are useful in that they require slightly different strategies and methods. Common to these categories is an ideal value and the desire to get as many units as possible as close as possible to this ideal. This requires getting the average as close as possible to the ideal. It further requires minimizing the variation around the average. *Optimization of the average* is to achieve the most desirable average. *Variation reduction* is to reduce the variation around this average. *Optimization* jointly refers to optimization of the average and variation reduction. Optimization of the average and variation reduction are inseparably linked and must be achieved simultaneously.

Three sources of variation

From the customer perspective, variation in the product performance results from usage and deterioration variation as well as manufacturing variation.

1. *Manufacturing variation.* The variation in product performance up until the time it is delivered to the customer. It generally results from fluctuations in the process parameters and materials, wearing and changes in tooling, and changes in the methods, operators, and

manufacturing environment. However, manufacturing variation can also result from the effect of storage and transportation. Reducing manufacturing variation requires achieving stable and capable processes.

2. *Usage variation.* The variation in product performance due to the manner and conditions under which the product is used.

3. *Variation due to deterioration.* The variation in product performance resulting from product deterioration and wear.

The goal

The goal of optimization and variation reduction is to design product, develop the processes, and improve these processes so that *every unit of product performs exactly as required, every time, for all manners and conditions of use.*

The importance of reducing variation

Reducing variation reduces the number of defects, provides wider operating windows, causes more units to be closer to the ideal value resulting in more satisfied customers, and increases manufacturing capability spurring the development of new products.

The Taguchi loss function generally better estimates the loss because of off-target product. Specification limits serve as a guide to disposing of product, once made. They are an inspection tool. But just because it is best to release a unit barely within the specification limits, does not mean it is desirable to produce such a unit.

Benefits

The methods of optimization and variation reduction improve quality, reduce costs, and shorten development time. Improved quality not only means fewer defects, but includes improved performance, better reliability, wider range of usage conditions, and so forth. These methods offer a competitive advantage which is rapidly becoming a prerequisite to staying in business.

2

Three Case Studies

To set the stage for the rest of the book, this chapter is devoted to three case studies. The purpose of these case studies is to bring the process of optimization and variation reduction to life. You will get to look over the shoulder of experts and see what they might do in a variety of situations. Subsequent chapters will explain the why and how. These case studies illustrate the key concepts, strategies, and methods covered in subsequent chapters. Each case study illustrates a different stage of development:

Hinge case study: product design

Heat-sealer case study: process development

Multi-head filler case study: manufacturing

The case studies are based on actual projects. As such, they are realistic. They do not, however, always reflect a single project. The actual products, companies involved, and so on, are frequently disguised. Frequent reference will be made to these case studies throughout the book.

2.1   Hinge Case Study

The first case study illustrates the methods for performing optimization and variation reduction during *product design*. This case study involves the design of the lower front door hinge of an automobile.*

---

*This case study is based on the article "Lincoln Door Hinge Experimental Design Using Taguchi Methods" by Hasan Mutlu and Edgar Hammer published in the transactions of the 1984 Ford Supplier Symposium on Taguchi methods. The program given in this article was used to generate the data.

The characteristic of interest is the closure force. If the closure force is too much, the door will be difficult to close. If the force is too little, the door will not stay open when it should. The closure force is measured in pounds of torque. The acceptable range for closure force is very narrow. Therefore, the designer would like to target the closure force at the desired value, reduce the variability of closure force, and minimize changes in closure force due to wear of components (especially the springs).

A design has been proposed. While this design determines the basic principles, there are still numerous design parameters for which targets and tolerances must be determined. The following 13 design parameters were selected for further study. Also given are suggested ranges.

A	Pivot to top of pie	37.5 to 38.5
B	Pivot to same notch	64.8 to 66.0
C	Top of pie to bottom of notch	5.4 to 7.4
D	Top of pie to bottom opposite notch	5.4 to 7.4
E	Pivot to opposite notch	64.8 to 66.0
F	Angle per D hole	6° to 10°
UC	Coefficient of friction top of pie hole	0.1 to 0.5
H	Pivot to roller	37.9 to 38.4
K	Spring constant	−20% to 20%
L	Width of spring	36.0 to 38.0
M	Roller contact point	14.5 to 18.5
P	Spring prebend	0° to 9°
f	Residual friction	0.1 to 0.3

A program was developed based on a mathematical model that iteratively determines torque given these 13 parameters. The traditional approach is to adjust the input parameters one at a time in order to determine how to set these parameters to obtain the desired torque. The *one-at-a-time* approach begins with the parameters thought to be most important and proceeds depending on previous results. Once targets have been identified to optimize the average, tolerances are set to reduce the variation to an acceptable level.

An alternate approach will be demonstrated that offers two advantages. First variation is considered in selecting targets for the design parameters. This frequently allows variation to be reduced without tightening the design parameter tolerances thereby resulting in lower-cost designs. The second advantage is that multiple options for achieving the target are generally identified which allows the low-cost option to be selected.

This alternate approach involves running a screening experiment to identify the key design parameters, augmenting the screening experiment in order to model the effect these key design parameters have on torque, and performing a variation transmission analysis to identify proper targets and tolerances for the key design parameters.

Screening experiment

Ultimately a model of the effect that the design parameters have on the torque is desired. An equation of the form:

$$\text{Torque} = c_0 + c_1 A + c_2 B + \ldots + c_{13} f + q_1 A^2 + q_2 B^2 + \ldots$$
$$+ q_{13} f^2 + i_{1,2} AB + i_{1,3} AC + \ldots + i_{12,13} Pf + \ldots$$

will be used to model this effect. Subscripted terms represent constants. The other terms, A, B, f, ..., represent the design parameters. The c_0 term is the *intercept term*; terms like $c_1 A$ are called *linear terms*; the $q_1 A^2$ terms are called *quadratic terms*; and $i_{1,2} AB$ terms are called *two-way interaction terms*. Other terms such as *cubic terms* $c_3 A^3$ and *three-way interactions* $j_{1,2,3} ABC$ can also be added if needed. An equation of this form can be made to fit as closely as desired over the region of study.

The purpose of the screening experiment is to identify which of the 13 design parameters one must really be concerned with, that is, belong in the equation. In addition, interactions between these key design parameters should be identified. Interactions, frequently missed using the one-variable-at-a-time approach, are very important when it comes to optimizing the average and reducing variation. Interactions are explained in Chap. 3.

The screening experiment requires running the 33 combinations of the design parameters given in Table 2.1. This requires running the torque simulation program 33 times. The results thus obtained are also given in this table. Using these data, the effects of the 13 design parameters were calculated and used to rank the design parameters in order of importance. The results are shown in Table 2.2. The effect is the change in torque that results from changing the design parameters from their low values to their high values. The design parameters in order of importance are L, K, B, f, A, H, C, D, UC, E, P, F, and M.

In addition, two groups of interactions were identified with effects greater than 3. These are shown toward the bottom of Table 2.2. Each group of interactions consists of three interactions. For example, the term $L*f$ represents the two-way interaction between L and f. On the basis of the data, one cannot distinguish between the interactions within a group. One or more of the interactions is important. All six interactions are possible and will be considered in the next stage. On

TABLE 2.1   Torque Screening Experiment

Trial Number	Design Parameters													Torque
	A	B	C	D	E	F	UC	H	K	L	M	P	f	
1	38.5	64.8	5.4	5.4	66.0	10	0.5	38.4	-20	38.0	14.5	0	0.1	39.8
2	38.5	66.0	5.4	5.4	64.8	10	0.5	37.9	20	36.0	14.5	0	0.3	24.3
3	38.5	66.0	7.4	5.4	64.8	6	0.5	38.4	-20	38.0	18.5	0	0.1	20.6
4	38.5	66.0	7.4	7.4	64.8	10	0.1	38.4	20	36.0	14.5	0	0.1	25.2
5	38.5	66.0	7.4	7.4	66.0	10	0.5	38.4	20	38.0	18.5	9	0.3	67.0
6	37.5	66.0	7.4	7.4	66.0	6	0.5	37.9	20	38.0	14.5	0	0.1	47.7
7	37.5	64.8	7.4	7.4	66.0	6	0.1	38.4	-20	38.0	18.5	9	0.1	59.5
8	38.5	64.8	5.4	7.4	66.0	6	0.1	38.4	20	36.0	18.5	0	0.1	54.2
9	38.5	66.0	5.4	5.4	66.0	10	0.1	37.9	20	38.0	18.5	9	0.1	41.5
10	37.5	66.0	7.4	5.4	64.8	10	0.5	37.9	-20	38.0	14.5	9	0.3	41.3
11	38.5	64.8	7.4	7.4	64.8	10	0.5	37.9	-20	38.0	18.5	9	0.1	20.1
12	37.5	66.0	5.4	7.4	66.0	10	0.5	38.4	-20	36.0	18.5	0	0.3	43.6
13	37.5	64.8	7.4	5.4	66.0	10	0.5	38.4	20	38.0	14.5	9	0.1	50.8
14	38.5	64.8	5.4	7.4	64.8	6	0.5	38.4	20	38.0	14.5	9	0.3	91.3
15	37.5	66.0	5.4	5.4	66.0	6	0.1	38.4	-20	38.0	18.5	9	0.3	89.1
16	37.5	64.8	7.4	5.4	64.8	10	0.1	38.4	20	38.0	18.5	0	0.3	97.2
17	37.5	64.8	5.4	7.4	64.8	10	0.5	37.9	20	38.0	18.5	0	0.1	71.7
18	37.5	64.8	5.4	5.4	66.0	6	0.5	37.9	-20	38.0	18.5	9	0.3	62.8
19	38.5	64.8	5.4	5.4	64.8	10	0.1	38.4	-20	36.0	18.5	9	0.3	39.4
20	37.5	66.0	5.4	5.4	64.8	6	0.5	38.4	20	36.0	18.5	9	0.1	37.4
21	38.5	64.8	7.4	5.4	64.8	6	0.1	37.9	20	38.0	14.5	9	0.1	47.3
22	37.5	66.0	5.4	7.4	64.8	10	0.1	38.4	-20	38.0	14.5	9	0.1	49.1
23	38.5	64.8	7.4	5.4	66.0	6	0.5	37.9	20	36.0	18.5	0	0.3	32.5
24	38.5	66.0	5.4	7.4	64.8	6	0.1	37.9	-20	38.0	18.5	0	0.3	41.0
25	38.5	66.0	7.4	5.4	66.0	6	0.1	38.4	-20	36.0	14.5	9	0.3	21.6
26	37.5	66.0	7.4	7.4	64.8	6	0.1	37.9	20	36.0	18.5	9	0.3	42.8
27	38.5	64.8	7.4	7.4	66.0	10	0.1	37.9	-20	38.0	14.5	0	0.3	51.5
28	38.5	66.0	5.4	7.4	66.0	6	0.5	37.9	20	36.0	18.5	0	0.1	16.3
29	37.5	66.0	7.4	5.4	66.0	10	0.1	37.9	-20	36.0	18.5	9	0.1	16.8
30	37.5	64.8	7.4	7.4	64.8	6	0.5	38.4	-20	36.0	14.5	0	0.3	46.1
31	37.5	64.8	5.4	7.4	66.0	10	0.1	37.9	20	36.0	14.5	9	0.3	78.6
32	37.5	64.8	5.4	5.4	64.8	6	0.1	37.9	-20	36.0	14.5	0	0.1	31.2
33	38.0	65.4	6.4	6.4	65.4	8	0.3	38.15	0	37.0	16.5	4.5	0.2	46.2

TABLE 2.2   Torque Effects Table

Design Parameter	Effect
L	21.1
K	18.6
B	-15.5
f	15.1
A	-14.5
H	10.3
C	-7.7
D	7.0
UC	-4.5
E	3.0
P	2.1
F	1.0
M	-0.2
Interaction Group (L*f,H*K,A*D)	5.4
Interaction Group (K*L,H*f,D*UC)	4.8
Combined Quadratic Effects	-0.7

the other hand, the other 72 possible interactions have been demonstrated to be sufficiently small and so can be safely ignored.

Also of interest are the quadratic effects. The screening experiment provides an estimate of the combined effect of all the quadratic effects. This is given at the bottom of Table 2.2. Since this combined effect is small, quadratic effects and beyond may be safely ignored. All that remains in order to model torque is to estimate the effects of the six interactions identified in the table.

Augmenting to form a model

In order to estimate the six interactions, data must be collected for 18 additional combinations of the design parameters. The required combinations and the resulting data are shown in Table 2.3. Using these data, the effects of the six interactions were calculated. The results are shown in Table 2.4. Of these six interactions, only the K^*L interaction has an effect greater than 3. This interaction will be included in the model. Using all of the data previously collected the following equation was fit to the data:

$$\text{Torque} = 97.7 - 14.51\,A - 12.95\,B - 3.855\,C + 3.505\,D + 2.467\,E$$
$$+ 0.257\,F - 11.35\,\text{UC} + 20.56\,H - 3.42\,K + 10.54\,L$$
$$+ 0.105\,KL - 0.0475\,M + 0.2378\,P + 75.3\,f$$

The effect of the design parameters can also be shown in the form of plots. Figure 2.1 shows the effects of all design parameters except K and L. Each of these plots assumes all other design parameters are at their center value. Because of the interaction between K and L, these two design parameters must be plotted together. Their joint effect is shown in the contour plot in Fig. 2.2 and the interaction plots in Fig. 2.3. These plots also assume all other design parameters are set to their middle value. These plots help illustrate the nature of interactions. Because of the K^*L interaction, the effect of changing K depends on where L is set and vice versa.

TABLE 2.3 Torque Augment Data

Trial Number	Design Parameters													Torque
	A	B	C	D	E	F	UC	H	K	L	M	P	f	
1	38.5	64.8	5.4	7.4	64.8	6	0.1	37.9	-20	36.0	14.5	0	0.1	25.2
2	38.5	64.8	5.4	5.4	64.8	6	0.1	37.9	-20	36.0	14.5	0	0.1	20.7
3	37.5	64.8	5.4	7.4	64.8	6	0.1	37.9	-20	36.0	14.5	0	0.1	35.7
4	37.5	64.8	5.4	5.4	64.8	6	0.1	38.4	20	36.0	14.5	0	0.1	57.4
5	37.5	64.8	5.4	5.4	64.8	6	0.1	38.4	-20	36.0	14.5	0	0.1	38.3
6	37.5	64.8	5.4	5.4	64.8	6	0.1	37.9	20	36.0	14.5	0	0.1	46.7
7	37.5	64.8	5.4	5.4	64.8	6	0.1	37.9	-20	36.0	14.5	0	0.1	62.6
8	37.5	64.8	5.4	5.4	64.8	6	0.1	37.9	-20	38.0	14.5	0	0.1	47.7
9	37.5	64.8	5.4	5.4	64.8	6	0.1	37.9	-20	36.0	14.5	0	0.1	42.4
10	37.5	64.8	5.4	7.4	64.8	6	0.5	37.9	-20	36.0	14.5	0	0.1	30.6
11	37.5	64.8	5.4	7.4	64.8	6	0.1	37.9	-20	36.0	14.5	0	0.1	35.7
12	37.5	64.8	5.4	5.4	64.8	6	0.5	37.9	-20	36.0	14.5	0	0.1	26.5
13	37.5	64.8	5.4	5.4	64.8	6	0.1	37.9	20	38.0	14.5	0	0.1	71.6
14	37.5	64.8	5.4	5.4	64.8	6	0.1	37.9	20	36.0	14.5	0	0.1	46.7
15	37.5	64.8	5.4	5.4	64.8	6	0.1	37.9	-20	38.0	14.5	0	0.1	47.7
16	37.5	64.8	5.4	5.4	64.8	6	0.1	38.4	-20	36.0	14.5	0	0.3	51.2
17	37.5	64.8	5.4	5.4	64.8	6	0.1	38.4	-20	36.0	14.5	0	0.1	38.3
18	37.5	64.8	5.4	5.4	64.8	6	0.1	37.9	-20	36.0	14.5	0	0.3	42.4

TABLE 2.4 Interaction Effects Table

Interaction	Effect
K*L	4.20
L*f	1.85
H*K	1.80
H*f	0.85
D*UC	-0.20
A*D	0.00

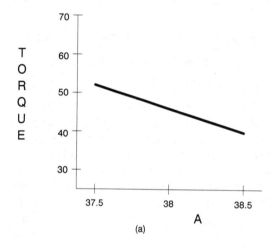

(a)

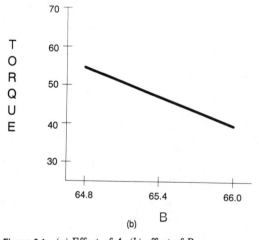

(b)

Figure 2.1 (a) Effect of A; (b) effect of B.

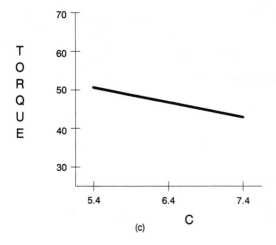

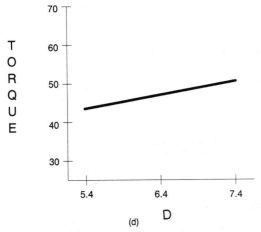

Figure 2.1 (*Continued*) (*c*) Effect of *C*; (*d*) effect of *D*.

One of the criteria of interest is to minimize the effect of component wear. In particular, one is interested in guarding against changes over time of the spring constant K. The interaction plot in Fig. 2.3*a* indicates that setting $L = 36.0$ reduces the slope of K's effect. This produces a smaller change in torque as a result of a change in K. Setting $L = 36.0$ results in a 40 percent reduction in the effect of K changing. If K deteriorates at a constant rate, the hinge will perform 40 percent longer. Likewise setting $K = -20$ makes the design less sensitive to changes in L. This may not be of benefit if L is tightly controlled.

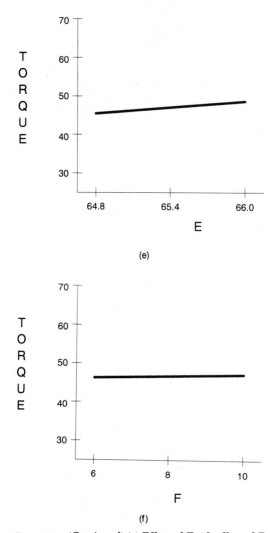

Figure 2.1   (*Continued*) (*e*) Effect of *E*; (*f*) effect of *F*.

Variation transmission analysis

The previous plots can be used to determine targets for the design parameters. Let these targets be denoted t_A, t_B,..., t_f. Numerous combinations of these targets will result in the same torque value. Therefore other criteria may be considered including cost. One important criterion is variation.

In production, the design parameters will each vary to some small degree. Let σ_A, σ_B,..., σ_f represent the variation of the design param-

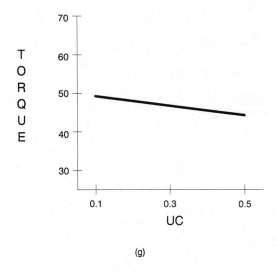

(g)

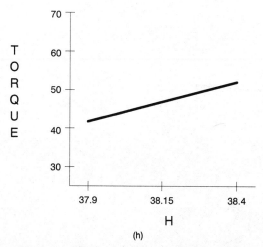

(h)

Figure 2.1 (*Continued*) (*g*) Effect of UC; (*h*) effect of *H*.

eters. Based on statistical theory and the equation determined in the previous section, the resulting average torque, μ_{torque}, and torque variation, σ_{torque}, are as follows:

$$\mu_{\text{torque}} = 97.7 - 14.51\,t_A - 12.95\,t_B - 3.855\,t_C + 3.505\,t_D + 2.467\,t_E$$
$$+ 0.2575\,t_F - 11.35\,t_{\text{UC}} + 20.56\,t_H - 3.42\,t_K + 10.54\,t_L + 0.105\,t_K\,t_L$$
$$- 0.0475\,t_M + 0.2378\,t_P + 75.3\,t_f$$

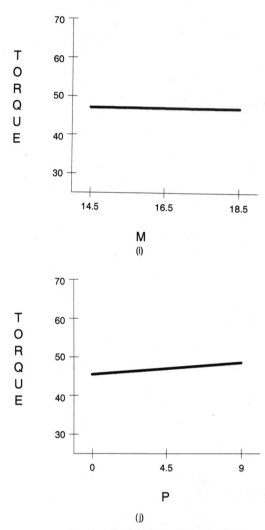

Figure 2.1 (*Continued*) (*i*) Effect of *M*; (*j*) effect of *P*.

$$\sigma^2_{\text{torque}} = 210.5\,\sigma^2_A + 167.7\,\sigma^2_B + 14.86\,\sigma^2_C + 12.29\,\sigma^2_D + 6.086\,\sigma^2_E$$
$$+\ 0.06631\,\sigma^2_F + 128.8\,\sigma^2_{\text{UC}} + 422.7\,\sigma^2_H + 11.70\,\sigma^2_K + 111.1\,\sigma^2_L$$
$$+\ 0.002256\,\sigma^2_M + 0.05655\,\sigma^2_P + 5670\,\sigma^2_f + 2.213\,\sigma^2_L\,t_K + \dots$$
$$+\ 0.7182\,\sigma^2_K\,t_L + 0.01102\,(\sigma^2_K\,\sigma^2_L + \sigma^2_L\,t^2_K + \sigma^2_K\,t^2_L)$$

Estimates of the amounts that the design parameters will vary are

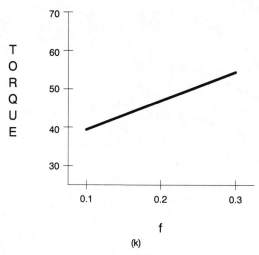

Figure 2.1 (*Continued*) (*k*) Effect of *f*.

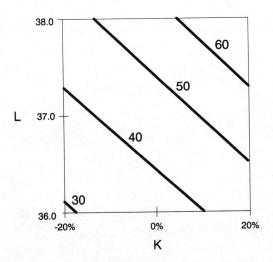

Figure 2.2 Contour plot of torque.

$$s_A = 0.16 \qquad s_B = 0.2 \qquad s_C = 0.33 \qquad s_D = 0.33$$

$$s_E = 0.2 \qquad s_F = 0.66 \qquad s_{UC} = 0.066 \qquad s_H = 0.083$$

$$s_K = 7.3 \qquad s_L = 0.33 \qquad s_M = 0.66 \qquad s_P = 1.5$$

$$s_f = 0.033$$

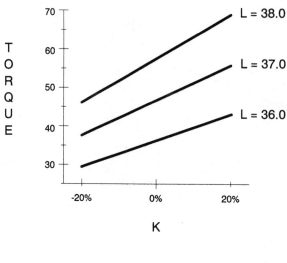

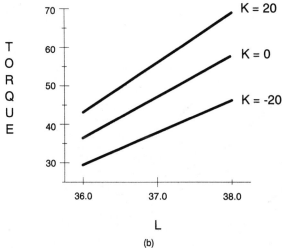

(b)

Figure 2.3 (a) $K*L$ interaction plot; (b) $K*L$ interaction plot.

Plugging these values into the above equation for $\sigma_A, \ldots, \sigma_f$ gives

$$\sigma_{\text{torque}} = \sqrt{660.8 + 0.2410\, t_K - 38.27\, t_L + 0.001200\, t_K^2 + 0.5873\, t_L^2}$$

Torque variation depends on the targets selected for K and L. A contour plot showing the relationship between these targets and the resulting variation is shown in Fig. 2.4. Selecting $K = -20$ percent and $L = 36$ minimizes the variation. In this case the reduction is rather minor, an 18.5 percent reduction from worst case. Selecting this com-

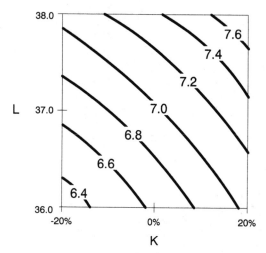

Figure 2.4   Contour plot of variation.

bination of values makes the design less sensitive to variation in K and L.

Targeting K and L affects both the average and variation. Such parameters are called VAPs or *variation adjustment parameters*. VAPs are generally targeted to minimize the variation. Targeting the other 11 design parameters affects only the target. The other parameters should be targeted so as to bring the average torque on target. Since there are more parameters than required, those parameters affecting cost the most should be set to reduce costs. Those parameters with the smallest impact on cost should be targeted to bring the average torque on target.

The equation for σ_{torque} can also be used to determine the contributions of each of the design parameters to the total variation. Figure 2.5 shows how much of the total variation is contributed by each of the design parameters under the worst case targets: $K = 20$ and $L = 38$. Parameters K and L contribute the most variation. Figure 2.5 follows the familiar Pareto shape, the majority of the variation resulting from just two parameters: K and L. Those few parameters contributing the most to the total variation are called VIPs or *variation inducing parameters*. In this case K and L are the VIPs. Setting $K = -20$ and $L = 36$ reduces the variation transmitted by the two VIPs. The result is shown in Fig. 2.6. The total variation is reduced from 7.73 to 6.30, an 18.5 percent reduction. While this is not a large reduction, it is essentially free and even this size of reduction in the variation can result in dramatic reductions in levels of defects.

Further reductions in variation require tightening tolerances on the

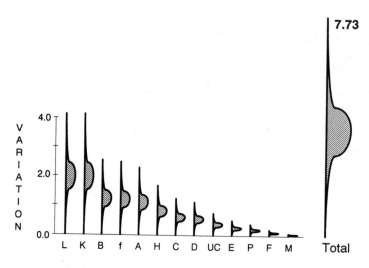

Figure 2.5   Transmitted variation ($K = 20$, $L = 38$).

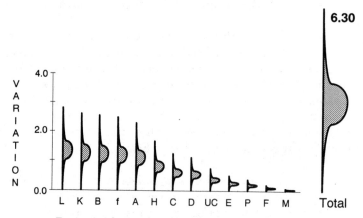

Figure 2.6   Transmitted variation ($K = 20$, $L = 36$).

design parameters. The five parameters L, K, B, f, and A are all contributing about equally. These are now the VIPs. Figure 2.7 shows what happens if the variation of each of these five parameters is reduced by 20 percent. The total variation is reduced from 6.30 to 5.04, an additional 20 percent reduction. This chart no longer follows the traditional Pareto shape. It is instead indicative of a balanced system. Further improvements will be increasingly more difficult and expensive.

This case study demonstrates how optimization and variation reduction can be accomplished early on during product design. The keys to

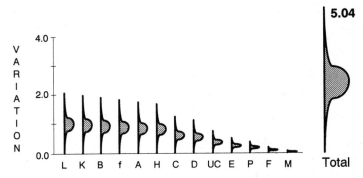

Figure 2.7 Transmitted variation (25 percent reduction in *K, L, B, f, A*).

reducing variation in a cost-effective fashion are identifying the VAPs and targeting them to minimize the variation, and identifying the VIPs and tightening their tolerances. The tolerances of non-VIPs should be widened to reduce costs. If one already has an equation, the screening experiment and augmentation may be skipped and the variation transmission analysis applied directly. If one does not have either a simulation or equation, the screening experiments and augmentation are required. However, collecting the data requires the construction of prototypes with different combinations of the design parameters whose performance can be measured.

2.2 Heat Sealer Case Study

This second case study illustrates the methods for performing optimization and variation reduction during *process development*. It involves the development of a heat-sealing process to form the top seal of a plastic bag. Forming the top seal closes the bag sealing its contents inside. The top seal is a tear seal. It must be torn open to remove the contents of the bag. Of interest is the seal strength. Too weak a seal can result in the bag breaking open during shipping and storage. Too strong a seal makes the bag difficult to open. Specification limits for seal strength have been set at 20 lb and 32 lb. The developer would like to target the process at 26 lb, reduce the variability of seal strength, make the process insensitive to material and process variations, and establish a procedure for controlling the process.

The plant already has a heat sealer which is believed capable of performing the job. The manufacturer of the heat sealer has provided the following recommended cycle:

Temperature – hot bar = 190°F

Temperature – cold bar = 100°F

Dwell time = 0.8 s*

Pressure = 100 lb

Cooling air pressure = 30 lb

Material thickness = 14.5 mils

The heat sealer works by clamping the material to be sealed between two bars. The top bar, called the hot bar, provides heat to melt the plastic materials and cause them to flow together to form the seal. The top bar also moves up and down to allow the material to be moved. The bottom bar is stationary and has cooling water running through it allowing its temperature to be controlled. When the top bar comes down to make contact with the material, it is lowered until it exerts a preset pressure on the material. It is then held there for a preset time. Before moving the material, cooling air is blown on the seal to facilitate hardening.

Process capability study

In order to evaluate the heat sealer, a *process capability study* was performed using the recommended cycle. Twenty groups of five samples were collected over a 4-h trial run. The data are shown in Table 2.5. The average and standard deviation of each group are also shown in Table 2.5. The standard deviation, covered in Part 2, is a measure of variation. These data were used to construct the average and standard deviation control charts shown in Figs. 2.8 and 2.9.

The *average control chart* is simply a plot of the averages of the 20 groups. The control limits represent the extent that the group averages should vary if the process does not shift. Points outside these control limits indicate that the process is shifting over time. As all points fall within the control limits, there is no evidence of any shifting. When all points remain within the control limits, the process is said to be stable. The *standard deviation control chart* is a plot of the standard deviations for the 20 groups. The fact that all points fall within the control limits means that the variation is not changing over time.

Since the process has proved to be stable, the 100 samples can be plotted in a histogram. The result is shown in Fig. 2.10. The histogram is centered at 26 lb. However, the histogram is wider than the specification limits. Processes whose variation is larger than the spec-

---

*Editor's note: The unit seconds is abbreviated throughout the book as s.

TABLE 2.5 Heat-Sealer Process Capability Data

GROUP	SAMPLES					AVERAGE	STD. DEV.
1	28.2	22.1	23.2	22.5	24.5	24.10	2.47
2	26.8	26.5	26.7	27.7	28.3	27.20	0.77
3	28.8	28.2	24.5	28.2	24.9	26.92	2.05
4	23.7	23.7	25.3	24.2	25.9	24.56	0.99
5	22.0	28.9	24.9	27.2	29.7	26.54	3.13
6	27.1	27.1	27.2	30.2	29.2	28.16	1.45
7	28.1	27.2	27.2	26.3	28.3	27.42	0.80
8	26.8	24.8	25.4	27.3	27.6	26.38	1.22
9	24.0	28.0	25.3	26.3	28.5	26.42	1.87
10	19.7	26.3	27.2	27.0	23.0	24.64	3.24
11	24.3	28.8	22.5	28.7	26.8	26.22	2.77
12	26.5	21.1	24.5	23.2	26.4	24.34	2.28
13	24.9	24.9	27.9	29.5	26.2	26.68	2.00
14	28.0	26.6	26.6	26.0	23.0	26.04	1.85
15	25.3	28.3	27.2	18.0	24.5	24.66	4.02
16	28.2	27.7	23.2	28.7	27.7	27.10	2.22
17	28.1	26.7	27.5	23.1	23.2	25.72	2.40
18	27.8	25.5	25.4	25.8	26.3	26.16	0.98
19	24.8	22.8	29.4	28.7	24.5	26.04	2.86
20	29.1	28.2	28.0	27.5	27.3	28.02	0.70

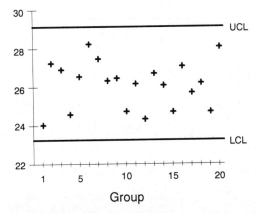

Figure 2.8 Control chart of averages.

ification limits are said to be not capable. A measure of process capability is the *capability index,* C_p, which for the heat sealer is

$$C_p = \frac{\text{USL} - \text{LSL}}{6s} = \frac{32 - 20}{6(2.2)} = 0.91$$

where USL is the upper specification limit of 32, LSL is the lower specification limit of 20, and s is an estimate of the process variation calculated from the data. Values of C_p less than 1.5 are unacceptable. Such processes are said to be not capable. Values of 2 or greater are

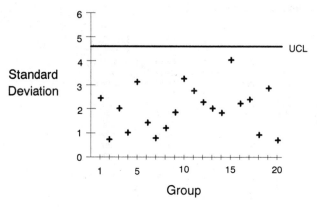

Figure 2.9   Control chart of standard deviations.

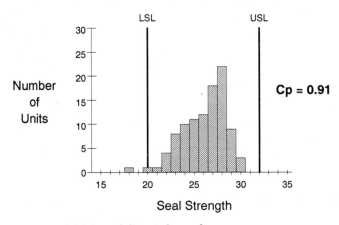

Figure 2.10   Initial capability study results.

excellent. For the heat sealer, C_p is 0.91, which is very low. This indicates that the process is not capable of holding the required specifications.

In the final analysis, the heat sealer has proved stable but not capable. The fact that the process is stable means that the process is consistent over time. However, the fact that the process is not capable means that the process is consistently producing defects. One might decide to try a different type of sealer. However, in this case it was decided to try to improve the existing sealer.

Screening experiment

In order to reduce the variation, it is first imperative to understand the heat-sealing process. This requires identifying the key parameters affecting seal strength, and understanding the effect these key inputs have on seal strength. With this understanding in hand, improvements can be identified that will reduce the variation.

The first step in understanding the heat-seal process is to identify the key parameters affecting seal strength. The tool for doing this is a *screening experiment*. A screening experiment will identify which of a long list of candidate parameters are the ones that are in fact critical to the process. In addition, a screening experiment will help identify interactions. Interactions play a key role in reducing variation.

In addition to the six parameters suggested by the manufacturer of the heat sealer, it was decided to examine two additional parameters: material temperature and room temperature. The complete list of parameters to be studied along with suggested ranges are as follows:

HB	Temperature – hot bar	150 to 200°F
CB	Temperature – cold bar	80 to 120°F
D	Dwell time	0.5 to 1.0 s
P	Pressure	50 to 150 lb
C	Cooling air pressure	0 to 30 lb
TH	Material thickness	14 to 15 mils
MT	Material temperature	70 to 110°F
RT	Room temperature	70 to 80°F

The screening experiment required running the 18 trials given in Table 2.6. For each trial, the machine was set to the required combination of HB, CB, $D, \ldots$, RT. The process was then run until it stabilized. Finally ten bags were selected and measured for seal strength. The

TABLE 2.6   Heat-Seal Screening Experiment

Trial Number	Process Parameters								Seal Strength	
	HB	CB	D	P	C	TH	MT	RT	Average	Std. Dev.
1	175	100	0.75	100	15	14.5	90	75	28.5	0.94
2	200	80	0.5	50	30	15.0	70	80	25.1	1.05
3	200	120	0.5	50	0	14.0	110	80	27.4	0.80
4	200	120	1.0	50	0	15.0	70	70	11.3	2.94
5	200	120	1.0	150	30	15.0	110	80	15.7	6.49
6	150	120	1.0	150	0	14.0	110	70	24.3	2.45
7	200	80	1.0	150	0	14.0	70	80	11.8	5.71
8	150	120	0.5	150	0	15.0	70	80	11.8	2.42
9	200	80	1.0	50	30	14.0	110	70	11.3	7.87
10	200	120	0.5	150	30	14.0	70	70	28.9	0.84
11	150	120	1.0	50	30	14.0	70	80	16.9	1.87
12	150	80	1.0	150	30	15.0	70	70	20.6	1.84
13	200	80	0.5	150	0	15.0	110	70	31.7	1.14
14	150	120	0.5	50	30	15.0	110	70	12.2	4.08
15	150	80	1.0	50	0	15.0	110	80	18.6	1.88
16	150	80	0.5	150	30	14.0	110	80	15.9	4.18
17	150	80	0.5	50	0	14.0	70	70	10.5	4.46
18	175	100	0.75	100	15	14.5	90	75	28.2	0.91

averages and standard deviations of these groups of ten samples are also reported in Table 2.6.

Using these data, the effect of each of the process parameters was calculated. The effects the process parameters have on the average seal strength are given in Table 2.7. These effects represent the amount that seal strength changes as a result of adjusting the parameters from their low values to their high values. Pressure, dwell time, temperature of the hot bar, and material temperature all have significant effects. The effects of the other four parameters are small, if they exist at all, when compared to the noise. In addition, an interaction between dwell time and the temperature of the hot bar has been identified. This interaction is denoted $D*HB$. The estimated effect of this interaction, -12.85, is dramatically larger than the effect of any of the individual parameters. Understanding this interaction is critical to the understanding of the heat sealer.

The screening experiment estimates the linear effects of the individual process parameters. This is sufficient for identifying the key parameters. But it does not provide the level of understanding that will be required later on. While the screening experiment cannot estimate the nonlinear effects (quadratic, cubic, and so forth) of the individual parameters, it can provide an estimate of the combined effect of all the nonlinear terms. The resulting estimate of -10.15 is large, indicating strong quadratic effects exist. The data already collected will have to be supplemented with new data in order to identify the particular quadratic effects involved.

The effects that the design parameters have on the seal-strength standard deviation are given in Table 2.8. Both dwell time and the $D*HB$ interaction affect the variation. Since targeting of both dwell time and temperature of the hot bar affects the variation, these two parameters are VAPs. Generally VAPs are targeted to minimize the variation. In addition, quadratic effects are present requiring additional data to be collected.

The screening experiment identified four key process parameters:

TABLE 2.7   Seal-Strength Average: Significant Effects

Design Parameter		Effect
D*HB	Dwell Time * Hot Bar Interaction	-11.62
-	Combined Quadratic Effects	-9.98
D	Dwell Time	-4.12
HB	Temperature - Hot Bar	4.05
P	Pressure	3.42
MT	Material Temperature	2.52

TABLE 2.8   Seal-Strength Standard Deviation: Significant
Effects

Design Parameter		Effect
D*HB	Dwell Time * Hot Bar Interaction	3.28
-	Combined Quadratic Effects	2.20
D	Dwell Time	1.51

HB, D, P, and MT. The screening experiment also determined that
two of these parameters, HB and D, are VAPs.

Response surface study

Now that the screening experiment has determined the key process
parameters, a *response surface study* can be run to help understand
the relationship between these key parameters and seal strength. The
response surface study will provide plots of the effects of the key parameters as well as an equation.

The data already collected during the screening experiment can be
reused. However, the response surface study also requires additional
data to be collected. In order to determine which quadratic effects exist, the 12 additional trials given in Table 2.9 must be run. The resulting data are also given. The effects for the average and standard deviation are given in Tables 2.10 and 2.11, respectively. In addition to the
effects previously found, both dwell time and temperature of the hot
bar have quadratic effects affecting the average, and dwell time has a
quadratic effect affecting the standard deviation.

Also as part of a response surface analysis, a *lack-of-fit test* is performed. The lack-of-fit test indicates whether the model fit to the data
is adequate. The model in this case consists of linear, quadratic, and

TABLE 2.9   Additional Data for Response Surface Study

Trial Number	Process Parameters								Seal Strength	
	HB	CB	D	P	C	TH	MT	RT	Average	Std. Dev.
19	175	-	0.75	50	-	-	70	-	24.8	0.76
20	175	-	0.5	100	-	-	70	-	25.1	2.70
21	200	-	1.0	100	-	-	90	-	13.4	4.17
22	175	-	1.0	150	-	-	90	-	22.2	3.62
23	200	-	0.75	150	-	-	90	-	26.3	2.07
24	150	-	0.75	100	-	-	70	-	20.5	3.05
25	200	-	1.0	100	-	-	90	-	8.9	4.74
26	175	-	1.0	150	-	-	90	-	25.6	3.56
27	200	-	0.75	150	-	-	90	-	27.7	2.04
28	175	-	0.5	100	-	-	70	-	24.8	2.52
29	150	-	0.5	50	-	-	90	-	8.9	3.40
30	175	-	0.75	50	-	-	70	-	24.5	0.74

TABLE 2.10   Response Surface Effects Table for Seal-
Strength Average

Design Parameter		Effect
D*HB	Dwell Time * Hot Bar Interaction	-11.88
HB*HB	Temperature - Hot Bar (quad.)	-5.66
D*D	Dwell Time (quad.)	-4.90
D	Dwell Time (linear)	-4.10
HB	Temperature - Hot Bar (linear)	4.05
P	Pressure (linear)	4.00
MT	Material Temperature (linear)	2.55

TABLE 2.11   Response Surface Effects Table for Seal-
Strength Standard Deviation

Design Parameter		Effect
D*HB	Dwell Time * Hot Bar Interaction	3.14
D	Dwell Time (linear)	1.43
D*D	Dwell Time (quad.)	1.02

two-way interaction terms. The model passes the lack-of-fit test indicating further terms, such as cubic or higher-order interactions, do not
have to be added to the model.

Now that a good model has been obtained, it is time to examine the
plots in order to understand the effect that the key parameters have
on seal strength. There are four key parameters: temperature of the
hot bar, dwell time, pressure, and material temperature. The first two
are also VAPs, as they also affect the variation. The second two affect
just the average. Since the primary concern is excessive variation, it
was decided to try to target the two VAPs, temperature of the hot bar
and dwell time, in order to minimize the variation and then adjust the
other two key parameters, pressure and material temperature, in order to bring the average seal strength on target.

The place to start is with the plot given in Fig. 2.11. This plot shows
the affect that temperature of the hot bar and dwell time have on the
variation. The lowest possible standard deviation is 1.02 obtained
when temperature of the hot bar is 200°F and dwell time is 0.625 s. As
the standard deviation was 2.2 during the capability study, this represents over a 50 percent reduction in the variation.

The second plot, Fig. 2.12, shows the effect of temperature of the hot
bar and dwell time on the average. If temperature of the hot bar is set
to 200°F and dwell time is set to 0.625 s, the resulting average is

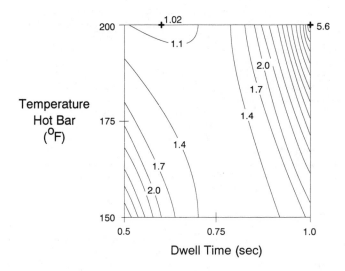

Figure 2.11   Contour plot of seal-strength standard deviation.

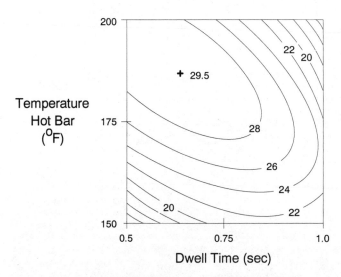

Figure 2.12   Seal-strength average (P = 100 lb, MT = 90°F).

around 28 lb. This is 2 lb too high. This plot assumes that pressure is set to 100 lb and that material temperature is set to 90°F. Therefore, these two key parameters must be adjusted to bring the average on target.

Figure 2.13 shows the effect of pressure and material temperature on the average, assuming the temperature of the hot bar is set to 200°F and dwell time is set to 0.625 s. Setting pressure equal to 80 lb targets seal

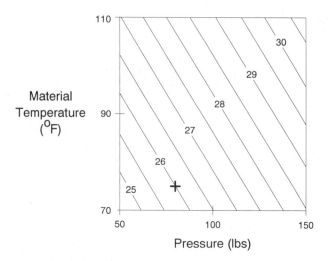

Figure 2.13   Seal-strength average (HB = 200°F, D = 0.625 s).

strength at 26 lb while allowing material temperature to be equal to the room temperature (75°F). This avoids the need for a preheating chamber. Based on the findings so far, the following recommendations can be made:

- Set HB = 200°F and D = 0.625 s in order to minimize variation.
- Set P = 80 lb to put the average on target.
- Set MT = RT to reduce costs. Also set CB, C, TH, and RT to low-cost values.
- Adjust the process average using P, if necessary.

These recommendations satisfy the four objectives laid out initially:

1. Target the process at 26 lb.

2. Reduce seal-strength variation. This was accomplished by setting HB = 200°F and D = 0.625 s. However, the possibility of tightening tolerances to further reduce the variation has not been explored.

3. Make the process insensitive to material and process variation. Setting HB = 200°F and D = 0.625 s makes the process less sensitive to variation of both temperature of the hot bar and dwell time. This is evident in Fig. 2.12. This point is in a region where the contour lines are far apart.

4. Establish control procedures. Pressure has been determined to be the proper adjustment parameter for targeting of the average. Tolerances for the process parameters have not yet been established.

The major task left to be accomplished is the setting of tolerances. In addition to the plots, an equation for seal strength can be obtained. The resulting equation is:

Seal strength = $- 431.35 + 3.933$ HB $+ 273.9\,D + 0.03803\,P$

$$+ 0.06120\text{ MT} - 0.008947\text{ HB}^2 - 75.72\,D^2 - 0.9640\text{ HB }D$$

The HB^2 and D^2 terms are the quadratic terms. The HB D term is the HB*D interaction. This equation can be used to perform a variation transmission analysis. As part of the variation transmission analysis, tolerances for the process parameters can be established.

Variation transmission analysis

So far it has been determined that setting temperature of the hot bar to 200°F and dwell time to 0.625 s minimizes the seal-strength variation. But it is not understood why this works as it does. In particular, the cause of the seal-strength variation has not been determined. Understanding the cause of the seal-strength variation might result in even further reductions of the variation. *Variation transmission analysis* can be used to understand the cause of variation.

Variation transmission analysis requires an equation such as the one obtained for seal strength. It assumes that the averages of the process parameters are t_{HB}, t_D, t_P, and t_{MT}, respectively, and that these parameters vary around their averages with standard deviations σ_{HB}, σ_D, σ_P, and σ_{MT}. Based on these assumptions the standard deviation of seal strength σ_{SS} can be determined to be

$$\sigma_{\text{SS}}^2 = (3.933\,\sigma_{\text{HB}})^2 + (273.9\,\sigma_D)^2 + (0.03803\,\sigma_P)^2 + (0.0612\,\sigma_{\text{MT}})^2$$

$$+ (-0.008947)^2\,(4\,t_{\text{HB}}^2\,\sigma_{\text{HB}}^2 + 2\,\sigma_{\text{HB}}^4) + (-75.72)^2\,(4\,t_D^2\,\sigma_D^2 + 2\,\sigma_D^4)$$

$$+ (-0.964)^2\,(\sigma_{\text{HB}}^2\,\sigma_D^2 + t_{\text{HB}}^2\,\sigma_D^2 + t_D^2\,\sigma_{\text{HB}}^2)$$

$$+ 4\,(3.933)\,(-0.008947)\,t_{\text{HB}}\,\sigma_{\text{HB}}^2 + 4\,(273.9)\,(-75.72)\,t_D\,\sigma_D^2$$

$$+ 2\,(3.933)\,(-0.964)\,t_D\,\sigma_{\text{HB}}^2 + 2\,(273.9)\,(-0.964)\,t_{\text{HB}}\,\sigma_D^2$$

$$+ 4\,(-0.008947)\,(-0.964)\,t_{\text{HB}}\,t_D\,\sigma_{HB}^2 + 4\,(-75.72)\,(-0.964)\,t_{\text{HB}}\,t_D\,\sigma_D^2$$

σ_{SS} depends on t_{HB}, t_D, σ_{HB}, σ_D, σ_P, and σ_{MT}. It does not depend on t_P and t_{MT}. Adjusting temperature of the hot bar and dwell time affects the variation. These two parameters are therefore VAPs. Adjusting pressure and material temperature does not affect the variation. This agrees with the results obtained from analyzing the observed variation.

In addition to an equation, a variation transmission analysis requires information on how much each of the process parameters is varying. The following estimates of the variation of the process parameters were obtained by measuring the process parameters during the course of normal production:

$$s_{HB} = 2°F$$

$$s_D = 0.08 \text{ s}$$

$$s_P = 1 \text{ lb}$$

$$s_{MT} = 4°F$$

Plugging these values into the above equation for σ_{HB} through σ_{MT} gives

$$\sigma_{SS} = \sqrt{\begin{array}{c} 542.57 - 3.9426 \, t_{HB} - 561.27 \, t_D + 0.0071622 \, t_{HB}^2 \\ + 150.50 \, t_D^2 + 2.0067 \, t_{HB} \, t_D \end{array}}$$

A contour plot showing the effect that adjusting temperature of the hot bar and dwell time has on seal-strength variation is shown in Fig. 2.14. Selecting HB = 186°F and D = 0.625 s minimizes the variation. The resulting variation is estimated to be 0.75. This recommendation, while differing somewhat from the previous recommendation, is in general agreement with the results obtained by observing the variation directly. This should be the case whenever the variation during the course of the study is representative of actual manufacturing conditions. Variation transmission analysis can, however, be particularly

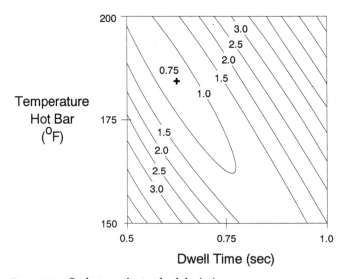

Figure 2.14   Seal-strength standard deviation.

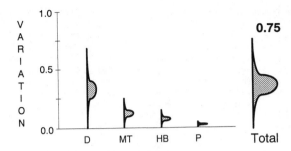

Figure 2.15 Transmitted variation (HB = 186°F, D = 0.625 s).

advantageous when this is not the case and the observed variation is meaningless.

Variation transmission analysis can also be used to examine the contributions of the individual inputs to the total variation. This allows tolerances to be established. The equation for σ_{SS} shows the total variation resulting from variation of the four key process parameters. It can also be used to determine the contribution of the individual inputs. The results when HB = 186°F and D = 0.625 s are shown in Fig. 2.15. The total variation is shown along with the individual contributions of the four process parameters. Most of the variation results from the dwell-time variation. Dwell time is therefore the primary source of variation. Such parameters are called VIPs. Reducing the variation further requires tightening the tolerances on dwell time. This can be accomplished by replacing the timing mechanism with a more accurate but also more expensive one. The result would be to reduce σ_D to 0.04 s. Figure 2.16 shows the resulting reduction in seal-strength variation. Based on the estimated improvement, it was decided to implement the more accurate timing mechanism.

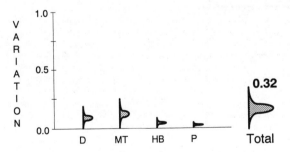

Figure 2.16 Transmitted variation after reducing dwell-time variation.

TABLE 2.12   Heat-Sealer Process Capability Data

GROUP	SAMPLES					AVERAGE	STD. DEV.
1	25.8	27.7	26.8	26.3	25.3	26.38	0.93
2	26.5	26.8	27.2	26.0	26.8	26.66	0.44
3	26.5	26.0	26.7	26.1	27.0	26.46	0.42
4	27.3	25.5	25.7	26.6	27.1	26.44	0.81
5	26.6	26.3	27.4	25.2	26.2	26.34	0.79
6	25.8	26.8	26.0	26.6	26.2	26.28	0.41
7	24.4	27.0	27.2	27.1	27.3	26.60	1.23
8	24.7	25.9	26.8	29.0	25.3	26.34	1.68
9	26.4	25.1	25.7	27.4	27.4	26.40	1.02
10	27.9	26.1	26.6	27.1	26.7	26.88	0.67
11	27.4	25.8	26.4	27.0	26.1	26.54	0.65
12	27.2	26.3	27.4	27.2	27.1	27.04	0.43
13	26.1	25.0	26.9	27.9	28.5	26.88	1.40
14	27.5	25.7	27.4	25.4	25.9	26.38	0.99
15	26.9	25.5	25.7	27.1	26.6	26.38	0.72
16	26.6	25.5	26.0	27.0	25.2	26.06	0.75
17	27.0	25.4	26.4	26.5	25.4	26.14	0.71
18	26.8	26.5	26.8	28.3	27.2	27.12	0.70
19	26.4	25.9	25.9	27.3	26.8	26.46	0.60
20	26.3	27.2	27.6	27.5	25.3	26.78	0.97

Final process capability study

In order to verify the expected improvements, a second capability study was run. The study was run the same as before. The data are given in Table 2.12. The average and standard deviation control charts are given in Figs. 2.17 and 2.18. As all points are within the control limits on both plots, the process is stable. Therefore, the process capability can be determined.

Figure 2.19 shows a histogram of the results. While the process is

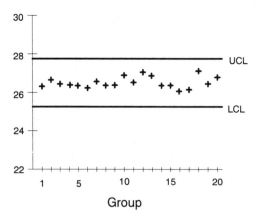

Figure 2.17   Control chart of averages.

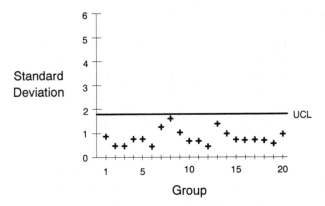

Figure 2.18 Control chart of standard deviations.

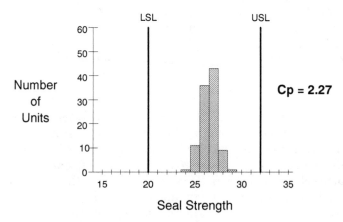

Figure 2.19 Final capability study results.

slightly off center, all units are easily within the specifications. The process is capable. The new process capability index is

$$C_p = \frac{\text{USL} - \text{LSL}}{6\sigma} = \frac{30 - 20}{6(0.88)} = 1.89$$

An acceptable C_p, $C_p \geq 1.5$, has been achieved.

2.3 Multi-head Filler Case Study

The problem

Ideally optimization and variation reduction should be performed during product and process design so that at start-up the objectives are achieved. However, sometimes things are missed that later surface during *manufacturing.* Further, there are many existing products and processes where optimization and variation reduction was never attempted during the design phase. In these cases, optimization and variation reduction must be performed during manufacturing. The same methods applied during design can also be applied during manufacturing. However, during manufacturing the process can be observed for extended periods of time. This allows a different set of methods to be applied that frequently reduce the time required to solve the problem.

The third case study, the multi-head filler, illustrates the use of these additional optimization and variation reduction methods for process improvement. The multi-head filler is used to fill small vials with reagents. Common fill volumes are 5, 10, and 20 ml. The problem is excessive variation as shown in the histogram in Fig. 2.20. This histogram represents the results of 80 vials drawn at random from a single production lot. The target fill volume for this lot is 10 ml. Specification limits are always ±10 percent of target. Therefore, for this 10-ml fill, the specification limits are 9 to 11 ml. Because of the excessive variation, 34 percent of the vials fall outside these limits.

The process

The multi-head filler, shown in Fig. 2.21, consists of ten syringes (A) mounted between two horizontal bars. The top bar (B) is stationary. The bottom bar (C) moves up and down. On each stroke of the machine, ten vials are filled. The motor (D) moves the left end of the curved drive arm (E) up and down. This in turn moves the straight drive arm (F) and the bottom bar (C) up and down.

Fill volume can be controlled by either changing the size of the sy-

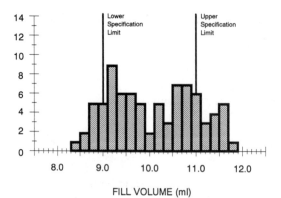

Figure 2.20   Histogram of lot BZ1089-45.

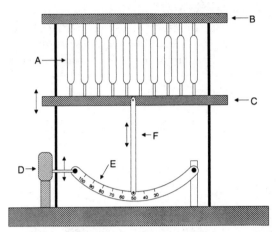

Figure 2.21   Multi-head filling machine.

ringes or by adjusting stroke length. Syringes are available in 5-, 10-, 20-, and 40-ml sizes. Stroke length can be adjusted by changing the point of attachment between the straight drive arm (*F*) and the curved drive arm (*E*). The stroke length can be adjusted from 30 percent up to around 110 percent of full stroke. Full stroke (100 percent) with a 40-ml syringe will result in a 40-ml fill. Half stroke (50 percent) with the same 40-ml syringe will result in a 20-ml fill.

The syringe, shown in Fig. 2.22, draws its solution from a common solution tank. Each of the ten syringes works by drawing solution in through one opening on the down stroke, and then pushing

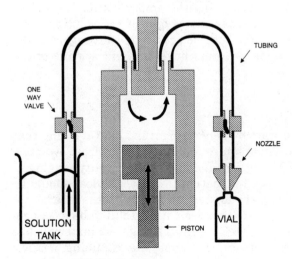

Figure 2.22   Individual syringe.

this solution out a second opening on the up stroke. Two one-way valves keep the solution flowing in the right direction. Critical factors determining the fill volume are stroke length, syringe diameter, and amount of back flow. The theoretical formula relating these three parameters is

$$V = 16.387 \left(\frac{\pi}{4}\right) D^2 S - B$$

where V = volume, ml
D = syringe diameter, in
S = stroke length, in
B = amount of back flow, ml

The constant 16.387 converts the volume from cubic inches to milliliters. The constant π is equal to 3.14159. At full stroke (100 percent) the stroke length is 3 in. The nominal syringe diameters are

Syringe size	Nominal diameter
5 ml	0.3599 in
10 ml	0.5089 in
20 ml	0.7197 in
40 ml	1.0178 in

These nominals result in the rated fill volumes when running full stroke and assuming no back flow.

Fill volume is measured by weighing a filled bottle, emptying and drying the bottle, and then measuring the empty bottle. The difference between these two weights is the weight of the solution. This weight is then multiplied by the specific gravity of the reagent to determine its volume. Different reagents have different specific gravities.

Possible causes

It is often worthwhile to start by generating a list of everything that might affect fill volume. This requires obtaining input from everyone involved in the process including manufacturing, quality, engineering, and the material experts. In creating this list, all ideas should be considered. This is not the place to start evaluating these ideas.

To help generate and organize the ideas, it is useful to have categories. For the multi-head filler such categories might be materials (solution and vials), machine (motor, drive arms, valves, tubing, nozzles, and syringe mountings), tools (syringes), methods, man* (operators), environment, and measurement. These categories include the four Ms: machine, materials, methods, and man. Also included is the fifth M, measurement, to allow for the fact that measurement variation may count for at least some of the observed variation. In addition, tooling has been separated from machine, and environment has been added.

Using these categories, a multidiscipline team generated the following list of items that might affect fill volume:

- *Materials.* Solution temperature and viscosity, the presence of bubbles, and the height of the solution in the holding tank. Variation of the specific gravity of the reagent. Tendency of solution to gum up valves. Too narrow an opening in vials and improper centering of vials under nozzles. Moisture or contamination of vials.

- *Machine.* Variations in stroke length because of variations in motor stroke or sloppy fitting of drive arms. Wobble in bottom bar because of improper tolerances with side guide bars. Difficulty of adjustment. Valve leakage and sticking. Differences in connecting tubes, nozzles, and alignment of attachments for syringes.

- *Tools (syringes).* Inside diameter, warping and sticking, leakage, and other dimensional variations.

- *Method.* Cleaning procedure, setup procedure, and stroke adjustment procedure.

- *Man.* Improper stroke adjustments and running damaged syringes.

- *Environment.* Temperature and humidity.

- *Measurement.* Accuracy limitation of scale, improper calibration, improper drying of bottles for empty weight, calculation errors, and operator errors.

All these ideas can be summarized in a cause and effect diagram as shown in Fig. 2.23.

Constructing a cause and effect diagram is a good way of quickly becoming familiar with the process. It brings to light the numerous possibilities and conflicting viewpoints. Everyone feels satisfaction in having their views considered. Open communication helps to build a team spirit. However, the cause and effect diagram does not solve the problem. To maintain the cooperation and feeling of progress without breaking into fractions requires a systematic approach whereby

---

*Editor's note: *Man* is traditionally used and in no way reflects gender.

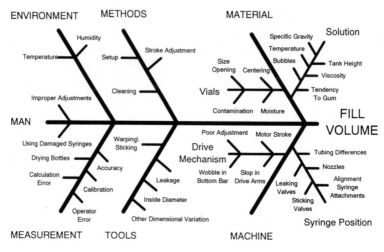

ENVIRONMENT   METHODS   MATERIAL

Figure 2.23   Cause and effect diagram.

everyone's ideas will be duly considered, and ideas are fairly evaluated, being eliminated only on the basis of hard data.

Diagnostic process

So how does one proceed next? One possibility is to take actions to study and fix each of the potential causes listed in the *cause and effect diagram*. Each potential cause could be assigned as an action item. For efficiency, only the most likely potential causes might be assigned. While this procedure will solve the problem, so long as the cause is on the cause and effect diagram, considerable effort is wasted fixing things that are not broken. A much better way is to first diagnose the cause(s) of the problem.

Consider the game of 20 questions. One player picks an object and tells the other players whether it is an animal, vegetable, or mineral. The other players then ask yes and no questions to try to determine the object. They must determine the object within 20 questions or they lose. Starting by asking, "Is it a phone?", "Is it a TV?", and "Is it a house?" will eventually determine the object. But it is not very likely the object will be determined in the allotted 20 questions. This is akin to fixing each of the possible causes on the cause and effect diagram.

The best strategy is to ask questions that roughly divide the possible objects in half, thus eliminating half of the remaining objects. This leads to questions like "Is it bigger than a bread box?" and "Are they currently living?" Using this strategy, within 20 questions over three million objects can be determined. Using this same process, one can quickly diagnose the cause of the excessive filling variation.

Diagnosing the cause of excessive fill variation differs from 20 questions in several important ways:

- The number of objects we are sorting among is much smaller. There are only 35 potential causes listed in the cause and effect diagram.

- One is not allowed 20 questions. Each question corresponds to the collection and analysis of data. Typically one to four such questions is reasonable.

- One is not limited to yes and no questions. Questions can be asked with many different answers. The first question might determine whether the primary cause is material, machine, tool, method, man, measurement, or environment. The next question might determine the next branch. Within two or three questions the cause of the problem can easily be isolated.

- Not all questions may be asked. Each question requires collecting and analyzing data. It is difficult to devise a study that could determine which of the seven primary branches the cause lies on. But other questions that are just as effective can be asked so that it is still possible to isolate the cause of the problem within two to three questions.

- More than one cause may exist. This means that some questions may result in two different branches being identified as containing causes.

Part of learning optimization and variation reduction consists of learning which questions can be asked and how to collect the data to get an answer. The process should always begin by looking at the data that are already available and determining which questions they can answer. Then special studies can be designed to gather new information not previously available. It is not necessary to list all the possible causes before beginning the diagnostic process any more than one needs a list of all possible words in order to play 20 questions. The cause and effect diagram is not a requirement. It is, however, generally beneficial in that it fosters teamwork, open communication, and a structured approach.

A key element of the diagnostic process is to recognize the symptoms that will be exhibited by each of the potential causes. A change in specific gravity should affect all ten syringes since they are drawing from the same solution tank and should persist for the entire batch (corresponding to one filling of the solution tank). Wobble in the bottom bar should cause differences among the syringes. Possibly the center syringes will have smaller fills than the end ones. It is also possible that those at one end may fill higher than those at the other end.

Moisture in vials should cause a sporadic problem not associated with any particular syringe.

Recognizing the symptoms associated with each potential cause allows one to isolate the cause in a manner similar to that used by a doctor for diagnosing a disease. A doctor compares the observed symptoms with the symptoms of the potential diseases. By simply asking questions the doctor can eliminate a large number of diseases. This may narrow the field to just a couple of possibilities for which the doctor orders tests to complete and confirm the diagnosis.

Using this strategy the cause(s) of the fill-volume variation will first be diagnosed. The diagnostic process will begin with two sources of information already available: quality control (Q.C.) inspection results and a start-up study. Then specific studies will be devised to answer further questions in order to complete the diagnosis.

Q.C. inspection data

The final inspection of each lot requires the testing of 80 samples. In order to pass the inspection, no more than two samples can exceed the specification limits. Since runs are 8-h* long, a random sample of five vials is collected and measured every half hour. One thing that can be done with these data are to plot them in the order collected. This would indicate whether at least a part of the variation is the result of shifting of the process over time. A time plot constructed from the Q.C. inspection data for lot BZ1089-45 is shown in Fig. 2.24. Such a plot is called a Multi-Vari chart. The time periods 1 to 16 on the bottom axis correspond to the half-hour time periods ½, 1, 1½,..., 8 h. For each time period five samples are plotted, one above the other and connected with a vertical line. In addition, the middle value of each time period is circled. These circled points are called medians. The medians are connected to help highlight any time trend.

Looking at the median line in Fig. 2.24, it appears that the first two time periods are slightly lower than the others. Looking at the vertical bars, it appears the time periods 3 to 8 are slightly higher than 9 to 16 with period 14 standing out as an oddball. It is difficult, however, to judge what are significant effects and what is simply normal variation within the data. Help in making these decisions is available in the form of control charts.

Before proceeding with the control charts, it should be noted that the data used for the time plot in Fig. 2.24 are the same data used for the histogram in Fig. 2.20. The data are listed in Table 2.13. The last two columns give the average and range of the five samples from each period.

---

*Editor's note: The unit hours is abbreviated throughout the book as h.

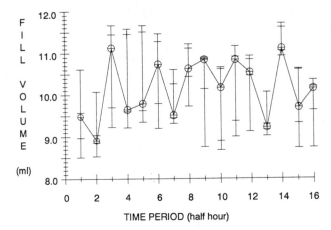

Figure 2.24   Multi-Vari chart of lot BZ1089-45.

TABLE 2.13   Q.C. Inspection Data for Lot BZ1089-45

PERIOD	SAMPLES					AVERAGE	RANGE
1	10.62	8.98	9.67	9.52	8.45	9.45	2.17
2	8.89	8.54	8.91	10.08	9.02	9.09	1.54
3	9.19	11.62	11.07	11.48	9.71	10.61	2.43
4	11.45	9.20	11.54	9.62	9.65	10.29	2.34
5	11.62	11.52	9.75	9.67	9.37	10.39	2.25
6	11.45	10.75	9.75	11.31	9.19	10.49	2.26
7	10.24	9.41	10.63	9.50	9.33	9.82	1.30
8	11.10	10.64	11.26	9.74	10.40	10.63	1.52
9	10.89	10.90	10.88	10.14	8.74	10.31	2.16
10	10.12	10.70	8.66	10.66	8.88	9.80	2.04
11	10.90	11.15	10.81	9.37	8.98	10.24	2.17
12	10.48	10.56	10.83	9.11	10.95	10.39	1.84
13	9.19	9.17	10.08	9.02	9.30	9.35	1.06
14	11.63	11.71	11.09	10.94	11.03	11.28	0.77
15	9.71	8.75	9.29	10.64	10.59	9.80	1.89
16	10.18	8.72	10.15	10.36	9.57	9.80	1.64

The average is determined by adding the five values together and dividing by 5. For example, the average for period 1 is calculated as follows:

$$\text{Average} = \frac{10.62 + 8.98 + 9.67 + 9.52 + 8.45}{5} = 9.45$$

The range is calculated by subtracting the smallest value from the largest. For period 1, the largest value is 10.62 and the smallest value is 8.45. Therefore the range is

$$\text{Range} = 10.62 - 8.45 = 2.17$$

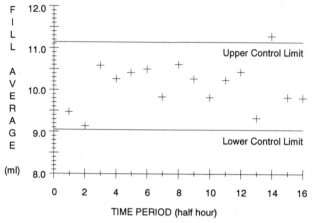

Figure 2.25   Average chart of lot BZ1089-45.

Figures 2.25 and 2.26 give average and range control charts for the data above. The average chart is simply a time plot of the period averages. The range chart is a time plot of the period ranges. The charts also contain control limits to aid their interpretation. The control limits were calculated using the data. The method of calculating these limits is fully explained in Part 3. The method of calculation is not important here. What is important is how to interpret the charts using the control limits.

A point outside the control limits indicates that during that time period the process was clearly different from the majority of the other time periods. An average above the upper control limit or below the

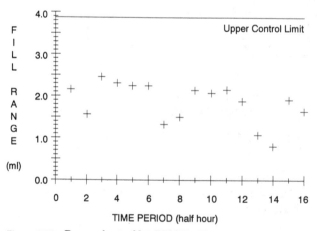

Figure 2.26   Range chart of lot BZ1089-45.

lower control limit indicates that the process average was different during that time period. A range above the upper control limit indicates the process had become more variable. No lower control limit is shown for the range because the sample size is insufficient to reliably detect a decrease in the variation. The range chart in Fig. 2.26 indicates that the variation within the time periods is stable over time. No time period has a variation that is noticeably larger than the others.

The average control chart does have one point out of the control limits. Period 14 certainly has a higher average fill volume than the majority of the other time periods. The fact that periods 1 and 2 appear slightly lower than the preceding periods is not confirmed by the chart. This may still be the case. However, the evidence is not conclusive. We have learned that there is little shifting over time. Most of the variation is occurring within the time periods. But how does this help us determine the cause of the variation? Based on the above results approximately one-third of the potential causes can be eliminated from further consideration. To understand how, some additional background in components of variation is needed.

Any time product can be segregated into groups by some criteria (time, syringes, cavities, etc.). The variation can be split into two components of variation: *within-group variation* and variation due to *group-to-group differences*.

Total variation = within-group variation + group-to-group differences

Figure 2.27 shows how this is done.

The total variation is represented by a *histogram* of all the samples. The within-group variation is represented by individual histograms of

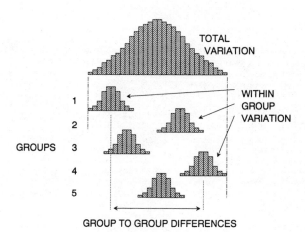

Figure 2.27 Components of variation: large group differences.

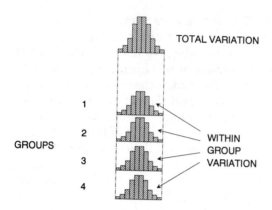

Figure 2.28 Components of variation: small group differences.

each group. The variation due to group-to-group differences is then represented by the differences among the group histograms. When the group-to-group differences are large, the results look like Fig. 2.27. The largest source of variation is causing the group differences. However, when the group-to-group differences are small, the results look more like Fig. 2.28. In this case the largest source of variation is causing within-group variation.

Having completed this background on components of variation, let us return to the multi-head filler. Figure 2.29 shows a schematic of a production lot. There are two natural groupings of the vials: by time

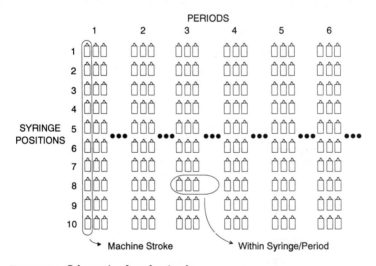

Figure 2.29 Schematic of production lot.

periods and by syringe positions. The result is that the total variation can be split into three components:

Total variation = within-period/syringe variation
    + period-to-period differences + syringe-to-syringe differences

Figure 2.30 shows how the total variation can be decomposed into these three components.

The fact that the variation can be split into components provides us with a powerful investigation tool. Most of the potential causes of variation will contribute to only one of these three components of variation. Some might contribute to several. By eliminating components that do not significantly contribute to the total variation, many potential causes can be eliminated.

Now the importance of the control charts should become apparent. These control charts indicate that most of the variation is associated with the *within-period variation*. The within-period variation is a combination of the *within-syringe/period variation* and the *syringe-to-syringe differences*. Those potential causes whose sole contribution is to *period-to-period differences* can be set aside for the time being. Of course, once other sources of variation have been eliminated, one of

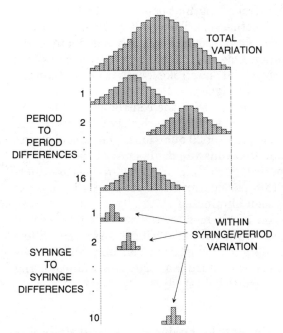

Figure 2.30 Components of variation: multi-head filler.

these causes may take over. But for the time being they can safely be set aside.

Which potential causes contribute to the period-to-period differences? One example is *changes of the solution height in the fill tank* where all syringes share a common fill tank and so should be equally affected. Therefore this potential cause cannot contribute to syringe-to-syringe differences. Further, the height changes little over short periods of time. Therefore this potential cause should not contribute to within-syringe/period variation. The solution height will, however, change significantly during a production run and thus may contribute to the period-to-period differences. A second example is *improper stroke length adjustments* where setting the stroke length too long or too short should affect all ten syringes equally since they are attached to common bars. Therefore this potential cause cannot contribute to syringe-to-syringe differences. Improper adjustments occur at specific points in time causing shifting that will for the most part be evident as period-to-period differences. Such a shift may contribute to the within-period variation only for the period during which the adjustment was made. These two potential causes and others like them can be eliminated for the time being.

Remaining are those potential causes affecting the within-period variation. Some of these potential causes contribute to syringe-to-syringe differences. One such potential cause is *wobble in bottom bar*. Wobble in the bottom bar might cause the stroke length at one end to be longer than that at either the center or the other end. The result would be consistent syringe-to-syringe differences. Other potential causes contribute to the within-syringe/period variation. One such example is *variations in stroke length between consecutive strokes*. If one stroke length is longer than the next one, all ten syringes will fill higher.

The diagnostic process was begun with the control charts. This diagnostic process should involve answering a series of questions to lead us to the cause, much like the game of 20 questions. The control charts allow the following question to be answered: "Is most of the variation associated with within-period variation or period-to-period differences?" The answer is within-period variation. As a result, many of the potential causes have been eliminated.

The obvious next question is, "Is most of the variation associated with within-syringe/period variation or syringe-to-syringe differences?" Fortunately other data sets exist that can help answer this question. These data were collected during a study run while starting up the process. So we next turn to this study.

Special start-up study. On the first lot produced, a special study was run. While the lot was being produced, samples were taken from all

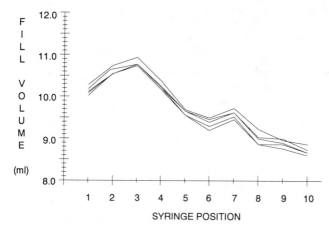

Figure 2.31   Plot of start-up data.

ten syringes on five consecutive machine strokes. The variation between these 50 samples would appear as within-period variation in the Q.C. inspection data. Figure 2.31 shows a plot of the data. The data are given in Table 2.14. The bottom axis contains the ten syringe positions. A line is drawn across the plot for each of the five machine strokes. These lines fall nearly on top of each other indicating the stroke-to-stroke variation (within-syringe/period variation) is small at least when compared to the differences among the syringes. The stroke-to-stroke variation is no larger than 0.4 ml.

The syringe-to-syringe differences are clearly the largest source of variation. These differences are as large as 2.4 ml. This accounts for most of the total variation. The first step in reducing the fill variation must therefore be to identify and eliminate the cause of these differ-

TABLE 2.14   Data for Special Start-up Study

SYRINGE POSITION	MACHINE STROKE					AVERAGE	RANGE
	1	2	3	4	5		
1	10.10	9.98	10.09	10.15	10.29	10.12	0.31
2	10.55	10.53	10.56	10.63	10.74	10.60	0.21
3	10.79	10.73	10.76	10.76	10.93	10.79	0.20
4	10.21	10.17	10.21	10.24	10.36	10.24	0.19
5	9.67	9.56	9.57	9.67	9.71	9.64	0.15
6	9.46	9.21	9.30	9.41	9.52	9.38	0.31
7	9.64	9.46	9.54	9.63	9.75	9.60	0.29
8	9.05	8.89	8.87	9.01	9.22	9.01	0.35
9	9.02	8.78	8.85	8.89	8.96	8.90	0.24
10	8.73	8.61	8.66	8.68	8.85	8.71	0.24

ences. Of all the potential causes listed in the cause and effect diagram, only a handful should result in syringe-to-syringe differences: using damaged syringes (bent, warped, sticking, or leaking), setup (assigning syringes to positions), cleaning, valve leakage and gumming (some valves may leak or stick more than others), inside diameter (different syringes may have slightly different inside diameters), wobble in bottom bar, tubing and nozzle differences, alignment of syringe attachments, and bubbles in particular lines. The other potential causes have essentially been eliminated, at least for the time being.

Further, Fig. 2.31 shows a pronounced downward trend across the syringes accounting for a majority of the syringe differences. Of the potential causes listed above, only one, wobble in the bottom bar, should result in such a slope. However, there are still many unanswered questions. Is the slope always present? Is the slope always of the same magnitude or are there other factors that can reduce the slope? For example, if certain syringes have slightly smaller diameters, maybe they can be placed on the end of the bar with the larger fills so that the two effects at least partially cancel out. Further investigation into syringe-to-syringe differences including the slope is required.

Tracking syringe-to-syringe differences.   In order to further investigate the syringe-to-syringe differences, a tracking system was set up. For each lot produced, samples from all ten syringes were taken on six different machine strokes. Two consecutive machine strokes were sampled at the beginning, middle, and end of the lot. Plots of the data from 16 lots are given in Figs. 2.33 and 2.34. These plots confirm the magnitude of the problem with many units falling outside the specification limits. Three different fill volumes are represented: 5, 10, and 20 ml. Take some time to closely examine the plots before reading further.

Probably the most noticeable item is that the slope is present for some lots and not for others. It is present for lots 67, 69, 71, 72, 73, 74, 76, 78, 80, and 82. The slope is absent for lots 68, 70, 75, 77, 79, and 81. The slope is present for some 5-ml lots and not for others. It is present for some 10-ml lots and not for others. It is present for all 20-ml lots. If the reason for the disappearance of the slope could be identified, a dramatic reduction in variation could be achieved. One operator identified a pattern. All lots without any slope present were half fills: either 5-ml fills using 10-ml syringes or 10-ml fills using 20-ml syringes. Figure 2.32 lays out the lots to make this pattern obvious.

During production the syringes were changed only when necessary. If the 20-ml syringes were on the machine and it was time to do a 10-

		SYRINGE SIZE			
		5	10	20	40
FILL VOLUME	5	Lots 71, 72, 73	Lots 75, 77 ———	AVOIDED	AVOIDED
	10	IMPOSSIBLE	Lots 74, 76	Lots 68, 70, ——— 79, 81	AVOIDED
	20	IMPOSSIBLE	IMPOSSIBLE	Lots 67, 69, 78, 80, 82	NO DATA

/ SLOPE

——— NO SLOPE

Figure 2.32   Breakdown of lots.

ml fill, the syringes were not changed. If instead it was time for a 5-ml fill, the syringes were changed since experience indicated one did not want to run much lower than a half fill. (See Figs..2.33 and 2.34.) Why does the slope disappear for half fills? Recall that earlier the suspected cause for the slope was wobble of the bottom bar. The left end of the bottom bar must be moving more than the right end. Figure 2.35 shows the position of the adjustment arms for full and half fills. For half fills the straight adjustment arm is straight up and down. For full fills the straight adjustment arm is tilted considerably. It would not be surprising if this tilting introduced more wobble.

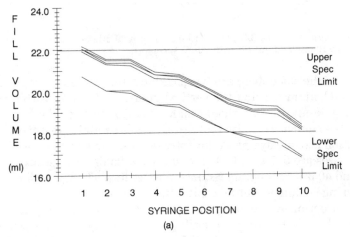

Figure 2.33   (a) Lot BZ1089-67 (20-ml fill with 20-ml syringes).

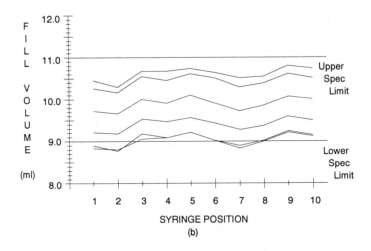

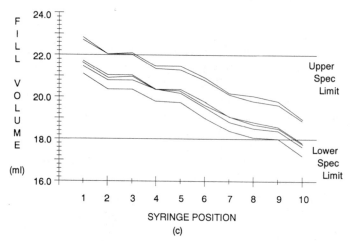

Figure 2.33 *(Continued)* *(b)* Lot BZ1089-68 (10-ml fill with 20-ml syringes); *(c)* lot BZ1089-69 (20-ml fill with 20-ml syringes).

To eliminate the slope there are two possible solutions. The first one is to replace the bottom bar and the vertical guides it slides on with ones with tighter tolerances. This should make it impossible for the bottom bar to wobble so much. This also requires a sizable capital investment. A second solution is to always run at half stroke. This can be done since the possible fill sizes are 5, 10, and 20 ml and the available syringe sizes are 5, 10, 20, and 40 ml. This option requires a procedural change with more frequent syringe changes, but no capital investment.

The second option was chosen. It was felt that by rearranging the production schedule to minimize syringe changes, this option would not result in any undue hardships. However, since a 20-ml fill with

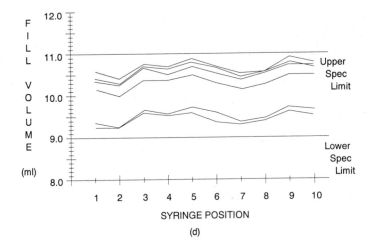

(d)

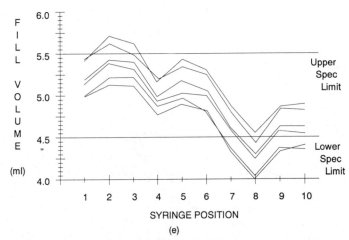

(e)

Figure 2.33 *(Continued)* *(d)* Lot BZ1089-70 (10-ml fill with 20-ml syringes); *(e)* lot BZ1089-71 (5-ml fill with 5-ml syringes).

40-ml syringes has not been previously run, a trial run was requested before final approval of this solution would be given. The results of this lot appear in Fig. 2.36. The slope is missing as hoped for.

Having solved one problem, the data from the 16 lots were examined further to see if other improvements could be made. Even those lots without a slope produced out-of-specification units. When centered the process makes good units all of the time. But there appears to be trouble getting or keeping the process centered. Questioning the operators leads to numerous complaints about the need for constant adjustments and the difficulty of making an adjustment. Complaints included:

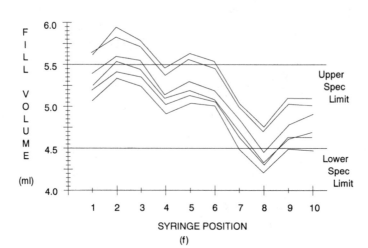

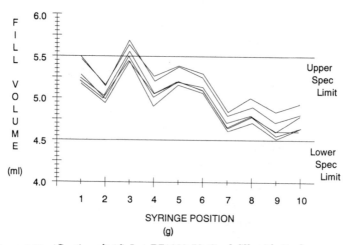

Figure 2.33 (*Continued*) (*f*) Lot BZ1089-72 (5-ml fill with 5-ml syringes); (*g*) lot BZ1089-73 (5-ml fill with 5-ml syringes).

"I would adjust the process up a little, but instead it would go down."

"We'd find a few high units so adjust down slightly. Then suddenly we would be producing all sorts of low units."

"I tried to set the process up just like yesterday. But a third of the vials were out of specification."

Lots 69 and 71 are probably indicative of the second complaint. The slope is such that bringing syringe 1 in pushes syringe 10 out and vice versa. But the other two complaints are indicative of a setup or ad-

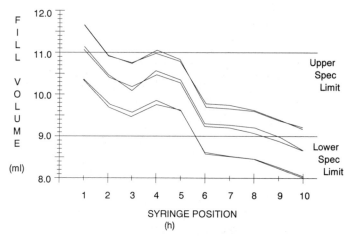

Figure 2.33 *(Continued)* *(h)* Lot BZ1089-74 (10-ml fill with 10-ml syringes).

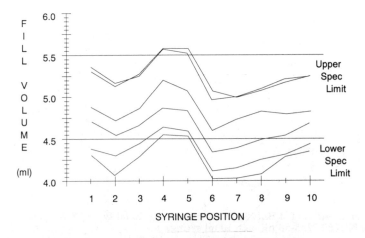

Figure 2.34 *(a)* Lot BZ1089-75 (5-ml fill with 10-ml syringes).

justment problem. Lot 75 is just such a lot. Originally the stroke length was adjusted to 50 percent since it was a half fill. The result was the two low machine strokes averaging 4.25 ml. A 20 percent upward adjustment was made to 60 percent. This, however, overcorrected the problem, resulting in the two high machine strokes. A downward adjustment was then made to 57 percent. This resulted in the middle two machine strokes being low and one of them producing defectives. Lot 77 is the next 5-ml fill with 10-ml syringes. This lot was started at 57 percent and ran perfectly.

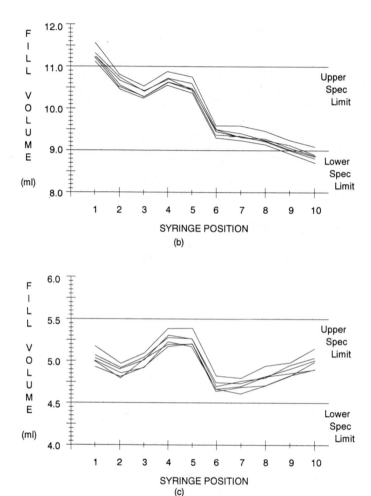

Figure 2.34   (*Continued*) (*b*) Lot BZ1089-76 (10-ml fill with 10-ml syringes); (*c*) lot BZ1089-77 (5-ml fill with 10-ml syringes).

Much of a run can be spent trying to get the process within the specification limits and the next lot may have to be set up differently. Because of this, it was decided to perform an evaluation of the setup and adjustment procedures.

Assembly/setup study. *Assembly/setup studies* consist of repeated disassembly and reassembly of different parts of a product or machine in order to determine those steps that have the largest effect on the product or machine performance. Using this approach, the setup and adjustment procedures may be investigated. The assembly/setup study will answer the following two questions:

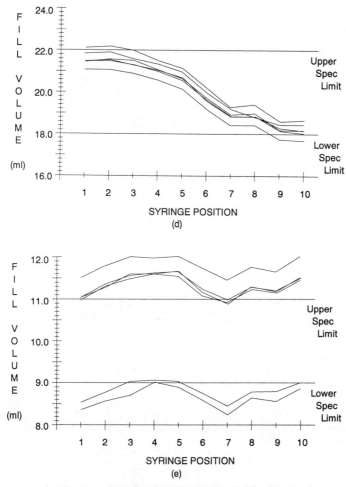

Figure 2.34 *(Continued)* *(d)* Lot BZ1089-78 (20-ml fill with 20-ml syringes); *(e)* lot BZ1089-79 (10-ml fill with 20-ml syringes).

1. Can the adjustment arm be moved and then set back to its original position without affecting the process?
2. Can the syringes be removed and replaced in their original positions without affecting the process?

The assembly/setup study consists of five parts:

1. *Initial samples.* Select samples from all ten syringes on three different machine strokes.
2. *Adjust arm.* Move adjustment arm and then restore to original setting. Select samples from all ten syringes on three different machine strokes.

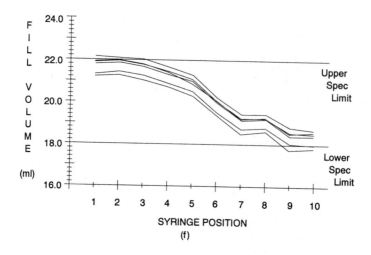

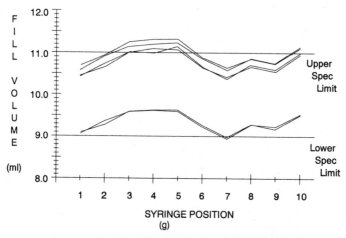

Figure 2.34 *(Continued)* *(f)* Lot BZ1089-80 (20-ml fill with 20-ml syringes); *(g)* lot BZ1089-81 (10-ml fill with 20-ml syringes).

3. *Adjust arm second time.* Move adjustment arm a second time and then restore to original setting. Select samples from all ten syringes on three different machine strokes.

4. *Change syringes.* Remove all ten syringes. Replace syringes back in their original positions. Select samples from all ten syringes on three different machine strokes.

5. *Change syringes second time.* Remove all ten syringes a second time. Replace syringes back in their original positions. Select samples from all ten syringes on three different machine strokes.

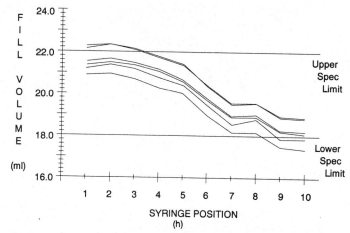

Figure 2.34 *(Continued)* (*h*) Lot BZ1089-82 (20-ml fill with 20-ml syringes).

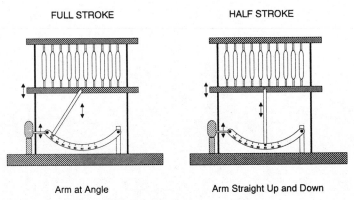

Figure 2.35 Position of adjustment arms.

The results of the assembly/setup study are plotted in Fig. 2.37. Shifts occur between the first and second sets of samples and between the second and third sets of samples. These correspond to the changes of the adjustment arm.

The assembly/setup study confirms that there is an adjustment problem. Adjustments may easily be off by 0.5 ml. When attempting to adjust the process up by 0.25 ml, the final result might be a downward shift of 0.25 ml or an upward shift of 0.75 ml. To correct this problem, two actions were taken. First, the attachment between the straight and curved drive arms was modified to allow fine adjustments to be made. The attachment was modified by adding a screw adjust-

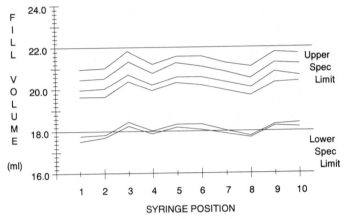

Figure 2.36 Lot BZ1089-87 (20-ml fill with 40-ml syringes).

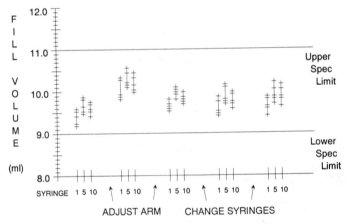

Figure 2.37 Assembly/setup study (20-ml fill with 10-ml syringes).

ment that allowed the relative position of the two arms to be adjusted without disconnecting and then reattaching the two arms. This change allows fine adjustments to be made accurately but does not necessarily ensure that the machine can be restored to the same conditions on the next run.

The second change was to add a gauge that measured the actual stroke length of the bottom bar on each stroke of the machine. This gauge coupled with the mechanism for making fine adjustments allows the stroke length to be restored to that of a previous run. Follow-up experimentation determined that the stroke lengths should be set as follows to get the desired fill volumes:

Fill volume	Stroke length	Percentage
5 ml	1.71 in	57%
10 ml	1.59 in	53%
20 ml	1.56 in	52%

The confirmation study. To date, the following changes have been made: The machine is always run around half stroke, eliminating the slope effect; and the adjustment mechanism has been modified to allow better targeting of stroke length. These changes have resulted in substantial improvements to the process. To help determine the magnitude of these changes and to help determine the next step, process capability studies were run for each of the three fill volumes. The results are shown in Figs. 2.38 to 2.43. The capability studies demonstrate a dramatic improvement over Fig. 2.20. However, the variation has not been reduced nearly enough. A few defectives are still being produced.

Figures 2.38, 2.40, and 2.42 indicate that, while the slope has disappeared, there are still significant syringe differences. There are also obvious stroke-to-stroke differences. These two problems are the target of further investigation in the next two sections.

Component swapping study. A *component swapping study* was run next to investigate the syringe-to-syringe differences. The purpose of the study was to determine whether the syringe-to-syringe differences were the result of the syringes themselves or associated with the positions. Position differences might result from valve differences or differences in the alignment of the syringe mounts. The procedure for

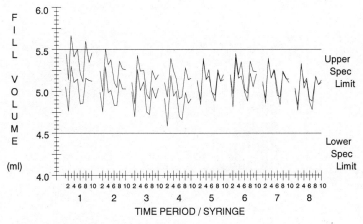

Figure 2.38 Capability study, 5-ml: lot BZ1089-92.

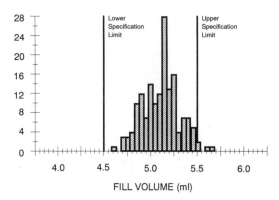

Figure 2.39   Capability study, 5-ml: lot BZ1089-92.

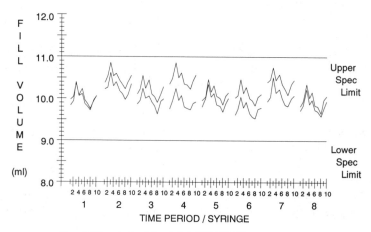

Figure 2.40   Capability study, 10-ml: lot BZ1089-93.

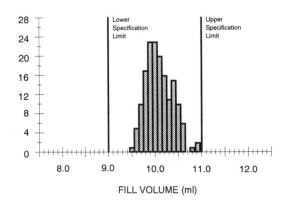

Figure 2.41   Capability study, 10-ml: lot BZ1089-93.

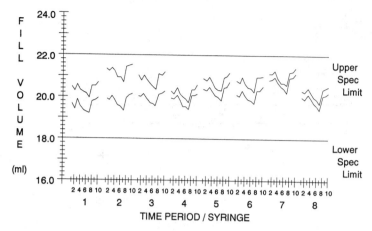

Figure 2.42   Capability study, 20-ml: lot BZ1089-94.

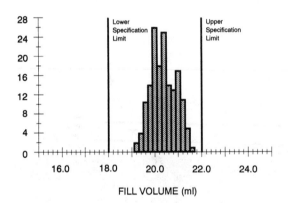

FILL VOLUME (ml)

Figure 2.43   Capability study, 20-ml: lot BZ1089-94.

running the study was to mark the syringes and the positions 1 to 10; place the syringes in the like-numbered positions and record the results for all ten syringes on two machine strokes over a short period of time; shift all ten syringes up one position (syringe 10 should be moved to position 1), and record the data for two more strokes; continue shifting syringes up one position, collecting data until each syringe has been in each position.

In total 200 data points were collected, two for each syringe-position combination. The study was run separately for a 5-ml fill, a 10-ml fill, and a 20-ml fill. The results for the 5-ml fill are plotted in Figs. 2.44 and 2.45. Figure 2.44 shows the averages for each of the syringes on the 5-ml fill. The fact that some of the averages exceed the decision limits indicates that at least some of the syringe-to-

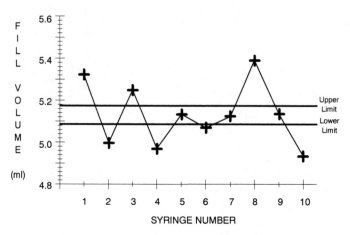

Figure 2.44   Syringe averages, 5-ml.

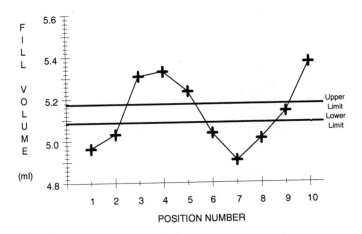

Figure 2.45   Position averages, 5-ml.

syringe differences are due to the syringes themselves. The syringes from high to low are 8, 1, 3, 9, 5, 7, 6, 2, 4, and 10. Figure 2.45 shows the averages for each of the positions on the 5-ml fill. The fact that some of the averages exceed the decision limits indicates that at least some of the syringe-to-syringe differences are due to position differences. The positions from high to low are 10, 4, 3, 5, 9, 6, 2, 8, 1, and 7.

One approach to reducing the syringe-to-syringe differences is to identify and eliminate both the cause of the syringe differences and the cause of the position differences. However, there is an alternate approach. The highest syringe could be placed in the lowest position, the second highest syringe in the second lowest position, and so on. This would not completely eliminate the syringe-to-syringe differences, but it would result in a sizable improvement and could be implemented immediately without incurring any cost. It simply requires changing the syringe assignment for setup to that given below:

Syringe Assignments for 5-ml Fills

Position	Syringe
1	1
2	9
3	2
4	4
5	6
6	5
7	8
8	3
9	7
10	10

The results for the 10-ml fill are plotted in Figs. 2.46 and 2.47. Figure 2.46 shows the averages for each of the syringes. Figure 2.47 shows the averages for each of the positions. Once again the syringe-to-syringe variation is the result of both the syringes themselves and

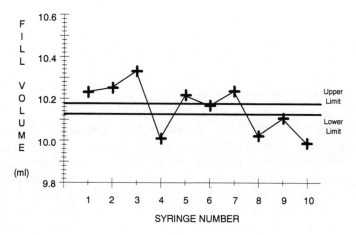

Figure 2.46   Syringe averages, 10-ml.

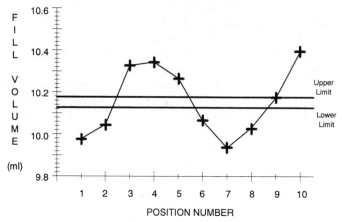

Figure 2.47   Position averages, 10-ml.

position differences. The syringes from high to low are 3, 2, 7, 1, 5, 6, 9, 8, 4, and 10. The positions from high to low are 10, 4, 3, 5, 9, 6, 2, 8, 1, and 7. This is the same order as the 5-ml fill, indicating the position effect does not depend on the syringe size. Therefore the best assignment of syringes to positions is

Syringe Assignments for 10-ml Fills

Position	Syringe
1	2
2	1
3	8
4	4
5	9
6	5
7	3
8	7
9	6
10	10

The results for the 20-ml fill are plotted in Figs. 2.48 and 2.49. Figure 2.48 shows the averages for each of the syringes. Figure 2.49 shows the averages for each of the positions. Once again the syringe-to-syringe variation is the result of both the syringes themselves and position differences. The syringes from high to low are 8, 1, 9, 2, 10, 3, 4, 6, 7, and 5. The positions from high to low are 10, 4, 3, 5, 9, 2, 6, 8, 1, and 7. This is almost the same order as for the 5- and 10-ml fills, further indicating that the position effect does not depend on the syringe size. Therefore the best assignment of syringes to positions is

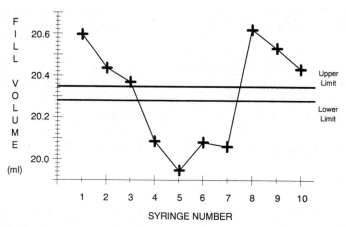

Figure 2.48 Syringe averages, 20-ml.

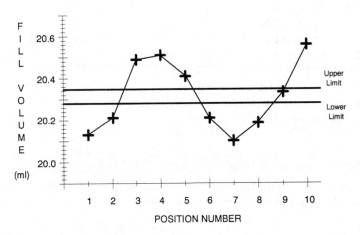

Figure 2.49 Position averages, 20-ml.

Syringe Assignments for 20-ml Fills

Position	Syringe
1	1
2	10
3	6
4	7
5	4
6	2
7	8
8	9
9	3
10	5

Changing the syringe assignments solves one problem. However there is still the problem of stroke-to-stroke variation.

Stroke-to-stroke variation. The suspected cause of the stroke-to-stroke variation is stroke length. To measure stroke length, a gauge was mounted between the top and bottom bars. Fifty measurements were taken and plotted on a histogram in Fig. 2.50. In order to determine the significance of the stroke-length variation, each of the values was plugged in for S, the stroke length, in the following equation:

$$\text{Fill volume} = 16.387 \left(\frac{\pi}{4}\right) D^2 S$$

D, the syringe diameter, was fixed at 0.5089, the nominal diameter for 5-ml fills. The 50 calculated fill volumes were plotted in the histogram shown in Fig. 2.51. The variation in fill volumes caused by the variation in stroke length is large enough to be of concern. It seems to match the stroke-to-stroke variation actually being observed.

To reduce the stroke-length variation, the machine was refurbished. Specifically, the drive arms were reworked to tighter tolerances to reduce any wobble. The variation in stroke lengths remaining after the machine was refurbished is shown in Fig. 2.52. The variation in stroke length has been cut nearly in half. This should in turn cut the fill-volume variation nearly in half.

Final results

To determine the amount of improvement made by these latest changes, the process capability studies were rerun. The results are

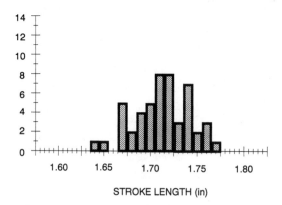

STROKE LENGTH (in)

Figure 2.50 Histogram of stroke lengths before change.

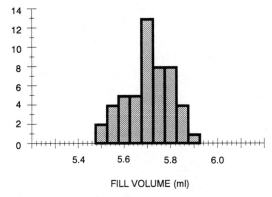

FILL VOLUME (ml)

Figure 2.51   Histogram of resulting fill volumes.

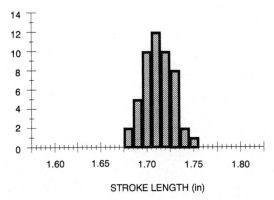

STROKE LENGTH (in)

Figure 2.52   Histogram of stroke lengths after change.

shown in Figs. 2.53 to 2.58. To date, the following changes have been made:

- The machine is always run around half stroke. This eliminates the slope effect.

- The syringes have been assigned permanent positions. This assignment matches the highest filling syringes with the lowest filling positions. This reduces, but does not totally eliminate, the syringe-to-syringe differences.

- The adjustment mechanism has been modified to allow better targeting of stroke length.

- The drive arms were refurbished to reduce the stroke-length variation.

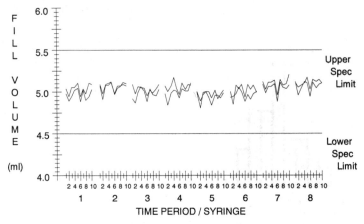

Figure 2.53 Capability study, 5-ml: lot BZ1089-104.

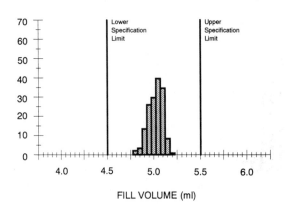

FILL VOLUME (ml)

Figure 2.54 Capability study, 5-ml: lot BZ1089-104.

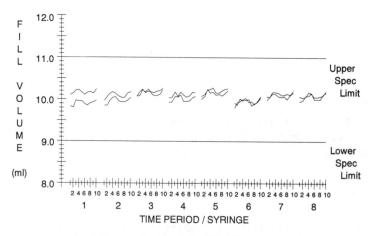

Figure 2.55 Capability study, 10-ml: lot BZ1089-106.

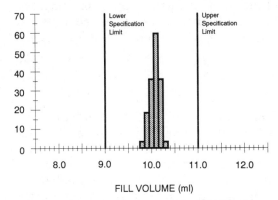

Figure 2.56   Capability study, 10-ml: lot BZ1089-106.

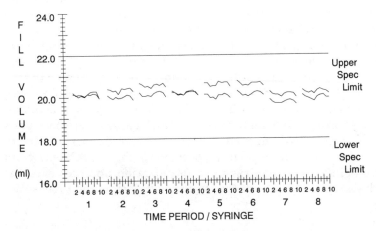

Figure 2.57   Capability study, 20-ml: lot BZ1089-109.

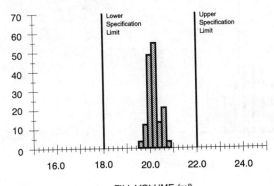

FILL VOLUME (ml)

Figure 2.58   Capability study, 20-ml: lot BZ1089-109.

The capability studies demonstrate that further significant improvements have been made. As a result of these two latest changes, the variation has now been reduced to a point where few, if any, defects are being made.

2.4 Summary

The reduction in variation as shown in Fig. 2.59 has been dramatic. Yet the methods employed are quite simple. They include cause and effect diagrams, histograms, Multi-Vari plots, control charts, capability studies, assembly/setup studies, and component swapping studies. Likewise, the solutions were frequently easy to implement, costing little. Running the machine at half stroke and assigning the syringes to optimal positions cost nothing. When machine improvements were required, only the specific parts of the machine needing fixing were modified: specifically the adjustment mechanism and the drive arms. Without having first diagnosed the cause of the problem, machine upgrades and replacements are generally more costly and less effective.

This case study is representative of efforts to improve an existing process. The diagnostic effort is driven by the search for differences: differences between time periods, differences between machine strokes, differences between syringes, differences between positions, and so on. Through these differences, problems are fixed. However, it is preferable to have prevented these problems from ever developing. This requires that optimization and variation reduction be addressed up front during product design and process development.

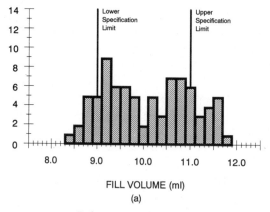

Figure 2.59 (a) Before.

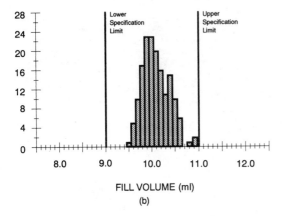

FILL VOLUME (ml)

(b)

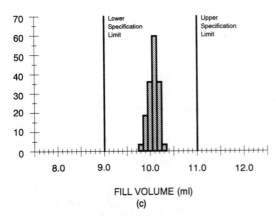

FILL VOLUME (ml)

(c)

Figure 2.59 (*Continued*) (*b*) Halfway; (*c*) after.

Understanding Variation

This chapter concentrates exclusively on variation. It is important to understand variation. False understanding and myths about variation are dangerous. They lead to inappropriate actions or to the failure to act. Once variation is firmly understood, Chap. 4 returns to the combined problem of optimizing the average and reducing variation.

3.1 Cause of Variation

Before one can begin reducing variation, one must first be able to answer the question, "What causes product and process variation?" To answer this question look at the system *input/output model* in Fig. 3.1. The system input/output model can be used to describe any system. The system produces certain outputs, be they product, invoices, sales, and so forth. In producing these outputs the system requires certain inputs like materials and work force. The system may also be affected by other inputs such as the environment. The system acts on the inputs to try to achieve the desired outputs.

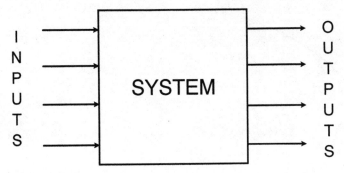

Figure 3.1 System input/output model.

A manufacturing process is a system. The inputs are the design parameters, material properties, machine parameters, and so on. The outputs are the desired characteristics and properties of the product. A product can also be viewed as a system. The product is intended to perform some function. For example, a copier is supposed to make copies. The outputs are the desired performance characteristics of the product. For a copier these might be resolution and blackness. The inputs are everything that affect the performance of the product. For a copier, these include paper weight, paper density, and humidity.

With the help of the system input/output model, we can answer the question, "What causes product and process variation?" Product and process variation, i.e., variation of the outputs, is caused by variations of the inputs. The system input/output model implies that there is some sort of relationship between the inputs and the outputs. Given this relationship, often in the form of an equation or plot, the variation transmitted to an output variable by an input variable can be determined. Figure 3.2 demonstrates how this might be done.

There are many inputs that might affect the system. Asking everyone what material properties, process parameters, tooling parameters, environmental conditions, and so on, can affect the process may lead to hundreds of suggestions. These suggestions will be referred to as the *candidate input variables*.

Candidate input variables: Those inputs that might affect the system

When generating a list of candidate key input variables, all things should be considered that affect the product's performance (Fig. 3.3). This includes design parameters as well as manufacturing parameters. It should also include factors in the user's environment as well as

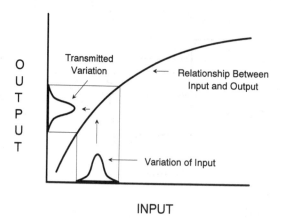

INPUT

Figure 3.2   Transmission of variation.

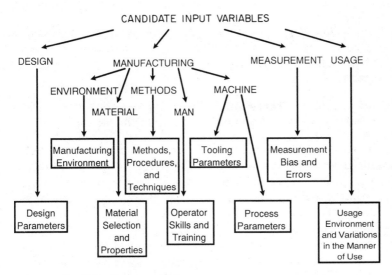

Figure 3.3   Candidate input variables.

variations in the manner the product is used. The following categories provide a checklist to help prevent areas from being overlooked. For each category several examples are given of variables that might affect the quality of an injection-molded part.

- Design parameters (part dimensions)

- Material selection and properties (type of plasticizer, strength of plastic, brittleness of plastic)

- Process parameters (machine temperature, mold time, pressure)

- Tooling parameters (mold dimensions)

- Methods, procedures, and techniques (procedure for shimming mold, procedure for shutting off mold cavities, cleaning frequency and procedure)

- Operator skills and training (ability to make adjustments)

- Manufacturing environment (room temperature, room humidity)

- Usage environment and variations in the manner of use (temperature, humidity, presence of corrosives)

- Measurement bias and errors (frequency and method of calibration, recording errors)

3.2 Key Input Variables

It is not hard to think of things that might affect the product or process. But not every candidate input variable will actually have an effect on the product or process. From this list of candidate input variables, a smaller list can be obtained containing only the input variables that actually affect the output. These will be referred to as the *key input variables.*

Key input variables: Those inputs that can affect the output, either by affecting the average or by contributing to the variation

Now it may seem that there are actually two distinct criteria for being a key input variable: (1) It can affect the average, or (2) it can contribute to the variation. These are not, however, really different criteria. Any input that can affect the average, can contribute to the variation. Likewise, any input that can contribute to the variation, can affect the average. Let us see why.

First, assume that adjusting an input causes the average of the output to shift. This implies that there is some sort of relationship between this input and the output. Changes in this input, as a result of this relationship, cause the output to change. Now suppose this same input were to fluctuate up and down by small amounts on its own. These fluctuations would cause variation in the output as illustrated in Fig. 3.4. Inputs that can cause the average to shift, can contribute to the variation.

Now assume just the opposite. Assume that an input is contributing to variation of the output. If this input is causing variation, it means that the small amounts by which this input is fluctuating naturally are in fact causing noticeable changes in the output. This again implies that there is some sort of relationship between this input and the output. Changes in this input cause changes in the output. Further,

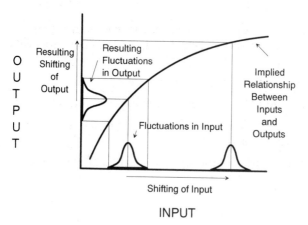

Figure 3.4   Key inputs can cause both shifting and variation.

the output must be very sensitive to this input for the output is reacting to even these small fluctuations. Therefore, if this input were adjusted by a much larger amount, one would expect a dramatic shift in the output's average. Again see Fig. 3.4.

Inputs that can contribute to the variation, can affect the average. The key input variables are therefore

- *All inputs that affect the average.* These are precisely the inputs required to optimize the average. The more key input variables identified and taken advantage of, the closer it is possible to get the average to the optimal.

- *All potential sources of variation.* When one is looking for potential sources of variation, one does not need to look further than the key input variables. This does not, however, imply that all key inputs are actually important sources of variation—only that they have the potential.

3.3   The VIPs

An important part of reducing variation is the identification of those key input variables that make significant contributions to the variation. These key input variables are called VIPs.* As stated previously, VIP stands for variation inducing parameters.

The VIPs: Those key input variables that make significant contributions to the variation of the output

For each key input variable, the *transmitted variation* can be determined. The resulting transmitted variation can be plotted as in Fig. 3.5. Such a plot is called a *Pareto chart*. Note that some of the inputs cause more variation to be transmitted than the others.

The Pareto principle,† also known as the 80/20 rule, states that 20 percent of the causes result in 80 percent of the effect. The Pareto rule applies to many things including causes of defects and distribution of wealth. Eighty percent of defective units are the result of 20 percent of the causes. Eighty percent of all wealth is held by 20 percent of the people. The Pareto principle also applies to transmitted variation. Eighty percent of the transmitted variation is the result of 20 percent of the key input variables. These 20 percent are the VIPs.

The Pareto principle alone demonstrates the importance of the

---

*Dorian Shainin calls these Red Xs.

†The Pareto principle was developed by Joseph Juran.

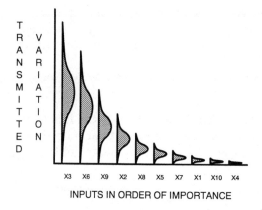

Figure 3.5   Pareto chart of transmitted variation.

VIPs. There is, however, a second effect that makes the VIPs doubly important.

This second effect is the *nonadditivity* of variation. The total variation is not a simple sum of the individual variations. Figure 3.6 shows the resulting total variation. The total variation is slightly larger than the largest individual variation. When dealing with defects, 80 percent of the defective units are the result of 20 percent of the causes. However, elimination of the other 80 percent of the causes still results in a 20 percent reduction of the defect rate. This is not the case with variation. As shown in Fig. 3.7, elimination of the variation transmitted from the other 80 percent of the key in-

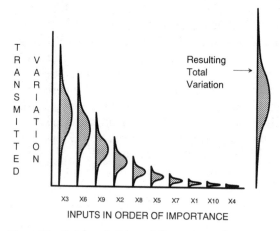

Figure 3.6   Total variation and its components.

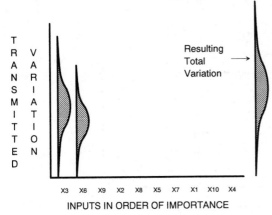

INPUTS IN ORDER OF IMPORTANCE

Figure 3.7   Effect of eliminating bottom 80 percent.

puts does little to reduce the total variation. This is the result of the nonadditivity of variation.

The key is to identify and eliminate the largest sources of variation, i.e., the VIPs. Without the VIPs, little progress will be made. The result of reducing the effects of the VIPs, on the other hand, can be dramatic. The result is illustrated in Fig. 3.8.

The relationship between the candidate input variables, key input variables, and the VIPs is summarized in Fig. 3.9. The status of key input variable is a permanent status, bestowed by nature. However, the status of VIP is like fame, only temporary. As improvements are made, VIP status is stripped from some key input variables. Other key input variables in turn take over as the new VIPs.

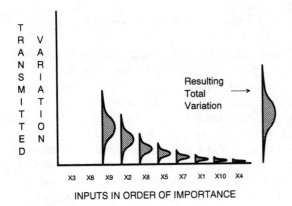

INPUTS IN ORDER OF IMPORTANCE

Figure 3.8   Effect of eliminating VIPs.

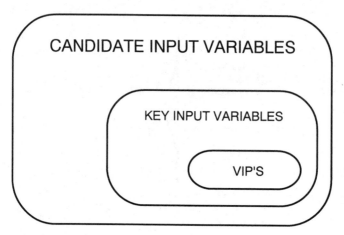

Figure 3.9   Candidate input variables.

3.4   Identifying Key Inputs and VIPs

There are two basic approaches for identifying key input variables and VIPs:

- Studying the inputs' effects
- Searching for differences

Studying the inputs' effects requires that the candidate input variables be purposely varied in order to identify the key input variables. Screening experiments, response surfaces, and other methods can be used. Once the key inputs have been identified, the transmitted variation of the inputs can be determined and compared to find the VIPs. This first approach can be tedious. Every candidate input must be considered. While screening experiments and other methods can examine a large number of inputs efficiently, considerable effort is still required.

The second approach, searching for differences, can often reduce this effort. If differences can be found, these differences provide valuable clues as to the key input variables and the VIPs. These differences can be differences over time, differences among cavities, differences between two units, differences among machines, and even differences within a unit. For example, suppose a sudden change in the process is found to have taken place shortly after 3 P.M. If the only change occurring around or shortly before 3 P.M. was a material change, a key input has been identified to be associated with material.

In some cases these differences go beyond just providing clues.

These differences may actually trap a key input, letting further experimentation and testing to be performed that can isolate the key input. Continuing the previous example, if samples of both lots of material are available, they could be sent to the lab for testing to identify how these materials differ. If more than one difference is found, experiments could be run to identify which difference is the key input. When searching for differences, if the difference identified is sizable compared to the total variation, the key input causing the difference must be a VIP, at least temporarily. Most differences, in order to be observable, are sizable. Therefore, the search for difference approach concentrates on VIPs.

The two basic strategies, studying the inputs' effects and searching for differences, have many variations and make use of dozens of tools. Part 3 is devoted to searching for differences. Part 4 is devoted to studying inputs' effects. Identifying the key inputs and VIPs, however, is not enough. Once identified, actions must be taken to reduce their transmitted variation in order to reduce the total variation.

3.5   Reducing Variation

Once a VIP has been identified, there are several approaches to reducing its effect. The obvious approach is to tighten control of the VIP to reduce its transmitted variation. However, this generally drives up costs. There are two other approaches that are more cost effective. This section presents the three approaches to reducing variation.

Approach 1: Reducing the variation of the VIPs

The transmitted variation can always be reduced by reducing the variation of the VIPs. In Fig. 3.10, the variation of a VIP is cut in half. The result is that the transmitted variation is also cut by about half. There are, however, two difficulties with this approach. First, reducing the variation of the VIPs means tighter control. Tighter control generally means higher costs. If a VIP is a material property, higher grade and therefore more expensive materials may be required. If a VIP is a process parameter, a new controller may be necessary. If a VIP is a product design parameter, a different method of manufacturing may be required.

The second difficulty is that for certain inputs reducing the variation may be undesirable from the customer's point of view. If usage temperature is a VIP, tightening down on usage temperature would limit the applicability of the product. The range for usage temperature

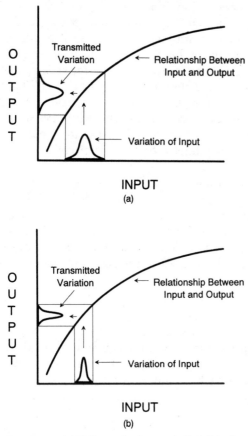

Figure 3.10   (a) Before reducing variation; (b) after reducing variation.

is a customer requirement and cannot be changed. Fortunately there are two other approaches that offer alternatives.

Approach 2: Making the system less sensitive to VIPs

A second way of reducing the transmitted variation of a VIP is to make the output less sensitive to the variation of the VIPs. This results in the variation of the output being reduced. However, the variation of the VIP remains the same. Making the output less sensitive to the variation of the VIP requires *nonlinear effects*. Figure 3.11 shows a VIP with a nonlinear effect. Adjusting this VIP to a part of the curve that is less steep results in the transmitted variation being reduced by

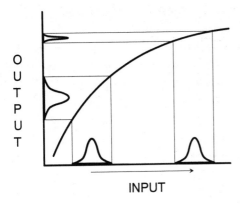

Figure 3.11 Effect of adjusting VIP.

INPUT

a factor of 4. Simply adjusting VIPs with nonlinear effects can cause the variation to increase or decrease.

A second type of nonlinear effect is called an *interaction*. An interaction involves two key inputs. The effect that one key input has on the output depends on the setting of the second key input.

Figure 3.12 illustrates an interaction affecting the heat sealing of plastics. The output of interest is seal strength. Two key inputs are seal temperature and seal time. These two key inputs interact since adjusting seal time changes the shape of the relationship between seal temperature and seal strength. One of these, seal temperature, is a VIP. When an interaction exists between a key input variable and a VIP, adjusting the key input variable can increase or reduce the variation transmitted by the VIP. In Fig. 3.13, adjusting seal time from ½ to 1 s cuts in half the variation transmitted by seal temperature.

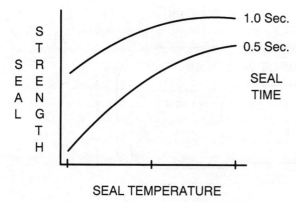

Figure 3.12 Interaction plot.

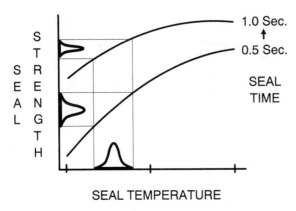

Figure 3.13   Effect of interaction with VIP.

Key input variables whose target affects the variation, VAPs, are either VIPs with nonlinear effects or key input variables that interact with a VIP. The possibilities are summarized in Fig. 3.14. Making the output less sensitive to the VIP has two advantages:

1. It is cost effective. Adjustments of VAPs are required rather than tighter controls.

2. It can be used to reduce the transmitted variation of a VIP for which it is undesirable to tighten. An example is usage humidity for a copier. If an interaction can be identified between humidity and some other key input, such as ink composition, ink composition can be adjusted to make the copier less sensitive to humidity.

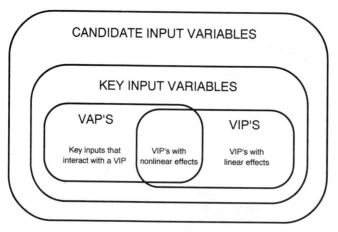

Figure 3.14   Categories of input variables.

Any nonlinear effect can be used to reduce variation. However, adjusting key inputs and VIPs to take advantage of these nonlinear effects will impact the average as well as the variation. Compromises may be necessary. In other cases there may not be any nonlinear effect of which to take advantage. So a third approach may still be necessary.

Approach 3: Changing the relationship between the inputs and outputs

The remaining approach is to simply change the relationship between the inputs and outputs to a more desirable one. Changing this functional relationship requires fundamental changes, generally of the product design, process design, and type of materials. For example, suppose one needed a 2-in spacer bar. Already in use in another product are 1-in spacer bars. To reduce parts inventory, it makes sense to use two 1-in spacer bars. Figure 3.15 shows a schematic.

The critical dimension is overall length. The formula for length is

$$\text{Length} = X + Y$$

The spacer bars are cut from roll stock. The accuracy of the cut is ± 0.0010 in. Thus, the variation of both X and Y is ± 0.0010 in. Using the method explained in Chap. 13, the total variation is ± 0.0014 in. The formula used for calculating the total variation is

$$\text{Length variation} = \sqrt{(X \text{ variation})^2 + (Y \text{ variation})^2}$$

$$= \sqrt{(0.0010)^2 + (0.0010)^2}$$

$$= 0.0014 \text{ in}$$

In order to reduce the variation in length, it was decided to go to a single 2-in spacer bar. A schematic is given in Fig. 3.16. Z also has a variation of 0.0010 in. The formula for the length and its resulting variation are now

$$\text{Length} = Z$$

$$\text{Length variation} = Z \text{ variation}$$

$$= 0.0010 \text{ in}$$

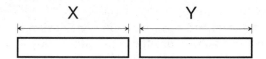

Figure 3.15 Schematic of two 1-in spacer bars.

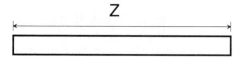

Figure 3.16 Schematic of one 2-in spacer bar.

The result is that the variation in length is reduced to ±0.0010 in, a 30 percent improvement. This improvement was gained through a design change that altered the functional relationship between the key input variables and length. This is an example of a general approach to reducing tolerance stack-up problems called *simplification.* The thrust of simplification is to reduce the number of parts by combining them whenever possible.

Changing the relationship between the inputs and outputs is frequently the most cost-effective approach. However, it is best applied early in the design cycle when changes are less expensive to make.

3.6 Robustness

Robustness means making the product and process less sensitive to variation of the key inputs. Robustness is an important concept popularized by Taguchi. It was the second approach presented for reducing variation. Because of the wide variety of uses of robustness, this section is devoted exclusively to illustrating a number of them. Both products and processes can be made robust. Robust products are products that are insensitive to the manufacturing process, usage conditions, materials, and their deterioration. Robust processes are processes that are insensitive to the materials, environment, and variation in machine parameters.

The uses of robustness are many. The product can be made robust to the process providing wider process windows. The product may be made robust to the materials. This might allow the use of lower-grade materials in order to reduce cost. It might also increase product reliability by making the product less sensitive to deteriorations in the materials. The product may be made robust to usage conditions increasing its applicability. The process may be made robust to materials resulting in fewer problems because of incoming materials. The process may be made robust to fluctuations in the process parameters, reducing the manufacturing variation and making the process easier to control.

Robustness is extremely important to the reduction of variation because it is widely applicable since nonlinear effects are almost always present. Using robustness, variation can be reduced without increasing costs. In fact, costs are frequently reduced. Tighter controls to reduce variation generally increase costs. It may be used to reduce the transmitted variation of a key input that is outside of the manufacturer's control. An example is usage conditions. It is not possible to tighten up on usage conditions without reducing the functionality of the product. Instead, interactions between usage conditions and other key inputs can be used to make the product insensitive to the variations in usage conditions.

3.7   Myths about Variation

Myths about variation abound. These myths are dangerous. They prevent appropriate actions from being taken to reduce variation. The understanding already gained goes a long way to ensuring appropriate actions. However, it is worth the time to look at several common myths and lay them to rest.

Myth 1: Physical barrier

Myth 1.   Variation may be the result of a physical barrier beyond which further improvement is impossible.

This myth portrays hopelessness. Nothing is being done because nothing can be done. It is dangerous in that it prevents appropriate actions from taking place that can result in real improvement. Myth 1 is supported by pointing to games of chance and to truly chance phenomena such as the decay of radioisotopes. However, in both these situations, the rules of the game or the random mechanism are fixed by the casino or nature and cannot be changed.

Suppose one wants to play roulette. Because the casino is running the game, the odds of a seven are determined. But back home in the plant the rules are not fixed. The rules are determined by the product design, the process design, the materials selected, the controls used, and so on. One can change the rules by changing materials, designs, and controls. These changes can amount to using a roulette wheel with all sevens and betting sevens. This is not to say no physical barriers have ever been encountered. They might exist. But in my experience, I have never encountered one. Claims of physical barriers are almost always the result of a lack of understanding of how to proceed. Myth 1 should be replaced by:

Fact 1.   Variation of the output is caused by variation of the VIPs. It can be reduced by reducing the variation of the VIPs, by making the product robust to the VIPs, or by changing the relationship between the key input variables and the outputs.

One place a physical barrier seems plausible is the miniaturization of computer chips. How long can it continue? At times it must seem we are stretching the limits. But, leading companies are already researching the use of X rays to make still finer lines allowing even smaller chips with more components. Even more recently, research into methods for moving individual atoms has proven fruitful. This might lead to chips that are less than a hundredth of their current size. Maybe the atom itself will prove to be the ultimate barrier to miniaturization. But today's chips are far removed from this barrier. Rapid improvements continue to be made.

Myth 2: Economic barrier

Myth 2. Variation may be an economic barrier beyond which further improvement is impossible.

A common belief is that once the process has been made stable, the variation remaining is the result of a large number of inputs, each with only a small effect. Further improvement is uneconomical because many things must be fixed with only small improvements resulting. This belief is frequently attributed to Walter Shewhart, the father of SPC. But Shewhart recognizes that even a stable process can be improved and in fact has a whole chapter devoted to just this topic.

> In this chapter we shall consider the problem of detecting the presence of a predominating cause or group of causes forming part of a chance system. Such a cause will be referred to as an assignable cause of Type II.*

Chance system is Shewhart's phrase for stable system. Myth 2 contradicts the Pareto principle and the nonadditivity of variation. It is just as dangerous as Myth 1 in that it also prevents appropriate actions from occurring. Myth 2 should be replaced by

Fact 2. Variation is dominated by a single or handful of causes called the VIPs.

Myth 3: Increases cost

Myth 3. Reducing variation increases costs.

This myth is related to the myth that improved quality costs more money. However, experience has indicated just the opposite, improving quality reduces costs through the elimination of waste. Improving

---

*Walter Shewhart, *Economic Control of Manufactured Product,* Quality Press, 1980, p. 321.

quality reduces scrap, rework, warranty costs, floor space to hold waste, the work force to transport waste, loss capacity currently producing defects and rejected batches, and on and on. As much as 25 percent of a plant's resources may be committed to the production, detection, and elimination of defects. The money invested in improving quality is recovered many times over. Quality pays.

Reducing variation improves quality. As a result, it reduces costs and pays for itself. Further, methods such as robustness and simplification can often be used to reduce the variation without any initial cost. The only change necessary may be to adjust certain input variables. The only thing better than a high return on investment is the same results with no investment. In this case, quality truly can be free.

Fact 3.   Reducing variation improves quality thereby reducing cost through the elimination of waste. Further, through robustness and simplification, variation reduction may actually be achieved without any initial costs.

3.8   Summary

Cause of variation

All variation is caused. The system input/output model demonstrates that variation of the output is caused by variation of the inputs. *Candidate input variables* are those inputs that might affect the system.

Key input variables

Key input variables are those inputs that can affect the average or can contribute to the variation. Inputs that can affect the average, can contribute to the variation. Inputs that can contribute to the variation, can affect the average. The key input variables are all the inputs required to optimize the average. The search for sources of variation may be restricted to the key input variables.

The VIPs

VIPs (variation inducing parameters) are the key input variables that make significant contributions to the variation of the output. Given the relationship between the key input variables and the outputs, the transmitted variation for each input can be computed. The Pareto principle implies that 20 percent of the key input variables results in 80 percent of the transmitted variation. These variables in the 20-percent range are the VIPs. Elimination of variation transmitted from the other 80 percent of the key input variables does little to reduce the total variation. This is the result of the nonadditivity of variation. Variation reduction requires identifying the VIPs and reducing the effects of the VIPs.

Identifying key inputs and VIPs

There are two basic approaches for identifying key inputs and VIPs: studying the inputs' effects and searching for differences. Studying the effects of the inputs requires that the candidate inputs be purposely varied in order to identify the key inputs and the transmitted variation of the key inputs be determined and compared in order to identify the VIPs.

The effort required may be considerably reduced by identifying differences that provide clues as to the key inputs and VIPs. Differences may exist over time, between streams of product, between individual units, between machines, and even within a unit. In all instances, these differences provide clues. However, in some cases these differences can actually trap a key input so that by special studies the key input can be clearly identified. Large differences are the result of VIPs.

Reducing variation

There are three basic approaches to reducing the variation transmitted by a VIP: (1) reducing the variation of the VIP, (2) making the system less sensitive to the VIP (called robustness), and (3) changing the relationship between the inputs and outputs. The transmitted variation can always be reduced by reducing the variation of VIPs. This generally adds cost. For inputs such as usage conditions, it may limit the applicability of the product.

For a VIP with a nonlinear effect, adjusting the VIP will increase and decrease the transmitted variation. For a VIP that interacts with a key input variable, adjusting the key input variable will increase and decrease the variation transmitted by the VIP.

Key inputs whose target affects the variation are called VAPs (variation adjustment parameters). VAPs are either VIPs with nonlinear effects or key inputs that interact with a VIP. Making the system less sensitive to VIPs is cost effective. It also can be used to reduce the effect of usage conditions. Nonlinear effects, however, may not be present. Changing the relationship between the inputs and outputs requires fundamental changes in the design or materials. It is frequently the most cost-effective approach. It is best applied early in the design cycle.

Robustness

Robustness means making the product and process less sensitive to changes in the key inputs. Robustness has a wide variety of uses which help to reduce costs as well as variation.

Myths about variation

Myth 1.   Variation may be the result of a physical barrier beyond which further improvement is impossible.

Fact 1.   Variation of the output is caused by variation of the VIPs. It can be reduced by reducing the variation of the VIPs, by making the product robust to the VIPs, or by changing the relationship between the key input variables and the outputs.

Myth 2.   Variation may be an economic barrier beyond which further improvement is impossible.

Fact 2.   Variation is dominated by a single or a handful of causes called the VIPs.

Myth 3.   Reducing variation increases costs.

Fact 3.   Reducing variation improves quality thereby reducing cost through the elimination of waste. Further, through robustness and simplification, variation reduction may actually be achieved without any initial costs.

Strategies for Optimization and Variation Reduction

4.1 Strategies for Reducing Variation

The basic strategies for reducing variation have been introduced in Chap. 3. They are changing the relationship between the inputs and outputs to a more favorable one, making the product or process robust to variation of the VIPs, and reducing the variation of the VIPs. The process of designing a product or process can be thought of as consisting of three stages: *system design, parameter design,* and *tolerance design.** During each stage, one of the above strategies for reducing variation can be applied. These stages and the corresponding strategy for reducing variation follow.

System design. System design is the stage during which the basic design concept is fixed. For example, in designing a pump, the principle on which the pump is to operate must be determined. Will the pump use pistons and valves, push the fluid by pinching off a tube and sliding the point of pinching along the tube, or one of the dozen of other possibilities? During system design the number and function of the parts are determined. It is during system design that the relationship between the inputs and outputs is determined. Steps to obtain a desirable relationship must be done at this stage.

Parameter design. During parameter design, targets are set for each input. These targets should be set to reduce variation by making the design robust to the VIPs. This is accomplished by targeting the VAPs

---

*This terminology and breakdown of the design process were suggested by Taguchi.

to minimize the variation. There may also be other considerations such as optimizing the average, reducing costs, and increasing the production rate.

Tolerance design. Once optimal targets have been determined, tolerances for the inputs need to be set in order to assure that variation is reduced to acceptable levels. Tolerance design reduces variation by reducing the variation of the VIPs. Tolerance design can also loosen tolerances on non-VIPs in order to reduce costs.

The stages and associated strategies for reducing variation are summarized in Table 4.1.

TABLE 4.1   Strategies for Variation Reduction

DESIGN STAGES	REDUCE VARIATION
SYSTEM DESIGN	Change the relationship between the inputs and outputs to a more favorable one.
PARAMETER DESIGN	Target VAP's to minimize variation by making the product/process more robust to the VIP's.
TOLERANCE DESIGN	Tighten tolerances of VIP's.

4.2   Strategies for Optimizing the Average

There are only two basic strategies for optimizing the average. They are (1) changing the relationship between the inputs and outputs to a more favorable one, and (2) adjusting the targets of the key input variables to move the average closer to target. These strategies are only applicable to the first two stages of the design process:

System design. It is during system design that the relationship between the inputs and outputs is determined. Steps to obtain a desirable relationship must be done at this stage.

Parameter design. During parameter design, targets are set for each input. Targets should be set for each of the key input variables to optimize the average. There may also be other considerations such as reducing variation, reducing costs, and increasing the production rate.

TABLE 4.2   Strategies for Optimization and Variation Reduction

DESIGN STAGES	OPTIMIZE THE AVERAGE	REDUCE VARIATION
SYSTEM DESIGN	Change the relationship between the inputs and outputs to a more favorable one.	Change the relationship between the inputs and outputs to a more favorable one.
PARAMETER DESIGN	Adjust key input variables so as to move the average closer to target.	Target VAP's to minimize variation by making the product/process more robust to the VIP's.
TOLERANCE DESIGN		Tighten tolerances of VIP's.

Tolerances have little affect on the average. Therefore nothing can be done to optimize the average during tolerance design. In Table 4.2, the strategies for optimizing the average have been added to those for reducing variation.

Combining the strategies for optimizing the average and reducing the variation requires that VIPs are identified and their tolerances tightened during tolerance design. It may also be possible to relax tolerances on non-VIPs without adversely affecting quality in order to reduce costs. The secret is to tighten only the critical parameters and then only to the degree necessary.

A combined strategy for parameter design requires splitting the inputs into three categories:

1. *Variation adjustment parameters (VAPs)*.   These are the inputs whose targeting affects the variation. Specifically, they are the VIPs with nonlinear effects along with any key input variables that interact with VIPs. The VAPs are generally set to minimize the transmitted variation. However, they also affect the average and costs. Sometimes compromises are necessary.

2. *Target adjustment parameters*.   These are the inputs that affect the average without affecting the variation. They are key input variables that are not VAPs. The target adjustment parameters are used to bring the product/process on target. If they are not enough, compromises with the variation adjustment parameters may be necessary. If there are multiple ways of achieving target, some target adjustment parameters can be set to their most economical level.

3. *Economic adjustment parameters*.   These are the candidate input parameters that affect neither the average nor variation. They should always be set to their most economical level.

The strategies for optimizing the average and reducing the variation apply to product design, process design, and manufacturing. There are, however, important differences in when and how these strategies can be applied. The next three sections outline these differences.

4.3   Objectives during Product Design

Product design includes determining the product dimensions and characteristics as well as the selection of materials. Table 4.3 shows which strategies can be applied during product design. Recall that there are actually three sources of variation that must be reduced. The only strategy that cannot be applied to all the objectives is tolerance design. Tolerance design cannot be used to reduce usage variation, which is a customer requirement and cannot be changed. To optimize the average and reduce variation during product design, the following objectives should be undertaken:

During system design to optimize the average:

- Select a design concept that allows one to drive the average closest to target.
- Select materials that allow one to drive the average closest to target.

During system design to reduce manufacturing variation:

- Select a design concept that is robust to the process and materials.
- Select materials that are robust to the manufacturing process.
- Simplify the design by reducing the number of parts and connectors. This is especially effective against tolerance stack-up problems.

TABLE 4.3   Strategies for Product Design

DESIGN STAGES	OPTIMIZE THE AVERAGE	REDUCE VARIATION		
		Manufacturing Variation	Usage Variation	Deterioration Variation
SYSTEM DESIGN	YES	YES	YES	YES
PARAMETER DESIGN	YES	YES	YES	YES
TOLERANCE DESIGN		YES	X	YES

- Design product to be manufactured using processes with demonstrated stability and capability.
- Use materials from suppliers who can consistently produce defect-free product. Suppliers should provide evidence of the stability and capability of their process.

During system design to reduce usage variation:

- Select a design concept that is robust to the manner and conditions of use.
- Select materials that are not affected by (robust to) the expected range of usage conditions.

During system design to reduce variation due to deterioration:

- Select a design concept that is not prone (is robust) to wear and deterioration.
- Select materials that are not prone (are robust) to deterioration and wear.

During parameter design to optimize the average:

- Set key input variables to get the average as close as possible to ideal.

During parameter design to reduce manufacturing variation:

- Use nonlinear effects and interactions among design parameters to widen (robustness) product tolerances.
- Use interactions among design parameters and process parameters to widen (robustness) processing windows.
- Use interactions among design parameters and materials to widen (robustness) material specifications.
- Use interactions among materials and manufacturing conditions to reduce (robustness) transmitted variation.

During parameter design to reduce usage variation:

- Use interactions among design parameters and usage factors to make design robust to usage factors.
- Use interactions among material properties and usage factors to make design robust to usage factors.

During parameter design to reduce variation due to deterioration:

- Use interactions among design parameters and dimensions subject to wear to make the product robust to changes in the dimension.
- Use interactions among design parameters and material properties to make the product robust to changes in the material properties.

During tolerance design to reduce manufacturing variation:

- Tighten tolerances of design parameters.
- Tighten tolerances on material specifications.

During tolerance design to reduce variation due to deterioration:

- Tighten tolerances on dimensions subject to wear.
- Tighten tolerances on materials subject to change.

In general, actions taken earlier on are more cost effective. Issues that may be easily solved during system design may add considerably to the cost of the product if solved using tolerance design.

4.4   Objectives during Process Development

Table 4.4 shows which strategies can be applied during process development. No actions are possible to reduce usage variation and variation due to deterioration during process development. These two sources of variation are determined by the product design and selection of materials. To optimize the average and reduce variation during process development, the following objectives should be undertaken:

During system design to optimize the average:

- Select a process concept that allows one to drive the average closest to target.

During system design to reduce manufacturing variation:

- Select a process concept that is robust to materials.

TABLE 4.4   Strategies for Process Design

DESIGN STAGES	OPTIMIZE THE AVERAGE	REDUCE VARIATION		
		Manufacturing Variation	Usage Variation	Deterioration Variation
SYSTEM DESIGN	YES	YES	X	X
PARAMETER DESIGN	YES	YES	X	X
TOLERANCE DESIGN		YES	X	X

- Select a process concept that is robust to manufacturing conditions and environment.
- Select known processes with demonstrated stability.
- Select processes whose capability matches the product specifications.

During parameter design to optimize the average:

- Set key processing variables to get the average as close as possible to ideal.

During parameter design to reduce manufacturing variation:

- Use nonlinear effects and interactions among process parameters to reduce (robustness) variation.
- Use interactions among process parameters and material properties to make the process robust to materials used.

During tolerance design to reduce manufacturing variation:

- Tighten tolerances of process parameters.

There are far fewer actions possible during process design. Further, the effectiveness of these actions is limited by many of the decisions made during product design and material selection. This stresses the importance of starting optimization and variation reduction during product design. It also suggests that product design and process development should be concurrent activities.

4.5 Objectives during Manufacturing

Once the product has been designed, the materials selected, and the process developed, it is manufacturing's job to produce product in which the average is as close to ideal as possible, and the variation is at a minimum. Table 4.5 shows the strategies available to manufacturing. Manufacturing can do little to reduce usage variation and variation due to deterioration. These are determined by the product design and materials. Further, manufacturing cannot generally change the system design of the product or process. All it can do is adjust process parameters, and tighten their control. According to Table 4.5, the following actions should be taken to optimize the average and reduce variation during manufacturing:

During parameter design to optimize the average:

- Set key process parameters to get the average as close as possible to the ideal.
- Search for new key process parameters that can get the average closer to the ideal.

TABLE 4.5   Strategies for Manufacturing

DESIGN STAGES	OPTIMIZE THE AVERAGE	REDUCE VARIATION		
		Manufacturing Variation	Usage Variation	Deterioration Variation
SYSTEM DESIGN	X	X	X	X
PARAMETER DESIGN	YES	YES	X	X
TOLERANCE DESIGN		YES	X	X

During parameter design to reduce manufacturing variation:

- Study the process parameters to identify any nonlinear effects and interactions. Use these nonlinear effects to reduce the variation transmitted by the VIPs.
- Determine whether interactions exist among process parameters and material properties. Use any interactions identified to help make the process robust to the materials.

During tolerance design to reduce manufacturing variation:

- Make the process stable by identifying and tightening control of key input variables which may be causing the average to shift up and down.
- Detect and compensate for shifting of the average by adjusting certain key process parameters.
- Make the process capable by identifying the VIPs. Tighten control of VIPs in order to reduce transmitted variation.

There is, of course, one other action taken by manufacturing to reduce variation: complaining about the poor product design, the aging and incapable process, and the inferior materials it is forced to use. The problem with complaining is that no one listens. Manufacturing complains about the product design. The product designers point to the materials instead. The materials group points back to manufacturing. No action results because everyone is convinced the problem is being caused by someone else. The methods given for optimization and variation reduction provide the remedy to this problem. Using these methods manufacturing can diagnose the cause of the problem. With hard evidence of the offending VIP, the proper group to solve the problem can be spurred to action. It is, however, manufacturing's responsibility to diagnose the problem. Simply voicing accusations is counterproductive.

4.6 The Complete System

In general, actions taken earlier on are more cost effective. Issues that may be easily solved during system design may add considerably to the cost of the product if solved using tolerance design. Steps taken during product design to make the product easier to manufacture by making it robust to the process and materials may result in considerable savings later on. As one progresses from product design to manufacturing, fewer and fewer options are available. Further, the effectiveness of these is often limited by decisions made previously. As illustrated in Table 4.6, the best place to start addressing optimization and variation reduction is system design of the product.

The lists of actions given may provide one with ideas about things that might be done differently. But more important, these actions should help one understand what everyone's role must be and how they fit into the overall system. Everyone involved with the product, from product designer to manufacturing, has a role in optimization (both optimizing the average and reducing variation). Optimization requires that product designers work with the process engineers. The process engineers must work closely with the plants. Purchasing must work with the designers and the plants. Materials engineers need to work with the designers, purchasing, and the plants. To quote

TABLE 4.6   Importance of Starting Early

- Fewer Options Are Available
- Effectiveness of Options Limited by Previous Decisions

- Costs Increase	PRODUCT DESIGN	PROCESS DEVELOPMENT	MANUFAC- TURING
SYSTEM DESIGN			▨
PARAMETER DESIGN			
TOLERANCE DESIGN			

W. Edwards Deming, "Optimization means cooperation." It is management's responsibility to create this cooperation.

The rest of this book deals with the methods for accomplishing the objectives laid out in Part 1. Part 3 covers the methods associated with searching for differences. Part 4 covers the methods associated with studying inputs' effects. In both approaches, one requires relevant and useful measures of the characteristics one is trying to optimize as well as methods for determining the average and variation. Part 2 deals with the issues of measurement.

4.7   Summary

Strategies for reducing variation

The design process can be thought of as consisting of three stages:

1. *System design.*   Select basic design concept.

2. *Parameter design.*   Set targets for inputs.

3. *Tolerance design.*   Select tolerances for inputs.

The three strategies for reducing variation are applied to these stages as follows:

1. *System design.*   Change the relationship between the inputs and outputs to a more favorable one.

2. *Parameter design.*   Make the product or process robust to variation of the VIPs by selecting targets for the VAPs that minimize variation.

3. *Tolerance design.*   Reduce the variation of the VIPs.

Strategies for optimizing the average

The stages and strategies for optimizing the average are system design—change the relationship between the inputs and outputs to a more favorable one; parameter design—adjust the targets of the key input variables to move the average closer to target; and tolerance design—the average is not affected by tolerance design.

For parameter design, the inputs should be divided into three categories:

1. *Variation adjustment parameters.*   These are the VIPs with nonlinear effects and any key input interacting with a VIP. They should be targeted to minimize the transmitted variation.

2. *Target adjustment parameters.*   These are the key input variables

that are not VAPs. They affect the average only. They are targeted to put the average on target.

3. *Economic adjustment parameters.* These are candidate input values that are not key input variables. They affect neither the average nor the variation. They should be set to minimize costs.

Objectives during product design

All strategies can be applied to each of the objectives with one exception: tolerance design cannot be used to reduce usage variation.

Objectives during process development

Usage variation and variation due to deterioration cannot be addressed during process development.

Objectives during manufacturing

During manufacturing the only strategies available are parameter design for the average and parameter design and tolerance design for reducing manufacturing variation. Manufacturing has the responsibility of diagnosing problems resulting from product and process design.

The complete system

Actions generally become more costly as one progresses through system design, parameter design, and tolerance design. As one progresses through product design, process development, and manufacturing there are fewer possible actions, and the effectiveness of these actions is limited by earlier decisions.

Optimization means cooperation. Everyone involved with the product, from product designer to manufacturing, has a role in optimization and variation reduction.

Measurement

Measuring Variation

It is impossible to fully understand a phenomenon that one cannot measure. Measurement provides the basis by which phenomena can be studied and ultimately understood. Before one can understand variation, determine its causes, and ultimately reduce variation, one first needs the means of measuring variation. That is the topic of this chapter. For many, Chap. 5 will be review. In which case it may be skimmed. However, do not miss the distinction between variation and deviation in Sec. 5.4. Also make sure you know how to determine the accuracy of estimates of variation as presented in Sec. 5.8.

5.1 What Is Variation?

Just like snowflakes, no two units of product are ever exactly alike. Each product is different from all others. Some of these differences may be large. Other differences may be so small as to not be of practical concern. Some differences may be so small as to defy accurate measurement. But always, the differences are there. This leads to the following definition:

Statistical variation. The differences, no matter how small, among ideally identical units of product.

In common usage, the word variation has several meanings. These alternate definitions are discussed in Sec. 5.4. However, whenever the term variation is used in this book, it refers to statistical variation as defined above.

5.2 Measurement of Statistical Variation

Statistical variation is defined as the differences among ideally identical units of product. If the characteristic of interest can be measured,

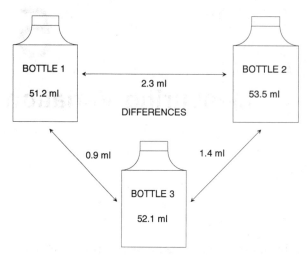

Figure 5.1   Statistical variation.

then several units of products can be measured and the results used to estimate these differences. Suppose that one is filling bottles with a solution and is interested in measuring the variation of the fill volumes. The results of measuring the fill volume of three bottles are shown in Fig. 5.1. The resulting fill volumes are 51.2 ml, 52.1 ml, and 53.5 ml. The differences among the bottles are therefore 0.9 ml, 1.4 ml, and 2.3 ml. These differences are estimates of the variation. They are estimates because they include measurement error and they are a sampling of the possible differences among all units of products.

The key to measuring variation is multiple measurements. The differences among these measurements provide estimates of the variation. The more measurements taken, the better the information on the variation. All the differences could be reported. However, generally the measurements are plotted in the form of a histogram or some summary of the differences is reported such as the largest difference or the average difference. These methods are explored in the next three sections.

5.3   Histograms

One way of summarizing variation is a histogram. An example of one is given in Fig. 5.2. The height of each bar represents the number of units that fall into the different ranges. The numbers on the bottom axis represent the midpoint of each range. For example, the bar above 51.0 ml extends up to 14. This means 14 units fell closest to 51.0 ml, that is, in the range from 50.75 to 51.25 ml.

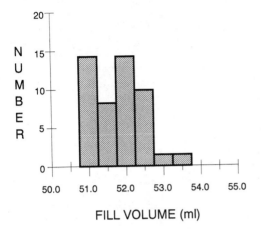

FILL VOLUME (ml)

Figure 5.2   Histogram of fill volume.

The following data were used to construct the histogram:

51.2	53.5	52.1	52.5	52.9
52.2	50.8	52.0	52.4	51.6
52.2	50.9	51.6	52.5	52.2
52.3	51.4	51.8	51.1	52.2
52.5	52.7	52.4	52.2	52.2
51.3	52.7	51.7	52.5	51.3
50.8	52.0	51.7	51.8	52.1
51.9	51.4	53.7	53.2	51.0
51.0	51.2	51.1	51.1	51.0
52.3	50.8	51.9	51.2	50.9

This data set contains 50 values. Typically 50 to 100 values are required to construct a histogram. Further guidance on sample sizes will be given in the individual sections dealing with different applications of histograms.

Histograms are easy to construct by hand. In addition, there are many software packages capable of constructing histograms. As many readers already know how to construct histograms and others will rely on software packages, the details of constructing a histogram will be delegated to App. 1 at the end of this chapter. The primary concern in this section will be the interpretation of histograms.

The most distinguishing feature of the histogram is its width. The width corresponds to the variation. In Fig. 5.2 the width is approximately 53.5 ml minus 51.0 ml or 2.5 ml. Methods of calculating more precise estimates of the variation are given in Sec. 5.6. A second important feature of the histogram is its center. In Fig. 5.2 the center is

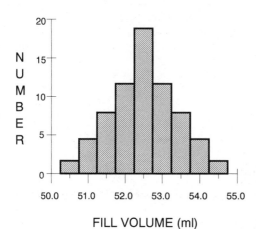

FILL VOLUME (ml)

Figure 5.3 Symmetric histogram.

around 52.0 ml. Methods of calculating more precise estimates of the central tendency are given in Sec. 5.5.

The center along with the spread of a histogram are generally adequate for summarizing it, especially when the histogram is symmetric as in Fig. 5.3. In some cases, however, the histogram will be noticeably skewed like those in Fig. 5.4. It can either be skewed left like the first histogram or skewed right like the second histogram. The direction of skewness corresponds to the direction of the longer tail. Skewness should generally be checked for. When skewness is present, some procedures in this book must be modified.

One final note on the interpretation of histograms. The histogram generally portrays a sample from a larger group of units. This larger group may be a batch or shipment of product, or an hour's production. Whatever the case, the histogram is simply an estimate of the group's variation. Selecting different samples from the same group will give slightly different histograms, so be careful not to overinterpret the histogram. Figure 5.5 contains four additional histograms constructed from different samples of the same batch of product as the histogram in Fig. 5.2. See how much they vary. Interpreting the high count, 54.5 ml, in sample 2 as an indication of right skewness would be incorrect. A general rule of thumb is that if moving just one or two points on the histogram could alter your conclusion, then you are overinterpreting the histogram.

5.4 Variation and Deviations

Statistical variation is defined as the differences among ideally identical units of product. Reducing statistical variation means reducing

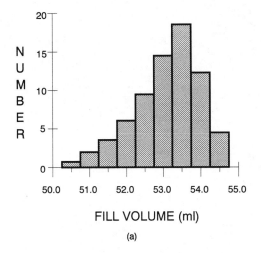

FILL VOLUME (ml)

(a)

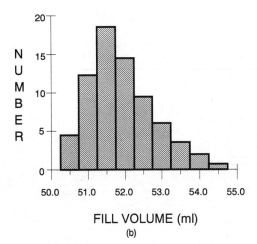

FILL VOLUME (ml)

(b)

Figure 5.4 (a) Skewed left; (b) skewed right.

these differences. The result is a more uniform product. However, more uniform does not necessarily mean higher quality. The product may be perfectly uniform and still have every unit defective. For this reason engineers tend to think not in terms of variation, but instead in terms of deviations.

Deviations are differences among the units of product and established goals. Deviations may be from specification limits, for example, 0.23 ml above the specification limit. Deviations may also be from a target value, for example, 1.56 lb below target. Deviations are what we are interested in reducing. However, these deviations are the result of the width of the histogram (statistical variation) and the distance between the center of the histogram and the target or specifica-

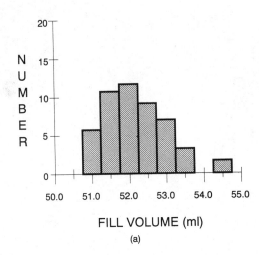

FILL VOLUME (ml)

(a)

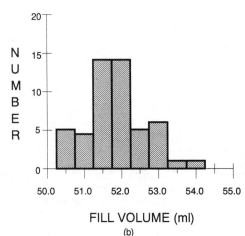

FILL VOLUME (ml)

(b)

Figure 5.5 (*a*) Sample 2; (*b*) sample 3.

tion limits. Therefore reducing deviations requires optimizing the average and reducing (statistical) variation.

In everyday usage, the words vary and variation have two meanings. The first meaning is that of statistical variation. For example, "The weather is extremely variable." There is no established goal. The differences of interest are those among different days. The second meaning of the words vary and variation is that of deviation. For example, "Five percent of the product varies from spec." Here there is an established goal, namely the specification limits. The differences of interest are those among the units of product and the specification limits. The units outside specifications may actually have resulted from either statistical variation or poor centering. Within this book, the words vary and variation will always refer to

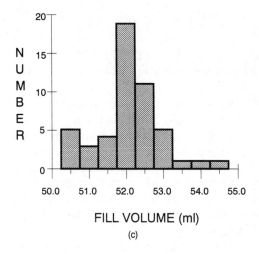

FILL VOLUME (ml)

(c)

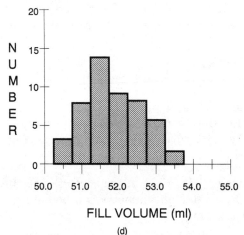

FILL VOLUME (ml)

(d)

Figure 5.5 (*Continued*) (*c*) Sample 4; (*d*) sample 5.

statistical variation. The words deviate and deviation will be used to refer to the second meaning.

5.5 Measures of Central Tendency

Summarizing a histogram can generally be accomplished using a measure of central tendency and a measure of variation. This section examines two measures of central tendency, namely the average and median.

The average

The *average* is the arithmetic average of all the samples. For example, if five bottles had fill volumes of 51.2, 53.4, 51.7, 53.1, and 52.5 ml, then the average is

$$\frac{51.2 + 53.4 + 51.7 + 53.1 + 52.5}{5} = 52.38 \text{ ml}$$

The average is calculated by summing the individual observations and then dividing by the number of observations. The average is also referred to as the *mean*.

The arithmetic average is the most commonly used measure of *central tendency*. It does, however, have certain drawbacks. First, the average may be misleading for nonsymmetric histograms. Generally one thinks of 50 percent of the units as below average and 50 percent as above average. This is the case so long as the histogram is symmetric. However, as in Fig. 5.6, with nonsymmetric histograms it is possible to have 70 percent below the average and only 30 percent above the average. Other cases can be even more extreme. Histograms of wages and wealth tend to match this shape.

The second drawback of the average is that it is sensitive to erroneous values. For example, if the first value above was instead reported as 57.2 as the result of a transcription error, the average would change to

$$\frac{57.2 + 53.4 + 51.7 + 53.1 + 52.5}{5} = 53.58 \text{ ml}$$

The average increases 1.2 ml because of a transcription error.

Despite these two drawbacks, the average is the most commonly used measure of central tendency. However, before using the average one should

Check for approximate symmetry. It is not appropriate to use the average for something like Fig. 5.6. Nonsymmetry can be detected by visible inspection of a histogram.

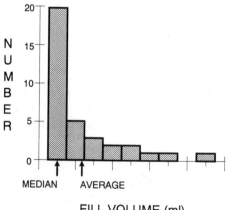

Figure 5.6 Average and median of a nonsymmetric histogram.

Screen for erroneous values. Erroneous values should be dropped from any calculations.

The median

The *median* is an alternate measure of central tendency. It is simply the middle value in the data set. Sorting the five values from before gives 51.2, 51.7, <u>52.5</u>, 53.1, and 53.4 ml. The median is therefore 52.5 ml. For an even number of values, the median is the average of the middle two values. The median is easy to interpret: 50 percent of the values are below the median and 50 percent above. For highly nonsymmetric histograms, the median should be reported instead of the average. As a result, median income should be reported instead of average income.

The median is also less sensitive to erroneous values. Sorting the five values with the transcription error gives 51.7, 52.5, <u>53.1</u>, 53.4, and 57.2 ml. The median changes by only 0.6 ml to 53.1 ml. This is half of the effect of the transcription error on the average.

The median offers one other advantage. The median can be graphically determined without any calculations. The median-range control chart explained in Part 3 requires periodically taking five samples, plotting the five values, and simply circling the middle one. This circled value is the median. No calculator is needed. The median is not, however, as accurate an estimate as the average. The loss of accuracy is minimal for small sample sizes (10 or less).

While the average is the most commonly used measure of central tendency, the median should be used for highly nonsymmetric histograms. The median is also frequently used to simplify calculations as in the median-range control chart.

5.6   Measures of Statistical Variation

The range

The *range* is the simplest measure of variation. It is simply the largest value minus the smallest value. The data on fill volumes used previously are 51.2, 51.7, 52.5, 53.1, and 53.4 ml. The largest value is 53.4 ml. The smallest value is 51.2 ml. The range is therefore,

$$53.4 - 51.2 = 2.2 \text{ ml}$$

While ranges are simple to compute, they can become complicated to interpret and use. The difficulty arises from the fact that ranges increase as more samples are taken. Figure 5.7 shows histograms of ranges based on different sample sizes. The ranges for the three sample sizes average around 4 ml for 5 samples, 4.5 ml for 20 samples, and 6 ml for 100 samples. Notice how the ranges tend to increase as the

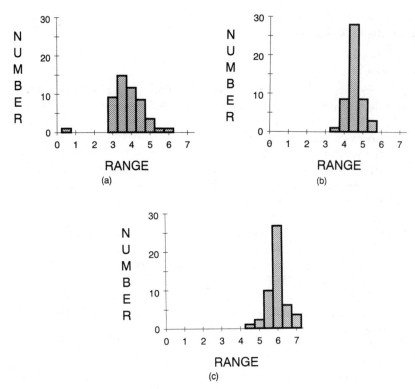

Figure 5.7   (*a*) Histogram of ranges: sample size = 5; (*b*) histogram of ranges: sample size = 20; (*c*) histogram of ranges: sample size = 100.

sample size goes up. The range based on 100 samples averages 50 percent larger than the range based on 5 samples. This means that in comparing ranges, one must be concerned about the number of samples the ranges were based on. Further, how does one interpret the range? What percentage of the product can be expected to be contained within the range? Again, the answer depends on the sample size. The range is also highly sensitive to erroneous values. It only uses the two most extreme points which are those most likely to be in error.

As a result of the difficulty in interpreting ranges, use of ranges is not appropriate in most instances. Ranges do, however, have one special niche: control charts. Control charts require the selection of samples of a fixed size on a periodic basis. The ranges of the samples are often plotted. This is perfectly acceptable since the only thing these ranges are compared to are control limits which are based on the sample size.

The standard deviation

The *standard deviation* is an alternate measure of the variation. It is more difficult to calculate. Methods of calculating the standard deviation are given in App. 2 at the end of the chapter. If one needs to calculate standard deviations frequently, the best thing is to purchase a calculator with statistical functions on it. If your calculator has two keys labeled σ_n and σ_{n-1}, always use σ_{n-1}. The methods of calculating the standard deviation shed little light on how to use it. This section will concentrate on interpreting the standard deviation.

While standard deviations are harder to compute than the range, they are easier to interpret and use. Figure 5.8 shows histograms of

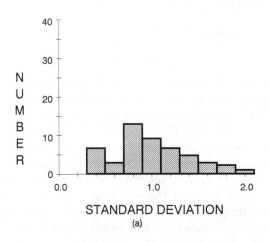

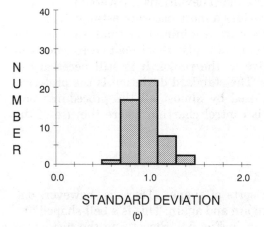

Figure 5.8 (*a*) Histogram of standard deviations: sample size = 5; (*b*) histogram of standard deviations: sample size = 20.

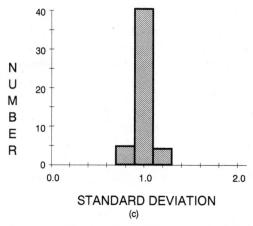

STANDARD DEVIATION
(c)

Figure 5.8 (*Continued*) (*c*) Histogram of standard deviations: sample size = 100.

the standard deviation based on different sample sizes. Unlike ranges, as the sample sizes increase the standard deviations do not tend to get larger. The only thing that happens when the sample size increases is that the standard deviations tend to get closer to the true value, in this case the value 1. This means that standard deviations can be safely used and compared without adjusting for their sample sizes.

There still remains a question of how to interpret standard deviations. Roughly speaking one would expect the width of a histogram based on 300 samples to be around 6 standard deviations wide. Therefore 1 standard deviation is approximately ⅙ the width of the histogram. More on interpreting standard deviations is covered in Sec. 5.7.

The standard deviation provides a more accurate estimate of variation than the range. The advantage is minimal for small sample sizes (10 or less). The standard deviation is also sensitive to erroneous values, although not as sensitive as the range. It is still necessary to screen out erroneous results. The standard deviation is the preferred measure of variation. It is used by almost all the procedures presented. The only exception is control charting where the use of the range is optional.

5.7 Normal Curve

Histograms can take on all sorts of shapes. There is, however, one shape that keeps appearing again and again. This is a bell-shaped histogram such as the one shown in Fig. 5.9. Smoothing the histogram results in the curve labeled the *normal curve*. The normal curve will prove extremely useful later on.

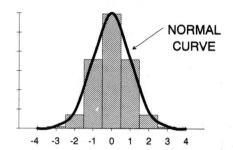

NORMAL
CURVE

Figure 5.9 Bell-shaped histogram.

The fact that so many histograms are bell-shaped is no accident. Look at the four histograms in Fig. 5.10. None look anything like a bell-shaped histogram. Now look at the histogram in Fig. 5.11. This is the histogram of

$$Y = A + B + C + D$$

The histogram of Y surprisingly looks very much like a bell-shaped histogram. Outputs of an equation tend to have bell-shaped histograms, even when the inputs have very different histograms. While

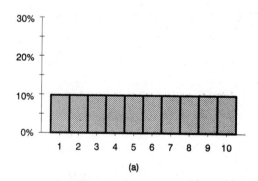

(a)

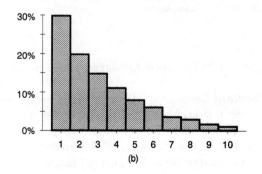

(b)

Figure 5.10 (a) Histogram of A; (b) histogram of B.

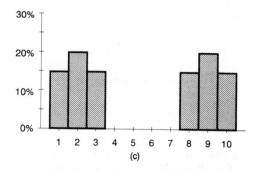

(c)

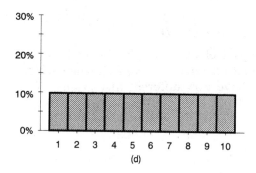

(d)

Figure 5.10 (*Continued*) (*c*) Histogram of *C*; (*d*) histogram of *D*.

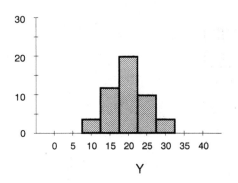

Y

Figure 5.11 Histogram of *Y* (50 samples)

the output does not always have a bell-shaped histogram, it is more frequently the case than not.

The normal curve is so important because it allows a more precise interpretation of the standard deviation. Using the Greek letter σ to represent the standard deviation, Fig. 5.12 shows that 68.3 percent fall within ± 1 standard deviation of the average, 95.4 percent fall within ± 2 standard deviations of the average, 99.7 percent fall within

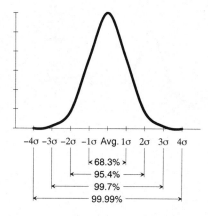

-4σ -3σ -2σ -1σ Avg. 1σ 2σ 3σ 4σ

‹68.3%›

‹—— 95.4% ——›

‹———— 99.7% ————›

‹———————— 99.99% ————————›

Figure 5.12   Normal curve.

±3 standard deviations of the average, and 99.99 percent fall within ±4 standard deviations of the average. A more complete listing is given in Table 5.1. Figure 5.13 gives the percentages in the lower tail only. These are equal to ½ of the percentage outside values in Table 5.1.

5.8 Accuracy of Estimates

The sample average $\overline{X}$ and standard deviation s are estimates of the actual center μ and variation σ. Just how accurate are these estimates? Using the normal curve, *confidence intervals* can be determined which contain the true values a specified percentage of the time.

TABLE 5.1   Normal Curve Percentages

Distance From Average	Percentage Within	Percentage Outside
±0.5σ	38.3%	61.7%
±1σ	68.3%	31.7%
±1.5σ	86.6%	13.4%
±2σ	95.4%	4.6%
±2.5σ	98.8%	1.2%
±3σ	99.7%	0.27% or 2700/million
±3.5σ	99.95%	465/million
±4σ	99.994%	63/million
±4.5σ	99.9993%	6.8/million
±5σ	99.99994%	0.6/million

Distance From Average	Percentage Below
-5σ	0.3/million
-4.5σ	3.4/million
-4σ	31/million
-3.5σ	233/million
-3σ	0.135%
-2.5σ	0.6%
-2σ	2.3%
-1.5σ	6.7%
-1σ	15.8%
-0.5σ	30.9%
0	50%

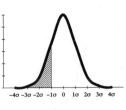

Figure 5.13   Lower normal curve percentages.

For example, the following are the data used to construct the sample 2 histogram in Fig. 5.5:

53.6	52.2	51.9	52.8	53.1
54.3	52.6	52.6	52.2	51.7
52.0	52.9	51.0	52.6	52.2
52.6	51.8	52.2	51.8	51.5
52.1	52.4	53.6	52.4	51.1
51.7	51.5	52.8	52.7	51.0
51.5	51.6	52.0	51.2	52.3
51.7	51.4	53.3	54.3	52.9
51.6	51.1	52.9	53.2	51.7
51.0	51.8	52.5	51.8	51.6

The average and standard deviation of this sample are

$\overline{X}$ = 52.206 ml

s = 0.80519 ml

The histogram of these data approximates a bell-shaped curve. Therefore confidence intervals are possible. The 95 percent confidence intervals are

Average.   With 95 percent confidence, the actual average is between 51.98 and 52.43 ml.

Standard deviation.   With 95 percent confidence, the actual standard deviation is between 0.6726 and 1.003 ml.

The sample average and standard deviation represent the best guess as to the actual center and variation. The confidence intervals represent all plausible values. The formulas for the confidence intervals are

$$\text{Average} = (\overline{X} - c_{\text{ave}}s, \overline{X} + c_{\text{ave}}s)$$

$$\text{Standard deviation} = (c_{\text{sd,lower}}s, c_{\text{sd,upper}}s)$$

The values for c_{ave}, $c_{\text{sd,upper}}$, and $c_{\text{sd,lower}}$ can be obtained from Tables 5.2, 5.3, and 5.4. These three terms depend on the number of samples taken and the desired level of confidence.

As an example, the data given earlier contain 50 samples. Looking in Table 5.2 under 95 percent, c_{ave} is 0.2842. The sample average and standard deviation are 52.206 ml and 0.80519 ml, respectively. The lower confidence interval for the average was calculated as follows:

$$\text{Lower confidence interval for average} = \overline{X} - c_{\text{ave}}s$$

$$= 52.206 - (0.2842)(0.80519)$$

$$= 51.98$$

Some rules of thumb based upon 99 percent confidence are:

For five samples. The true average can be 2 standard deviations in either direction of the sample average. The true standard deviation can be ½ to 4 times the sample standard deviation.

TABLE 5.2 c_{ave}: **Constants for Calculating Confidence Intervals for the Average**

Sample Size	Confidence Level		
	90%	95%	99%
2	4.464	8.985	45.01
3	1.686	2.484	5.730
4	1.177	1.591	2.920
5	0.9534	1.242	2.059
6	0.8226	1.049	1.646
8	0.6698	0.8360	1.237
10	0.5797	0.7154	1.028
15	0.4548	0.5538	0.7686
20	0.3866	0.4680	0.6397
25	0.3422	0.4128	0.5594
30	0.3102	0.3734	0.5032
40	0.2664	0.3198	0.4282
50	0.2371	0.2842	0.3790
60	0.2157	0.2583	0.3436
70	0.1993	0.2384	0.3166
80	0.1861	0.2225	0.2951
90	0.1752	0.2094	0.2775
100	0.1660	0.1984	0.2626
150	0.1351	0.1613	0.2130
200	0.1169	0.1394	0.1839
250	0.1044	0.1246	0.1642
300	0.09526	0.1136	0.1497
500	0.07370	0.08787	0.1156
1000	0.05206	0.06205	0.08161

TABLE 5.3 $c_{sd,upper}$: Constants for Calculating Upper Confidence
Interval for the Standard Deviation

Sample	Confidence Level		
Size	90%	95%	99%
2	15.95	31.91	159.6
3	4.415	6.285	14.12
4	2.920	3.729	6.467
5	2.372	2.874	4.396
6	2.089	2.453	3.485
8	1.797	2.035	2.660
10	1.645	1.826	2.278
15	1.460	1.577	1.854
20	1.370	1.461	1.666
25	1.316	1.391	1.558
30	1.280	1.344	1.487
40	1.232	1.284	1.397
50	1.202	1.246	1.341
60	1.180	1.220	1.303
70	1.165	1.200	1.275
80	1.152	1.185	1.253
90	1.142	1.172	1.235
100	1.134	1.162	1.220
150	1.106	1.128	1.173
200	1.090	1.109	1.147
250	1.080	1.096	1.129
300	1.072	1.087	1.117
500	1.055	1.066	1.088
1000	1.038	1.046	1.061

TABLE 5.4 $c_{sd,lower}$: Constants for Calculating Lower Confidence
Interval for the Standard Deviation

Sample	Confidence Level		
Size	90%	95%	99%
2	0.5102	0.4461	0.3562
3	0.5778	0.5207	0.4344
4	0.6196	0.5665	0.4834
5	0.6493	0.5991	0.5188
6	0.6721	0.6242	0.5464
8	0.7054	0.6612	0.5875
10	0.7293	0.6878	0.6177
15	0.7688	0.7321	0.6686
20	0.7939	0.7605	0.7018
25	0.8118	0.7808	0.7258
30	0.8255	0.7964	0.7444
40	0.8454	0.8192	0.7718
50	0.8594	0.8353	0.7914
60	0.8701	0.8476	0.8063
70	0.8786	0.8574	0.8184
80	0.8855	0.8654	0.8283
90	0.8914	0.8722	0.8367
100	0.8963	0.8780	0.8439
150	0.9137	0.8982	0.8692
200	0.9243	0.9107	0.8849
250	0.9318	0.9194	0.8959
300	0.9373	0.9259	0.9042
500	0.9507	0.9416	0.9243
1000	0.9646	0.9580	0.9453

For 50 samples. The true average can be 0.4 standard deviation in either direction of the sample average. The true standard deviation can be 20 percent below to 30 percent above the sample standard deviation.

The accuracy of estimates of the average depends on the sample standard deviation. If the standard deviation is small, accurate estimates can be obtained from only five samples. Good estimates of the standard deviation are harder to obtain. For five samples, the range of ½ to 4 times means that control charts of the standard deviation (also range) cannot detect any but the largest changes in the variation. Many charts cannot detect a decrease in the variation at all. Further, 30 percent and even 50 percent reductions in the variation can easily go undetected. The minimum number of samples required to get a decent estimate of the variation is 50. This still results in an error of 20 to 30 percent. This is why a minimum of 50 samples are required for a capability study. However, even with 50 samples, the C_p values calculated as part of capability studies can be off by as much as 20 to 30 percent. For this reason, 100 samples are preferred.

In many places it is standard practice to report just averages or to report just averages and standard deviations. These are not enough. Making accurate decisions requires confidence intervals. It is preferable that these confidence intervals be reported. Minimally, averages, standard deviations, and sample sizes should all be reported. Reporting these three numbers allows anyone who wants to, to calculate his or her own confidence intervals.

Suppose that the purpose of taking the data presented in this section was to demonstrate that the average was above 50 ml. If only the sample average, 52.206 ml, is reported, what conclusion can one draw? This sample average might be based on five samples with a sample standard deviation of 10 ml. In this case the 95 percent confidence interval is 39.8 to 64.6 ml. The true average could easily be below 50 ml. The best that can be said is that the odds of the true average being above 50 ml are greater than 50-50.

By reporting the 95 percent confidence interval, 51.98 to 52.43 ml, it is clear that the probability of the average being below 50 ml is extremely small. There is only a 2.5 percent chance of the true average being below 51.98 (the chance of being below 51.98 is the same as the chance of being above 52.43, namely 2.5 percent). Therefore, the probability of being below 50 ml is extremely small.

5.9   Summary

What is variation?

Before variation can be studied, one must first have the means of measuring it. No two units of product are ever exactly alike. *Statistical variation* is defined as the differences, no matter how small, among ideally identical units of product.

Measurement of statistical variation

Measuring variation requires multiple measurements in order to estimate the differences. These differences are generally plotted or summarized.

Histograms

A histogram provides a visual display of the variation. The width of the histogram represents the variation. A histogram can generally be summarized by its width and center. However, skewness should also be checked for.

It is easy to overinterpret histograms that are based on a small number of samples. A general rule of thumb is that if moving just one or two points on the histogram could alter your conclusion, then you are overinterpreting the histogram.

Variation and deviations

Reducing statistical variation does not necessarily lead to higher quality product. Perfectly uniform product may be achieved where every unit is defective. *Deviations* are differences between units of product and established goals. Examples are deviations from specification and deviations from target. Deviations are the result of the width of the histogram (statistical variation) and the distance between the center of the histogram and the target or the specification limits (central tendency).

In common usage, the words vary and variation have two meanings: statistical variation and deviation. In this book these words will always refer to statistical variation.

Measures of central tendency

The *average* is the most commonly used measure of central tendency. However, it has two drawbacks: (1) It is misleading for highly skewed histograms. The median should always be used in this case. (2) It is sensitive to erroneous values. The median may be used or the data should first be screened for erroneous values.

The *median* is an alternate measure of central tendency. It overcomes the two drawbacks of the average and can be the basis for simple graphical procedures requiring no calculations. It is not, however, as accurate an estimate as the average [the loss of accuracy is minimal for small sample sizes (10 or less)].

Measures of statistical variation

The *range,* while it is the easiest measure of variation to calculate, is the most difficult to interpret. Ranges increase as more samples are taken. This means that in comparing ranges, one must be concerned about the number of samples the ranges are based on. Ranges are very sensitive to erroneous values. The range is not appropriate in most instances. The only exception is in control charting.

The *standard deviation*, while more difficult to calculate, is much easier to use. Standard deviations provide more accurate estimates than the range but are still sensitive to erroneous values. Standard deviations are the preferred measure of variation in almost all instances.

Normal curve

The *normal curve* represents the frequently occurring bell-shaped histogram. While histograms come in many shapes, a surprising number closely resemble the normal curve. Outputs of equations frequently take the shape of the normal curve. Based upon the normal curve, statements about the number of units falling different distances from the average can be made. In particular, 99.4 percent of the product will fall within ±3 standard deviations of the average.

Accuracy of estimates

Whenever estimates of the average and variation are given, their accuracy should also be reported. Confidence intervals are a means of reporting the accuracy of estimates. Minimally the average, standard deviation, and sample size should be reported so that confidence intervals can be calculated. It is preferable to report the appropriate confidence intervals for the decisions to be made. Some rules of thumb follow:

- Five samples provide an estimate of the average that is accurate within 2 standard deviations. The true standard deviation is between ½ and 4 times the sample standard deviation.

- An estimate of the mean provided by 50 samples is accurate within 0.4 standard deviation. They provide an estimate of the standard deviation that is within 20 to 30 percent of the true value.

APPENDIX 1   Construction of Histograms

The following procedure was used to construct the histogram given in Fig. 5.2. The data used to construct the histogram are given in Sec. 5.3. The first step is to tally the number of occurrences of each value. A simple method for accomplishing this task is shown in Fig. 5.14. For example, the lowest value was 50.8 ml. Three units had this value as signified by the three *x*s next to the 0.8 below 50.0. This plot is in fact

Figure 5.14 (Tally sheet):

```
50.0
  .1
  .2
  .3
  .4
  .5
  .6
  .7
  .8  xxx
  .9  xx
51.0  xxx
  .1  xxx
  .2  xxx
  .3  xx
  .4  xx
  .5
  .6  xx
  .7  xx
  .8  xx
  .9  xx
52.0  xx
  .1  xx
  .2  xxxxxx
  .3  xx
  .4  xx
  .5  xxxx
  .6
  .7  xx
  .8
  .9  x
53.0
  .1
  .2  x
  .3
  .4
  .5  x
  .6
  .7  x
  .8
  .9
54.0
```

Figure 5.14   Tally sheet.

Figure 5.15 (Collapsing values):

```
50.0
  .1
  .2
  .3
  .4
  .5          50.5    0 values
  .6
  .7
  .8  xxx
  .9  xx
51.0  xxx      51.0   14 values
  .1  xxx
  .2  xxx
  .3  xx
  .4  xx
  .5          51.5    8 values
  .6  xx
  .7  xx
  .8  xx
  .9  xx
52.0  xx       52.0   14 values
  .1  xx
  .2  xxxxxx
  .3  xx
  .4  xx
  .5  xxxx     52.5   10 values
  .6
  .7  xx
  .8
  .9  x
53.0          53.0    2 values
  .1
  .2  x
  .3
  .4
  .5  x        53.5    2 values
  .6
  .7  x
  .8
  .9
54.0
```

Figure 5.15   Collapsing values.

a simple histogram turned on its side. However, it suffers from the fact that there are too many "bars."

The next step is to decide how to group the values into intervals in order to make the histogram more readable. A rule of thumb is that seven to ten bars generally look best. More bars may be used for larger sample sizes. Fewer bars are needed for smaller sample sizes. To determine the interval size, the range was calculated by subtracting the smallest value, 50.8 ml, from the largest value, 53.7 ml. The resulting range is 2.9 ml. It was decided to shoot for seven bars. Therefore, to estimate the interval size, the range of 2.9 ml was divided by 7 to get an approximate interval size of 0.41 ml. This was rounded to 0.5 ml. Based on this result interval midpoints were selected every 0.5 ml and the histogram collapsed as shown in Fig. 5.15. The resulting tallies were used to construct the histogram in Fig. 5.2.

A summary of the procedure used for constructing histograms is given below:

Sort and tally the values as in Fig. 5.14.

Determine the interval midpoints.

- Range equals the largest value minus the smallest value.
- Approximate interval size equals the range divided by the number of bars.
- Round the interval size.
- Pick midpoints at a selected distance apart.

Collapse the data as in Fig. 5.15 and plot.

There are many variations of this procedure that work equally well. Use the one that works best for you and the data at hand.

Exercise. Below is a data set consisting of 50 samples. Prepare a histogram using these data. Compare the results with of Fig. 5.5a. This histogram was constructed using the same data set.

53.6	52.2	51.9	52.8	53.1
54.3	52.6	52.6	52.2	51.7
52.0	52.9	51.0	52.6	52.2
52.6	51.8	52.2	51.8	51.5
52.1	52.4	53.6	52.4	51.1
51.7	51.5	52.8	52.7	51.0
51.5	51.6	52.0	51.2	52.3
51.7	51.4	53.3	54.3	52.9
51.6	51.1	52.9	53.2	51.7
51.0	51.8	52.5	51.8	51.6

APPENDIX 2   Calculating Standard Deviations

The standard deviation can be easily calculated using Fig. 5.16. The procedure is as follows:

1. Place the values in column 2.

2. Sum the values in column 2.

SAMPLE NUMBER	VALUE [1]	DEVIATION [4] (Subtract Average)	SQUARED [5] DEVIATION
1	51.2	-1.12	1.2544
2	53.4	1.08	1.1664
3	51.7	-0.62	0.3844
4	53.1	0.78	0.6084
5	52.2	-0.12	0.0144
.			
.			
.			
Sum	261.6 [2]	Sum	3.428 [6]
Average (Divide By N)	52.32 [3]	Variance (Divide By N-1)	0.857 [7]
		Standard Deviation (Square Root)	0.92574 [8]

Figure 5.16   Calculating standard deviations.

3. Divide this sum by the number of samples. This is the average.

4. Subtract this average from each of the values in the second column and place the differences in the third column. Column 3 represents the deviations from average.

5. Square each of the deviations in column 3 and place the results in column 4.

6. Sum the results of column 4. This sum is called the sum of the squared deviations.

7. Divide the sum of the squared deviations by the sample size minus 1. This value is called the variance.

8. Take the square root of the variance. This is the standard deviation.

The standard deviation is the square root of the average of the squared deviations. One way of thinking about the standard deviation is that it is approximately equal to the average deviation from the average.

The question always arises as to why in step 7 the sum of the squared deviations was divided by the sample size minus 1 instead of just the sample size. This is done to adjust for the fact that standard deviation should really be based on the deviations from the true average. However, the true average is unknown so an estimate of the average is substituted instead. The deviations from the estimated average tend to be slightly smaller than the deviation from the true average. Therefore it is necessary to divide the sum of squared deviations by a slightly smaller number: the sample size minus 1. Some calculators have keys for both σ_n, where the sum of squared deviations is divided by the sample size, and σ_{n-1}, where the sum of squared deviations is divided by the sample size minus 1. Always use σ_{n-1}.

6

Measuring the Three Sources of Variation

6.1 Capability Studies

In Chap. 1 it was shown that optimization and variation reduction, when applied to manufacturing variation, means the achievement of a stable and capable process (Fig. 6.1). *Capability studies* measure manufacturing variation. Capability studies consist of two parts. They first evaluate the stability of the process. Then they compare the process variation to the product specification limits.

Process capability studies

Capability studies require that samples from the process be selected and measured on a periodic basis over a specified period of time. Ideally 20 groups of five samples should be selected. This results in a total of 100 samples, enough to provide a decent estimate of the variation. One should never run a capability study with fewer than 50

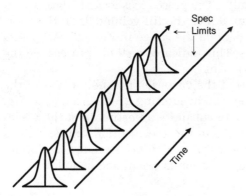

Figure 6.1 Stable and capable process.

TABLE 6.1 Filler Capability Study Data

Subgroup	Values					Average	Range	Std. Dev.
1	52.0	52.1	53.0	52.3	51.7	52.22	1.3	0.49
2	51.7	51.5	52.0	51.7	51.3	51.64	0.7	0.26
3	51.7	52.2	51.9	52.6	52.5	52.18	0.9	0.38
4	51.3	52.2	51.8	52.5	51.4	51.84	1.2	0.51
5	50.8	50.9	51.7	51.8	51.4	51.32	1.0	0.45
6	52.6	51.4	52.9	52.6	52.4	52.38	1.5	0.58
7	53.0	52.9	52.5	52.5	51.8	52.54	1.2	0.47
8	52.5	52.7	51.2	53.7	51.3	52.28	2.5	1.04
9	51.9	51.6	51.6	52.7	51.7	51.90	1.1	0.46
10	52.2	52.7	52.3	51.8	53.2	52.44	1.4	0.53
11	52.4	52.6	52.1	51.8	51.9	52.16	0.8	0.34
12	51.3	51.2	51.9	53.1	52.9	52.08	1.9	0.88
13	51.7	51.6	51.4	51.4	51.1	51.44	0.6	0.23
14	51.8	51.0	52.4	51.2	51.6	51.60	1.4	0.55
15	52.0	51.7	52.6	51.8	52.7	52.16	1.0	0.46
16	52.0	52.3	51.8	52.0	51.5	51.92	0.8	0.29
17	51.8	51.8	51.8	51.9	52.0	51.86	0.2	0.09
18	52.0	51.9	51.4	51.8	53.3	52.08	1.9	0.72
19	51.5	52.6	52.8	52.4	52.0	52.26	1.3	0.52
20	51.5	51.8	50.8	51.3	52.5	51.58	1.7	0.63
						51.99	1.22	0.538
						Grand Average	Average Range	Within Subgroup Std. Dev.

samples. Capability studies are typically run over 4 to 8 h of production.

Table 6.1 shows the results of a capability study run on a filling operation. Twenty groups of five samples were selected 15 min apart for 5 h. The specification limits are 50 to 55 ml. Once those data have been collected, they should be control charted. This requires calculating the averages and ranges of the groups and plotting them against time. It also requires calculating control limits and comparing the averages and ranges to these limits. The procedures for calculating control limits are covered in Chap. 9. For the fill-volume data, the average is control charted in Fig. 6.2 and the range in Fig. 6.3. All points are between the control limits. This indicates a stable process. So the process passes the first requirement.

The second requirement is that the variation fit safely between the specification limits. This can be seen by plotting a histogram as in Fig. 6.4. A more formal approach is to calculate an estimate of the variation and to compare this estimate to the specification limits. This is accomplished by calculating the within-subgroup standard deviation. The within-subgroup standard deviation is calculated as follows:

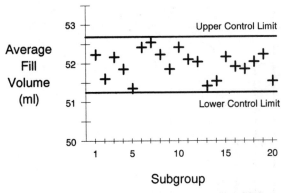

Subgroup

Figure 6.2 Control chart for average.

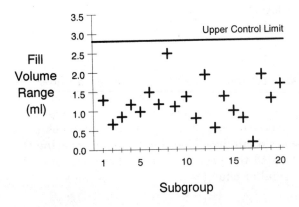

Subgroup

Figure 6.3 Range control chart.

- Calculate the standard deviation of each of the 20 groups
- Square these standard deviations
- Sum up these squared terms
- Divide this sum by 20 (the number of groups)
- Take the square root

For the data in Table 6.1, the within-subgroup standard deviation is calculated as follows:

$$\text{Within-subgroup standard deviation} = \sqrt{\frac{0.49^2 + 0.26^2 + \ldots + 0.63^2}{20}} = 0.538 \text{ ml}$$

The within-subgroup standard deviation measures the variation within the subgroups. It does not include the effect of any subgroup-

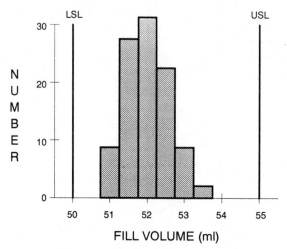

Figure 6.4   Histogram of fill volumes.

to-subgroup differences. It estimates the process variation under the assumption that no shifting, however slight, is occurring over time. But all processes change to some degree over time. Larger changes are detectable on control charts. However, even when the control chart is stable, smaller changes are occurring. Therefore, when comparing the within-subgroup variation to the specifications, allowances must be made for at least these smaller changes.

Capability indexes

Once an estimate of the within-subgroup variation is obtained, it must be compared to the specification limits. This is accomplished by calculating the capability index, C_p:

$$C_p = \frac{USL - LSL}{6\,s}$$

where USL is the upper specification limit, LSL is the lower specification limit, and s is the estimate of the within-subgroup variation.

For the data in Table 6.1,

$$C_p = \frac{55 - 50}{6(0.538)} = 1.55$$

How does one interpret C_p? In the numerator, USL − LSL is the width of the specifications. In the denominator, 6 s is the width of the process histogram. (See Fig. 6.5.) Therefore C_p compares the width of the specification limits to the width of the process histogram:

C_p = ½ (the width of the specification limits is half the width of the process histogram)

C_p = 1 (the width of the specification limits is equal to the width of the process histogram)

C_p = 2 (the width of the specification limits is twice the width of the process histogram)

Capability indexes measure how well the product requirements and process capabilities match. The larger the value of C_p, the better the match between product and process. Capability indexes are as much a measure of the manufacturability of the product as they are of the capability of the process. Capability indexes can be used to compare product/process matches as a means of identifying the poorest matches so that they receive top priority for improvement efforts. They can also be used to determine whether a particular match is acceptable. This requires some criteria for deciding which values of C_p are acceptable. Certainly a C_p of ½ is bad. A C_p of 2 looks good. But where is the dividing line?

Look at the C_p equals 1 diagram in Fig. 6.6. The specification limits are ±3σ from the center. The chart in Table 5.1 indicates 0.27 percent of the product should be defective (2700 defects per million) so long as the process remains perfectly centered at all times. However, even for stable processes, the average will change by small amounts. Mini-

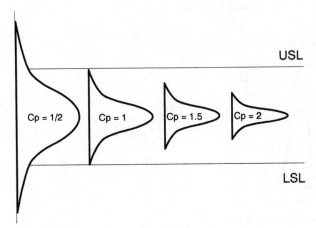

Figure 6.5   Capability index: C_p.

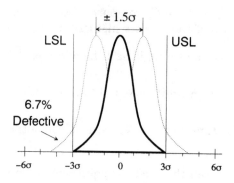

Figure 6.6 C_p = 1: less than 6.7 percent defective.

mally an operating window of $\pm 1.5\sigma$ should be allowed. Control charts (based on five samples) cannot reliably detect changes smaller than this. As shown in Fig. 6.6, if the process is running at the edge of the $\pm 1.5\sigma$ operating window, the process will produce 6.7 percent defective product. The exact value, 6.7 percent defective, was determined using Fig. 5.13. When C_p equals 1, the specification limits are $\pm 3\sigma$ wide. If the process is centered 1.5σ below the center of specification, the specification limit is just 1.5σ below the process average. Figure 5.13 indicates 6.7 percent of the product will be more than 1.5σ below the process average.

The defect rate reaches only 6.7 percent defective when the process is at the very edge of its $\pm 1.5\sigma$ operating window. A C_p of 1 assures that the process is less than 6.7 percent defective, so long as the process average remains within 1.5σ of the center of specification.

The story for a C_p of 1.5 is much better. As shown in Fig. 6.7, a C_p of 1.5 assures less than 0.135 percent defective or 1350 defects per million, so long as the process average remains within the $\pm 1.5\sigma$ operating window. A C_p of 1.5 or greater should be a requirement for new

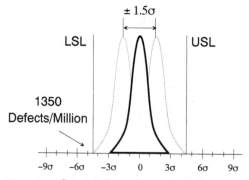

Figure 6.7 C_p = 1.5: fewer than 1350 defects per million.

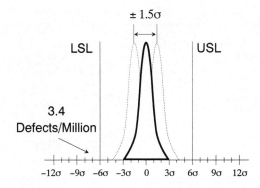

Figure 6.8 $C_p = 2$: fewer than 3.4 defects per million.

processes. However, even this minimal requirement is not met for most processes. Typically C_ps range from 0.7 up to 1.7. Even better is a C_p of 2. A C_p of 2 ensures fewer than 3.4 defects per million (Fig. 6.8), so long as the process average remains within the $\pm 1.5\sigma$ operating window. Achieving this level of performance is still rare, but not as rare as it used to be. In many industries, achieving a C_p of 2 will result in best of class and will provide a competitive advantage. However, the standards are rapidly changing. Motorola has set the goal of achieving C_ps of 2 or better on all their processes by 1991 as part of their Six Sigma program.

Six Sigma capability

Six Sigma capability means the specification limits are at least $\pm 6\sigma$ from the center (σ is the Greek letter sigma). Six Sigma capability is equivalent to a C_p greater than or equal to 2. Six Sigma means that, so long as the process remains within 1.5σ of target, there will be fewer than 3.4 defects per million for individual characteristics, fewer than 50 defects per million units for simple products (15 or fewer important characteristics), and at least 99.6 percent first-time yield for hardware consisting of 1200 or fewer important characteristics. Yield is the percent of units without any defects. *First-time yield* is the yield before any rework and inspection.

Six Sigma assures a single characteristic meets specification 99.99966 percent of the time (i.e., 3.4 defects per million). The chance that a unit of product with multiple characteristics is perfect is

$$\text{First-time yield} = 100 \times (0.9999966)^n$$

where n is the number of important characteristics. It is assumed each characteristic has probability 0.9999966 of being nondefective. Table 6.2 shows first-time yields for different ns.

TABLE 6.2   Six Sigma Quality Means

NUMBER OF KEY CHARACTERISTICS	FIRST TIME YIELD	DEFECT RATE
1	99.99966%	3.4 dpm
10	99.9966%	34 dpm
100	99.966%	340 dpm
1000	99.66%	3400 dpm or 0.34%
10000	96.7%	3.3%
100000	71.2%	28.8%

Six Sigma capability means good quality. By today's standards it means best in class. It should be your goal to achieve Six Sigma capability for every product and process.

Alternate capability indexes

The formula for C_p assumes that there are two specification limits and that the target is midway between them. Equivalent formulas for other cases are

- For an upper specification limit only:

$$C'_{pu} = \frac{USL - target}{3\,s}$$

- For a lower specification limit only:

$$C'_{pl} = \frac{Target - LSL}{3\,s}$$

- For two specification limits with an off-center target:

$$C'_{pk} = minimum\ (C'_{pu},\ C'_{pl})$$

When the target is mid-specification, C'_{pk} reduces to C_p.

For the fill-volume data in Table 6.1, the USL is 55 ml, the LSL is 50 ml, and the target is 52.5 ml. The within-subgroup standard deviation was previously determined to be 0.538 ml. Therefore,

$$C'_{pu} = \frac{55 - 52.5}{3(0.538)} = 1.55$$

$$C'_{pl} = \frac{52.5 - 50}{3(0.538)} = 1.55$$

$$C'_{pk} = \text{minimum } (1.55, 1.55) = 1.55$$

Because the target is mid-specification C'_{pk} is the same as C_p calculated previously.

C'_{pl} compares half the width of the histogram, 3σ, with the distance between the target and the lower specification limit. See Fig. 6.9. C'_{pk} compares half the width of the histogram with the distance between the target and the nearest specification limit. Regardless of the differences in their formulas, C_p, C'_{pu}, C'_{pl}, and C'_{pk} are all interpreted identically:

- Values of 2 or greater ensure fewer than 3.4 defects per million so long as the process is kept within 1.5σ of target. This is called Six Sigma capability. It is generally best in class.

- Values of 1.5 or greater ensure fewer than 1350 defects per million (0.135 percent defective) so long as the process is kept within 1.5σ of target. This should be a requirement of all new processes.

The above formulas all assume targets have been established. If targets have not been established, the average can be used instead. This leads to the following formulas:

$$C_{pu} = \frac{\text{USL} - \overline{X}}{3\,s}$$

$$C_{pl} = \frac{\overline{X} - \text{LSL}}{3\,s}$$

$$C_{pk} = \text{minimum } (C_{pu}, C_{pl})$$

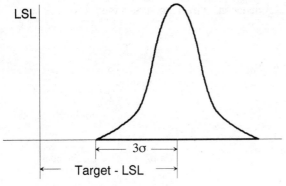

Figure 6.9 Interpreting C_{pl}.

For the fill-volume data, the average is 51.99 ml. Therefore,

$$C_{pu} = \frac{55 - 51.99}{3(0.538)} = 1.86$$

$$C_{pl} = \frac{51.99 - 50}{3(0.538)} = 1.23$$

$$C_{pk} = \text{minimum } (1.86, 1.23) = 1.23$$

C_{pu}, C_{pl}, and C_{pk} are interpreted in similar fashion as C_p, C'_{pu}, C'_{pl}, and C'_{pk}, but not identically. Values of 2 and 1.5 for C_{pu}, C_{pl}, and C_{pk} are interpreted almost the same:

- Values of 2 or greater ensure fewer than 3.4 defects per million so long as the process is kept within 1.5σ of the current average.

- Values of 1.5 or greater ensure fewer than 1350 defects per million (0.135 percent defective) so long as the process is kept within 1.5σ of the current average.

The difference between the *target-based capability indexes* (C_p, C'_{pu}, C'_{pl}, and C'_{pk}) and the *average-based capability indexes* (C_{pu}, C_{pl}, and C_{pk}) arises from the fact that the target-based capability indexes ignore centering. (See Fig. 6.10.) In fact C_p may equal 2 and the whole histogram fall outside the specification limits. The average-based capability indexes consider the effect of centering. When C_p is 2 and the average remains within the required 1.5σ of target, C_{pk} can range from 1.5 to 2. See Fig. 6.11. This demonstrates the fact that C_{pk} tends to be slightly smaller than C'_{pk}. C_{pk} considers centering in addition to the variation. C'_{pk} essentially assumes perfect centering. Typically C_{pk} runs 10 to 20 percent lower than C'_{pk}.

The target-based indexes are preferred when evaluating a process. They allow separate consideration of variation and centering, facilitating the decision-making process. The average-based indexes are-

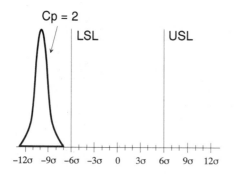

Cp = 2

LSL   USL

−12σ −9σ −6σ −3σ 0 3σ 6σ 9σ 12σ

Figure 6.10 C_p does not consider centering.

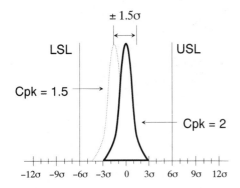

Figure 6.11 For $C_p = 2$, C_{pk} ranges from 1.5 to 2.

preferable for tracking process performance over time. They provide a single number evaluating both variation and centering.

Accuracy of C_ps

The C_ps calculated previously are estimates based on the sample average and within-subgroup σ. As with averages and standard deviations, confidence intervals can be calculated for C_p. The confidence intervals for target-based capability indexes are calculated as follows:

$$\frac{C_p}{c_{sd,upper}} \quad \text{and} \quad \frac{C_p}{c_{sd,lower}}$$

Both $c_{sd,lower}$ and $c_{sd,upper}$ are constants given previously in Tables 5.3 and 5.4. When looking up these constants, an adjusted sample size must be used. The adjusted sample size* is

Adjusted sample size = 1 + number groups × (number samples per group − 1)

The sample size is adjusted because the within-subgroup standard deviation is used to estimate the variation instead of the usual estimate. The within-subgroup standard deviation behaves like a standard deviation calculated from a single sample of the adjusted sample size. Tables 6.3 and 6.4 give additional values useful for calculating confidence intervals for C_ps. The confidence interval is exact for C_p, C'_{pu}, C'_{pl}, and C'_{pk}.

For the fill-volume capability study, C_p equals 1.55. This study consisted of 20 groups of five samples. The adjusted sample size is 1 + (20)(5 − 1) = 81. For 95 percent confidence, $c_{sd,upper}$ equals 1.183 and $c_{sd,lower}$ equals 0.8662. The 95 percent confidence interval for C_p is

---

*Statisticians use degrees of freedom = adjusted sample size − 1.

TABLE 6.3 $c_{sd, Upper}$

Number Groups	Samples/ Group	Effective Sample Size	Confidence Level		
			90%	95%	99%
6	5	25	1.316	1.391	1.558
10	5	41	1.228	1.280	1.390
15	5	61	1.179	1.218	1.300
20	5	81	1.151	1.183	1.251
10	10	90	1.141	1.171	1.233

TABLE 6.4 $c_{sd, Lower}$

Number Groups	Samples/ Group	Effective Sample Size	Confidence Level		
			90%	95%	99%
6	5	25	0.8118	0.7808	0.7258
10	5	41	0.8470	0.8210	0.7740
15	5	61	0.8711	0.8487	0.8077
20	5	81	0.8862	0.8662	0.8292
10	10	90	0.8919	0.8728	0.8375

$$\frac{1.55}{1.183} = 1.31$$

$$\frac{1.55}{0.8662} = 1.79$$

The confidence interval for average-based capability indexes is more complex. Useful approximations are

$$\frac{C_{pk}}{c_{sd,upper}} - \frac{c_{ave}}{6} \qquad \frac{C_{pk}}{c_{sd,lower}} + \frac{c_{ave}}{6}$$

$$\frac{C_{pu}}{c_{sd,upper}} - \frac{c_{ave}}{16} \qquad \frac{C_{pu}}{c_{sd,lower}} + \frac{c_{ave}}{16}$$

$$\frac{C_{pl}}{c_{sd,upper}} - \frac{c_{ave}}{16} \qquad \frac{C_{pl}}{c_{sd,lower}} + \frac{c_{ave}}{16}$$

Values for c_{ave} are given in Table 6.5. Values for c_{ave} were given previously in Table 5.2. When looking up c_{ave}, the total sample size should be used and not the adjusted sample size.

While these confidence intervals are approximate, they are accurate to within 0.02 for smaller values of C_p and to within 0.01 for larger values of C_p. They are wider than the previous confidence intervals because of the increased uncertainty from using an estimate of the average. For the fill-volume capability study, C_{pk} equals 1.23. For a study consisting of 20 groups of five samples and 95 percent confidence, $c_{sd,lower}$ equals 0.8662, $c_{sd,upper}$ equals 1.183, and c_{ave} equals

TABLE 6.5 C_{ave}

Number Groups	Samples/ Group	Total Sample Size	Confidence Level		
			90%	95%	99%
6	5	30	0.3102	0.3734	0.5032
10	5	50	0.2371	0.2842	0.3790
15	5	75	0.1923	0.2301	0.3053
20	5	100	0.1660	0.1984	0.2626
10	10	100	0.1660	0.1984	0.2626

0.1984. The resulting 95 percent confidence interval for C_{pk} is therefore,

$$\frac{1.23}{1.183} - \frac{0.1984}{6} = 1.01 \qquad \frac{1.23}{0.8662} + \frac{0.1984}{6} = 1.45$$

It is worth remembering the accuracy of C_p for two commonly run capability studies. For 95 percent confidence:

Number groups	Samples/ group	Accuracy
10	5	± 22%
20	5	± 15%

There is appreciable improvement going from 10 to 20 groups. For this reason, 20 groups are recommended. Still the accuracy of ±15 percent for 20 groups has less accuracy than most people assume. The accuracy for six groups of five is a whopping ±28 percent. Fewer than 10 groups (50 samples) is not recommended.

Unstable processes

Capability studies estimate future process performance, but only when such performance is consistent over time so as to allow for prediction of future performance. A stable process is predictable. It performs in a consistent manner. A capability study on a stable process measures the consistent performance of the process. It is the stability of the process that allows its capability to be measured. But many processes are unstable. What can we say about them? An unstable process changes. The average is shifting. The variation may be increasing and decreasing. The process has no well defined capability. The performance is changing and will continue to change with no guarantees as to how bad or good things might become in the future.

While it is impossible to provide a meaningful estimate of future process performance for an unstable process, it is possible to measure past performance and to estimate the process potential. Past performance can be measured by keeping a log of defects or by control charting the process. Such records provide ranges of process performance and estimates of extremes. But, as always with unstable processes, tomorrow is another adventure. The best way of estimating the process potential is to look into the past and find the best that the process has performed. If the process has never performed well enough to meet the specifications, it may not have the required potential. However, if for some period of time, no matter how fleeting, the process did the job, the process has the required potential. By identifying the factors causing the good performance, the process can be made to perform this way every day.

There is one situation where slightly more reliable estimates of the process potential can be obtained. Assume that one is performing a capability study and several points fell outside the control limits on the control chart for averages while all points were within the control limits for the range control chart. The process is unstable. The average is shifting over time. However, the within-subgroup standard deviation is consistent over time. An estimate of the within-subgroup standard deviation can be compared to the specification limits to estimate the process performance once all shifting has been eliminated. This can be accomplished by using the target-based capability indexes. These indexes do not use the average, which in this case cannot be reliably estimated. The resulting C_p value estimates the performance of the process once the process can be maintained within the required $\pm 1.5\sigma$ of target.

All estimates of process potential are fraught with danger. They provide estimates of process performance that can be realistically achieved. However, time after time, processes have been made to perform far better than the initial estimates of their potential. The only way of truly knowing the physical limitations of the process is to make the process stable and then improve its capability by identifying and reducing the variation transmitted by the VIPs until one runs up against a VIP for which it is not physically or economically feasible to reduce the transmitted variation further. Most processes can be made to perform far better than anyone imagines.

Long-term capability studies

Many texts and manuals on SPC provide an alternate procedure for running capability studies which will be referred to as a *long-term capability study*. The procedure given earlier will be referred to as a *short-term capability study* in this section only. Long-term capability studies are run identically to short-term capability studies except,

- Long-term capability studies are run over a longer period of time, generally days to weeks. The time period should be sufficient to include all sources of variation: different lots of material, different operators, and so on.

- Instead of calculating the within-subgroup standard deviation, the samples are combined into one large group and the total standard deviation calculated. The total standard deviation estimates both the within-subgroup variation along with the effects of any shifting between subgroups. It will be somewhat larger than the within-subgroup standard deviation.

Because the total standard deviation is larger than the within-subgroup standard deviation, C_p values for long-term capability studies will be smaller than for short-term capability studies. The interpretation of C_p values given previously only applies to short-term capability studies. Assuming the average varies uniformly throughout the $\pm 1.5\sigma$ operating window, C_ps from long-term studies will average 88 percent of the C_ps from short-term studies. Matching C_ps for long-term capability studies are as follows:

C_p from short-term capability study	Equivalent C_p from long-term capability study
2	1.76
1.5	1.32

Both long- and short-term capability studies recognize that even for stable processes differences between the subgroups will exist. Long-term capability studies attempt to measure this variation directly and include it in the estimated variation. Short-term capability studies conservatively allocate a $\pm 1.5\sigma$ operating window to allow for the subgroup differences.

Both types of capability studies can get the job done. This book favors the short-term capability studies because short-term capability studies are quicker and easier to run, it is difficult to assure that all sources of variation have been included in long-term capability studies, and the $\pm 1.5\sigma$ operating window is conservative. Companies should standardize on one or the other of the two types of capability studies so that C_p values are interpreted consistently. For this reason, this book only uses short-term capability studies. These will be referred to henceforth simply as capability studies.

6.2   Measuring Usage Variation

Usage variation is the variation in product performance that results from differences in the usage environment as well as from differences in the way various users use the product. Measuring usage variation requires identifying the usage factors affecting product performance and determining the conditions resulting in the most extreme performances. Take, as an example, the volume delivered by a pump. The pump is rated as capable of delivering 100 gal/min ± 10 gal. The specification limits are therefore 90 to 110 gal/min. A standard diameter hose must be used with the pump. However, the length of this hose can vary. This length might affect the flow rate. In addition there is concern about the effect of temperature on pump performance.

An *analysis of means* (ANOM) study was performed to investigate the effect of these two usage factors. Five different pumps were each run twice under four different usage conditions. The data are shown in Table 6.6. The averages for the four usage conditions are plotted in Fig. 6.12. In addition, two decision lines have been plotted. Complete coverage of the ANOM method including calculation of the decision lines is given in Part 3. Here the concern is how to interpret the decision lines. If one or more of the averages falls outside the decision lines, there is conclusive evidence that pump performance is effective by usage conditions. In Fig. 6.12, the first two averages corresponding to short hoses have significantly higher flow rates than the last two averages corresponding to longer hoses.

TABLE 6.6   Pump Usage Variation Data

		Usage Conditions				
		Short Hose		Long Hose		
		Low Temp	High Temp	Low Temp	High Temp	
Pump	1	96.9 100.9	99.4 103.2	91.5 92.9	91.7 92.4	
	2	106.6 101.5	102.5 104.3	97.2 96.2	95.2 97.3	
	3	101.1 99.3	103.1 101.6	92.7 92.0	96.3 94.7	
	4	103.7 102.9	103.7 103.6	94.1 99.6	99.0 94.8	Grand Average ↓
	5	103.3 104.2	100.8 102.6	94.9 96.3	95.5 94.5	
Average		102.04	102.48	94.74	95.14	98.60

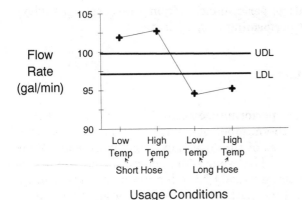

Usage Conditions

Figure 6.12 ANOM for pump usage variation.

The average flow rate for short hoses is 102.26 gal/min. The average for long hoses is 94.94 gal/min. Usage variation can be reported as

$$\text{Usage variation} = \overline{X}_{high} - \overline{X}_{low}$$

$$= 102.26 - 94.94$$

$$= 7.32 \text{ gal/min}$$

The within-subgroup standard deviation is 1.814 gal/min. Using this value, C_p can be calculated as follows:

$$C_p = \frac{\text{USL} - \text{LSL} - \text{usage variation}}{6\,s}$$

$$= \frac{110 - 90 - 7.32}{6(1.814)}$$

$$= 1.16$$

This C_p value is interpreted the same as before. Six Sigma or C_ps of 2 are desired. A C_p of 1.16 is not acceptable. Without considering usage variation, the C_p for the pump would be

$$C_p = \frac{110 - 90}{6(1.814)} = 1.84$$

Without considering usage variation the pump looks all right. However, as a result of differing hose lengths, many customers will experience out-of-specification performance. From the customer's viewpoint, the pump is not performing to specifications.

6.3 Measuring Variation Due to Deterioration

Deterioration in product performance results from wear and aging. *Wear* is determined by the number or length of time the product is used and by the harshness of this use. Tire wear is an example of deterioration due to wear. Tire wear is dependent on the number of miles driven. *Aging* is determined by the length of time the product has been in service and by the harshness of the product's environment. It does not depend on the amount or type of use. Rusting of automobiles is an example of aging. Rusting depends on the age of the car and the exposure of the car to salt and other corrosives. Rusting is not affected by the amount of driving and speed that the car is driven except as these affect exposure to salt and other corrosives.

Wear, related to the amount and harshness of use, can be measured by quickly cycling the product through a large number of usages under relatively harsh conditions. Tires can be run day and night, 7 days a week at 60 mi/h for 30 days on an abrasive surface to simulate their deterioration over 60,000 mi of normal usage. Aging, related to the length of service, can be measured by measuring the product performance over its useful life. If the effect of aging is linear, the rate of aging can be determined and multiplied by the useful length of the product. The time required to measure the effect of aging can also be decreased by *accelerated life testing*. Accelerated life testing requires testing different units under increasingly harsher conditions to be able to extrapolate the product performance under normal conditions.

The methods for measuring wear and aging are beyond the scope of this book. However, regardless of the method selected, an estimate of the deterioration in performance over the useful life of the product is desired. This estimate takes the following form:

$$\text{Variation due to deterioration} = \overline{X}_{\text{initial}} - \overline{X}_{\text{final}}$$

A C_p that accounts for all three sources of variation—manufacturing variation, usage variation, and variation due to deterioration—can be calculated as follows:

$$C_p = \frac{\text{USL} - \text{LSL} - \text{usage variation} - \text{variation due to deterioration}}{6s}$$

6.4 Summary

Capability Studies

Reducing manufacturing variation requires achieving stable and capable processes. Capability studies measure manufacturing variation. The recommended procedure is to select 20 groups of five samples and control chart the averages and ranges of these 20 subgroups to check for stability. If the process is stable, determine its capability by calculating the within-subgroup standard deviation. Use this estimate to compare the spread of the process with the width of the specification limits. This is accomplished by computing the capability index, C_p.

Capability indexes compare the match between the process capability and the product specifications. They are as much a measure of the manufacturability of the product as of the ability of the process to produce the product.

Alternate capability indexes exist for the cases of upper or lower specification limits only. Capability indexes also exist for considering the average along with the variation. Regardless of how the capability indexes are calculated, they are interpreted similarly.

C_ps of 1.5 or greater should be required to go into production. This assures less than 1350 defects per million for a single characteristic so long as the $\pm 1.5\sigma$ operating window is maintained. One should strive to achieve C_ps of 2 or greater for every process. This is called Six Sigma capability. Six Sigma assures fewer than 3.4 defects per million for an individual characteristic so long as the $\pm 1.5\sigma$ operating window is maintained. Six Sigma assures that product with 15 or fewer key characteristics are less than 50 defects per million. It assures that product with 1000 or fewer parts are perfect at least 99.66 percent of the time.

Confidence intervals can be calculated for the C_ps. For the recommended procedure (20 groups of five), C_p is accurate to within ± 15 percent. A stable process is required to obtain a reliable estimate of process capability. While there are several methods for estimating process potential for an unstable process, they have associated dangers.

The recommended procedure is sometimes called a short-term capability study. An alternate procedure, called a long-term capability study, is also available. Short-term capability studies are easier to run and just as reliable and so are preferable. However, many places already run the long-term studies. One should be aware that the C_p values resulting from a long-term study are somewhat smaller and need to be interpreted differently.

Measuring usage variation

Measuring usage variation requires measuring product performance under a variety of usage conditions and determining the worst-case conditions. C_ps adjusted for usage variation can be calculated. These C_ps reduce the width of the specification limits by the amount of the usage variation before dividing by the process spread.

Measuring variation due to deterioration

Deterioration results from wear (determined by the number or length of time used and the conditions of use) and aging (determined by the time and conditions of use). Wear, related to the number of usages, can be measured by quickly cycling the product through a large number of usages. Aging, related to length of usage, can be measured by life testing of the product. If, however, the product has a long expected life, it may be necessary to shorten the test time by using accelerated life testing. Accelerated life testing requires testing different units under increasing harsh conditions to be able to extrapolate the product performance under normal conditions. C_ps adjusted for deterioration can be calculated.

Evaluating Measurement Systems

7.1 Properties of Good Measures

Above all else, measurements should be *relevant*. The measurement should clearly capture some element of the product that is of concern to the customer. Having relevant measures means working on the right problem. Besides being relevant, the *measurement system* should also be stable and capable as shown in Fig. 7.1. All processes should be stable and capable. Taking measurements is itself a process involving a machine (tester), an operator, and materials (the unit to be measured). The output is the measurement. Therefore measurement systems, like all processes, must be stable and capable.

A *stable* measurement system is often called *reproducible*. The measurements should not change over time. The measurement should not be adversely affected by changes in operators and changes in the environment.

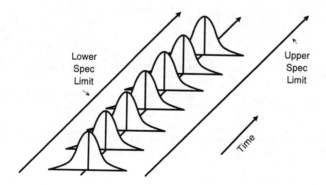

Figure 7.1 Stable and capable system.

A *capable* measurement system requires *sensitivity* [the variation around the average (*precision*) should be small relative to the specification limits or process variation] and *accuracy* (the average should be close to the true value).

For measurement systems, the target is the true value of the characteristic being measured. The distance between the average of the actual readings and this true value is called *bias*. Half of achieving a capable measurement system is to reduce this bias. A measurement system is said to be *accurate* if this bias is small (Fig. 7.2). Accuracy is required when making accept/reject decisions. However, in situations where the concentration is on detecting change (including most experiments), accuracy is not required. Stability assures meaningful results.

The second part of achieving a capable measurement system is to reduce the variation around the average. This variation is frequently referred to as the *measurement precision* or *repeatability*. Sensitivity is a comparison of the precision or repeatability with the requirements. One difficulty frequently arises in determining measurement sensitivity: there are often no explicit specification limits. There is, however, always an implicit requirement that the variation in the measurement system be small when compared to the process variation of the characteristic to be measured. Otherwise, the measurement system will be inadequate for investigating and controlling the process. When no explicit specifications are given, measurement capability is determined by comparing the measurement variation to the process variation.

One way of determining measurement capability is to compare the measurement precision to the product specification limits. For example, suppose shafts are being lathed to the tolerances 0.25 ±0.0005 in. If the measurement standard deviation is 0.0001 in, then C_p is

$$C_p = \frac{0.2505 - 0.2495}{6(0.0001)} = 1.67$$

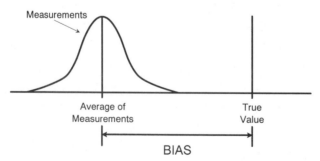

Figure 7.2   Accurate measurement system means small bias.

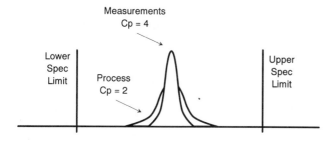

Figure 7.3 Sensitivity requires half the process variation or a measurement C_p of 4.

C_p is only 1.67, based on measurement variation alone. Adding process variation will only decrease C_p. Certainly, the measurement variation is large enough to cause problems as one attempts to achieve a process C_p of 2. To prevent measurement variation from hampering one's efforts at achieving Six Sigma capability, the C_p based on measurement variation alone should be 4 or greater (Fig. 7.3).

As a rule, the measurement standard deviation should be less than ½ of the process standard deviation. This assures that less than 20 percent of the total variation results from the measurement system. It was on this basis that measurement C_ps of 4 or greater were recommended for processes where one is attempting to achieve Six Sigma capability.

In summary, a measurement system should be relevant, stable (reproducible), and capable. Capable means accurate (small bias) and sensitive (precise or repeatable when compared to the specifications or process variation).

7.2 Measurement Capability Studies

When repeated measurements are possible on a single unit of product or reference standard, a capability study can be performed in the normal fashion. For example, Table 7.1 shows the data collected in order to determine the capability of a snap gauge. The snap gauge is used to measure the outside diameter of tubing. A reference tube was used with a known diameter of 0.2500 in. Five measurements were taken four times a day for 5 days by a single operator. The data are control charted in Figs. 7.4 and 7.5. All the averages and ranges are within the control limits. The snap gauge is therefore stable and its capability can be determined.

The within-subgroup standard deviation is

$$s = \sqrt{\frac{(0.0013)^2 + (0.0011)^2 + \ldots + (0.0017)^2}{20}} = 0.0019$$

TABLE 7.1   Snap Gauge Capability Data

Day	Time	Results					Average	Range	Std. Dev.
1	1	0.249	0.246	0.248	0.247	0.249	0.2478	0.003	0.0013
	2	0.250	0.248	0.247	0.248	0.249	0.2484	0.003	0.0011
	3	0.249	0.250	0.250	0.250	0.252	0.2502	0.003	0.0011
	4	0.248	0.250	0.248	0.250	0.244	0.2480	0.006	0.0024
2	1	0.246	0.251	0.252	0.249	0.251	0.2498	0.006	0.0024
	2	0.252	0.245	0.252	0.249	0.247	0.2490	0.007	0.0031
	3	0.251	0.249	0.253	0.247	0.248	0.2496	0.006	0.0024
	4	0.252	0.249	0.247	0.249	0.250	0.2494	0.005	0.0018
3	1	0.251	0.249	0.250	0.251	0.250	0.2502	0.002	0.0008
	2	0.248	0.255	0.250	0.252	0.252	0.2514	0.007	0.0026
	3	0.250	0.250	0.253	0.249	0.248	0.2500	0.005	0.0019
	4	0.251	0.250	0.247	0.249	0.250	0.2494	0.004	0.0015
4	1	0.249	0.252	0.249	0.250	0.251	0.2502	0.003	0.0013
	2	0.252	0.247	0.250	0.248	0.251	0.2496	0.005	0.0021
	3	0.252	0.250	0.252	0.248	0.253	0.2510	0.005	0.0020
	4	0.248	0.250	0.251	0.254	0.250	0.2506	0.006	0.0022
5	1	0.250	0.250	0.252	0.249	0.248	0.2498	0.004	0.0015
	2	0.251	0.248	0.247	0.247	0.248	0.2482	0.004	0.0016
	3	0.249	0.246	0.250	0.248	0.252	0.2490	0.006	0.0022
	4	0.249	0.249	0.253	0.251	0.250	0.2504	0.004	0.0017
							0.2496	0.0047	0.0019
							Grand Average	Average Range	Within Subgroup Std. Dev.

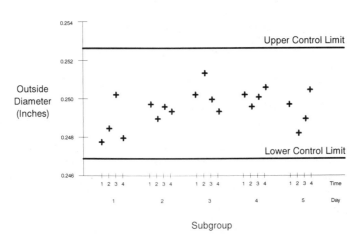

Figure 7.4   Control chart for average.

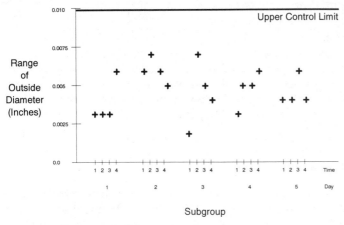

Figure 7.5   Range control chart.

This is the precision or repeatability of the snap gauge. The most commonly run tubing has a specification on outside diameter of 0.25 ± 0.03 in. The C_p based on the measurement standard deviation is therefore,

$$C_p = \frac{0.28 - 0.22}{6(0.0019)} = 5.26$$

Because the snap gauge's C_p is greater than 4, it is sensitive enough for this tubing.

The accuracy is evaluated by comparing the grand average of 0.2496 in to the standard's value of 0.25 in. The snap gauge is determined accurate because these two numbers are very close together. If actual product is used instead of a standard, accuracy could be evaluated by also measuring the product with a more accurate reference device. If none exists, it may be impossible to evaluate accuracy. The snap gauge passes the three tests for stability, sensitivity, and accuracy meaning the snap gauge has proven both stable and capable. If a wide variety of tubing diameters are run, this capability study should be repeated at other diameters to evaluate the snap gauge over the full range of interest.

What if repeated measurements are not possible? It might still be possible to run a measurement capability study if uniform material for testing can be obtained. As an example, a single tablet assay was being developed to measure drug potency. The assay involved dissolving the tablet and thus could not be repeated on the same tablet. To run the study 100 tablets were ground and thoroughly mixed. This material was divided into 100 piles and used for the study. This procedure eliminated any process-related variation. This same principle can be applied in many other places.

There are still cases, however, when repeated testing is not possible and uniform material cannot be obtained. In these cases measurement variation cannot be separated from process variation. A process capability study should be performed. However, it should be remembered that a portion of this variation is due to measurement variation. Attempts to reduce this variation should consider the measurement instrument along with the process.

7.3   Measurement Reproducibility Study

The ANOM method can be used to determine whether operators, the environment, or some other factor affects the instrument's reproducibility. These are all potential causes of instability. An example of such a study will be given for the snap gauge investigated previously. There is concern that the instrument can be affected by the operators. Five operators were selected for the study. The reference tube was measured by each of the five operators on five different occasions. A single snap gauge was used. The data are shown in Table 7.2.

The average reading for each operator is plotted in the ANOM chart in Fig. 7.6. ANOM is covered in detail in Part 3, including how to determine the decision lines (UDL and LDL). Two of the averages fall outside the decision lines. This signifies that the operators can in fact influence the readings. As a result, further training was provided to make the operators more uniform and a monitoring procedure was instituted to periodically check the operators against the reference standard.

TABLE 7.2   Operator Reproducibility Data

	Operators					
	1	2	3	4	5	
	0.2513	0.2483	0.2429	0.2482	0.2567	
	0.2482	0.2508	0.2492	0.2499	0.2573	
	0.2491	0.2505	0.2455	0.2507	0.2534	
	0.2499	0.2511	0.2464	0.2498	0.2541	Grand
	0.2489	0.2503	0.2468	0.2484	0.2564	Average
Average	0.24948	0.25020	0.24616	0.24940	0.25558	0.25016
Std. Dev.	0.0012	0.0011	0.0023	0.0011	0.0017	0.0016

Within Subgroup
Standard Deviation

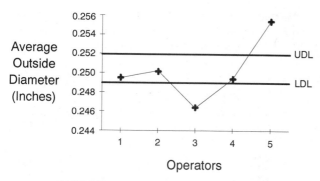

Figure 7.6   ANOM for operators.

The capability study run in the previous section failed to detect any instability of the snap gauge. However, it used only a single operator. The operator reproducibility study demonstrates that changing operators can cause shifting. Reproducibility studies are a good idea for any suspected factor. An alternate to ANOM is to use screening and response surface studies as in Part 4.

The above study used repeated tests of a reference standard. If repeated testing was not possible, a sample of 25 different units could have been used. To maximize the ability to detect operator differences, these units should be as uniform as possible. The units should be randomly assigned to the operators.

7.4   Instrument Bias Study

The ANOM method can also be used to determine whether a bias exists among different instruments. One of the instruments included in the study may be a reference standard. An example of such a study is given for the snap gauge investigated previously. There are five snap gauges which are to be compared. A single operator measured five tubes on each of the five gauges twice. The data are shown in Table 7.3.

The average reading for each gauge is plotted in the ANOM chart in Fig. 7.7. ANOM is covered in detail in Part 3 including how to determine the decision lines (UDL and LDL). Gauge 4 falls outside the decision lines. This signifies that this gauge is performing differently than the others. This gauge was repaired.

7.5   Attribute versus Variable Measures

An *attribute measure* is one whose results are reported on a pass/fail or go/no go basis. The distinguishing feature is that there are only two

TABLE 7.3   Instrument Bias Data

		Snap Gage					
		1	2	3	4	5	
Tube	1	0.2515 0.2470	0.2508 0.2502	0.2508 0.2552	0.2591 0.2611	0.2496 0.2492	
	2	0.2540 0.2531	0.2507 0.2512	0.2545 0.2513	0.2621 0.2606	0.2507 0.2518	
	3	0.2419 0.2511	0.2451 0.2467	0.2444 0.2472	0.2525 0.2561	0.2441 0.2459	
	4	0.2566 0.2546	0.2554 0.2565	0.2559 0.2586	0.2659 0.2637	0.2576 0.2576	Grand Average ↓
	5	0.2466 0.2486	0.2523 0.2516	0.2480 0.2528	0.2635 0.2589	0.2503 0.2542	
Average		0.25050	0.25105	0.25187	0.26035	0.25110	0.25297

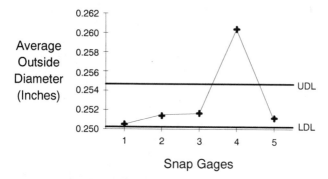

Figure 7.7   ANOM for instrument bias.

possible outcomes. Examples include checking for missing parts, checking for leakers, and gauging a part as in or out of specification. A *variable measure* is one that is reported as a number where numerous values are possible. It could be a count such as particles per milliliter solution, or it could be a reading such as breakforce in pounds. The distinguishing feature is that many different values are obtained and no single value accounts for more than say 30 percent of the units measured.

There are situations between these two extremes. More than two outcomes may be possible but one outcome accounts for the majority of the units measured. For example, a particle counter may report zero counts 90 percent of the time. The other 10 percent of the time nonzero counts are obtained. This type of data should not be treated as variable data. It can be treated as attribute data by classifying the results as zero and nonzero counts.

The methods of this book apply primarily to variable measurements. Both the average and variation can be estimated using variable measurements. VIPs can be separated from the key inputs. Parameter and tolerance design are possible. Variation can be reduced as well as the average optimized. With attribute data the effect of the average and variation cannot be separated. VIPs cannot be distinguished from key input variables. Important information is lost. With attribute data, the same level of performance is generally not achieved as with variable data.

Variable measures have several other important advantages over attribute data:

Fewer samples.   Variable measures require fewer samples than attribute measures to achieve the same results. Typically 50 to 100 samples would be required to prove that a new machine improves weld strength using a variable measure. For an attribute measure, classifying welds as pass/fail, several hundred to many thousands of samples are required.

Detect trends before defects.   Control charts of averages can detect changes and worsening conditions before things get so bad that defects are made. Control charts for attribute data only detect changes that result in defects.

In the drive toward zero defects, Six Sigma, and beyond to zero variation, variable measures are required whenever possible.

The type of measure, attribute or variable, is a property of the method of measurement selected, and not of the characteristic being measured. Seal strength can be measured on an attribute basis by putting 20 lb of pressure in the bag to see whether it ruptures. It can also be measured on a variable basis by measuring the force required to pull the seal apart using a tensile tester. Many measures currently reported as attributes could be converted to variable measures. The next section explains how to determine whether conversion is possible and how to accomplish the conversion.

7.6   Converting Attributes to Variables

Not all attributes can be converted to variables. How does one decide whether conversion is possible? This requires looking beyond the current measurement method to the actual mechanism causing the defect. Take missing caps as an example. A cap could be missing because the operator failed to put one on. The cap could also have fallen off due to poor tolerances resulting in a low removal force.

The first cause, operator failed to put the cap on, is an example of a defect caused by an error or omission. The cap is missing because of an operator error. The unit is either perfectly good or an error was made and the unit is defective. There is no in-between. Only these two possibilities exist. The effect of errors and omissions can only be measured on an attribute basis. The methods of this book are not appropriate for dealing with errors and omissions. The process should be mistake-proofed to eliminate this type of defect. Low-cost automatic 100 percent inspection methods are also effective against these defects.

The second cause, poor tolerances resulting in a low removal force, is an example of a *functional cause mechanism*. There is a functional relationship among several inputs and the output. In this case the inputs are the dimensions and the output is the removal force. As a result of this functional relationship and variation in the inputs, some units are better or worse than others. Some units are so bad they are considered defective. The effect of functional causes can always be measured using a variable measure. Functional causes should be dealt with using methods for optimization and variation reduction.

By now the answer to the question, "Can this attribute measure be converted to a variable measure?" should be apparent. One must examine the cause mechanism and determine whether defects are the result of errors or a functional relationship. If they are the result of errors or omissions, no conversion is possible. Mistake-proofing and low-cost automated 100 percent inspections are required to prevent defects. If they are the result of a functional relationship, conversion is possible. The methods of optimization and variation reduction are required to prevent defects. There may be several possible causes so that it cannot be determined which one is the actual cause. There may even be several causes, some errors or omissions and some functional relationships, acting simultaneously. In these cases, separate measures can be established for each cause and used to identify and deal with the actual cause(s).

For the missing cap problem, two possible causes were identified: operator failed to put cap on and poor tolerances resulted in a low removal force. An automated inspection could be set up immediately following the capping operation to test for the presence of a cap. Two electric eyes could be set at different heights so that one detected bottles and the other detected caps. If the bottle electric eye is triggered and the cap one is not, that bottle is missing a cap. These test results measure the effect of the first cause. Immediately following this testing station, samples could be periodically selected and the cap removal force control charted. This control chart measures the effect of the second cause.

A second example involves a filling operation. The operator places the bag on a nozzle, the bag is filled, and then the bag is removed by an operator and sealed. Of concern is the fill volume. There are two causes of out-of-specification fills: the operator and the machine. First, the operator could place the bag on the nozzle late or remove it early resulting in dramatic underfills or leave the bag on the nozzle for two cycles resulting in dramatic overfills. Second, the solution delivered by the filling machine varies. To track these two problems periodic samples were selected. Any units more than 6 standard deviations from the average were assumed out of specification due to the first cause. The incidents of these outliers were plotted. It ran around 0.5 percent. The remaining units were then used to control chart fill-volume variation. Allowing the operator-caused defects to be included in the control charting data could lead to confusing and misleading results.

Beware of defect classifications that are really a collection of different defects. Take leaking bags as an example. The leak rate is frequently reported. This may be appropriate for an overall measure of process performance. But when controlling and improving the process, the many possible causes of leaking bags must be dealt with individually. There may be seal delaminations, seal thin spots, channel leakers, puncture leakers, material cracking, material weak spots, and so on. Some of these causes, such as seal delaminations, can be converted to variables. Others cannot. The answer to the question, "Can this attribute be converted to a variable measure?" is often one of "For some causes, but not for all."

Errors and functional relationships are the two basic cause mechanisms leading to defects. From these, more complex cause mechanisms can be constructed. For example, another possible cause of missing caps is that some caps are snagging on the rim of the bottle packaging machine. If the cap snags and if the removal force is low, the cap will come off. This is a *complex cause mechanism*. It is a combination of two basic cause mechanisms. The first is an error: cap snags on packaging machine. The second is a functional relationship: removal force is low. Both contributing causes must act simultaneously to produce the defect. Removal of either cause will eliminate the defect.

Complex causal relationships can be broken down into a sequence of basic cause mechanisms. The functional causes can be measured using a variable measure. The answer to the question, "Can this attribute be converted to a variable measure?" is at other times one of "For some of the contributing causes, but not for all."

Once a functional-caused defect has been identified for conversion to a variable measure a wide variety of methods exist for performing the conversion. Some commonly used approaches are:

Stop converting to attribute. Many times variable data are already being taken but converted to attributes by comparing the values to the specification limits.

Stop gauging. When gauging is used to determine whether the unit is in or out of specification, gauging can be replaced with a measurement instrument.

Test to failure. Some tests place the product under controlled stress to see if it fails. Most units survive these tests. The number of failures is reported. The test procedure can be changed to place the product under increasing stress until it fails. The stress at failure is then reported (pressure, force, temperature, and so forth).

Rating scales. Standard rating scales can be established with guidelines for each rating. Frequently, limit samples are used to help define scale boundaries. A series of limit gauges could be used. The scale should be set up so that no more than 30 percent of the units receive any particular rating.

Panel of judges. This option also involves rating the units of product on a scale. However, in this case, no clear guidelines are established. Each judge is free to establish his or her own criteria. This approach requires using the same judges for all units tested. It is more appropriate for special studies than ongoing measurements.

This concludes Part 2 on measurement. Measurement has been covered in such detail because good measurements are essential to effective optimization and variation reduction. In some ways we have gotten ahead of ourselves. Many of the methods of optimization and variation reduction covered in the remaining two parts can be used for evaluating and improving measurements: control charts and ANOM to name a few. The use of these methods was illustrated in Part 2. However, complete coverage of these methods has been delayed until Parts 3 and 4.

7.7 Summary

Properties of good measures

All measures should have the following properties. They should be

Relevant. Represent some element of the product that is of concern to the customer.

Stable (reproducible). The measures should not change over time. They should not be adversely affected by changes in operators, environment, etc.

Capable. The measurements should be both accurate and sensitive. *Accurate:* The average of repeated measurements should be close to the true value. The difference between the true value and the average is called bias. Accuracy is required when making accept/

reject decisions. However, in situations where the concentration is on detecting change (including most experiments), accuracy is not required. Stability assures meaningful results. *Sensitive:* The measurement variation (precision, repeatability) should be small when compared to the specification limits or the size of the effect one is trying to observe. The measurement variation should be less than one-half the size of the process variation.

Measurement capability studies

Measurement systems are processes. Therefore capability studies can be run on the measurement systems. Measurement capability studies evaluate stability (reproducibility) and sensitivity (precision, repeatability). The evaluation of stability is limited to those factors allowed to vary during the capability study. If a standard is used instead of actual product, the measurement capability study also evaluates accuracy.

Measurement reproducibility study

ANOM can be used to evaluate whether operators, environment, or some other factor affects the instruments' reproducibility (stability).

Instrument bias study

ANOM can also be used to determine whether a bias exists among different measurement instruments. One of the instruments may be a standard.

Attribute versus variable measures

Attribute measures are measures whose results are reported on a pass/fail or go/no go basis. The distinguishing feature is that there are only two possible outcomes. *Variable measures* are measures whose results are reported as a number. The distinguishing feature is that many different values are obtained and no single value accounts for more than 30 percent of the units measured. Variable measures allow separate measures of average and variation making variation reduction possible, require smaller sample sizes, and can detect trends before defects result.

In the drive toward zero defects, Six Sigma, and beyond to zero variation, variable measures are required whenever possible.

Converting attributes to variables

Not all attribute measures can be converted to variable measures. Deciding whether conversion is possible requires looking beyond the current method of measurement to the cause of the defect.

There are two basic mechanisms causing defects: errors and functional relationships. The effect of errors and omissions can be measured only on an attribute basis. Defects caused by errors should be eliminated by mistake-proofing and low-cost automated 100 percent inspection. The effect of functional relationships can always be measured as a variable. Defects resulting from functional relationships should be eliminated by the methods of optimization and variation reduction.

When several causes exist or there is a complex cause mechanism (consisting of several errors and/or functional relationships), certain causes may be converted to variables while others cannot. Some strategies for converting an attribute to a variable are to stop converting to an attribute, to stop gauging, to test to failure, to use a rating system, and to employ a panel of judges.

Searching for Differences

8

Strategies for Identifying Differences

8.1 The General Strategy

Recall that there are two general approaches to identifying key input variables and VIPs: searching for differences and studying the input's effects. Searching for differences is the topic of this part. Studying the input's effects is covered in Part 4. The purpose of searching for differences is to provide clues to the key input variables and the VIPs. A difference exists because some key input variable is different. The nature of the difference provides clues to what that key input variable is. Searching for differences is especially effective at reducing variation. When a difference is found, the effect of the key input variable causing the difference is large and is at least temporarily acting as a VIP. Searching for differences identifies VIPs that can be used to reduce the variation. However, any VIP so identified is also a key input variable that can be used to help optimize the average. There are four categories of differences that should be searched for:

1. *Time differences.* The process may be changing over time. The average may be slowly trending downward. The variation may suddenly increase. The timing and pattern of these changes provide clues to the VIP. Control charts provide a useful tool for identifying and tracking time differences. Control charting is the topic of Chap. 9.

2. *Differences between streams of product.* Differences between different streams of product can also be used to identify VIPs; for example, differences between nozzles on a multistation filling machine, differences between cavities in injection molding, and differences between lines using supposedly identical equipment. Which streams differ and how they differ provide important clues. Multi-Vari charts,

ANOM, and variance decomposition studies are useful tools for identifying and studying stream-to-stream differences. These are the top-
ics of Chap. 10.

3. *Differences between individual units.* Even differences between
individual units of product can help identify VIPs. For example, two
supposedly identical motors may differ in horsepower. Something
must be different about either the components used or the manner of
assembly. Two injection-molded parts may have dramatically different strengths. Again, something must be different. Possibly a dimension or the built-in stresses. These unit-to-unit differences can be used
to help identify VIPs.

4. *Differences within a unit.* Finally, differences can exist even
within an individual unit. The left side of a bag may be stronger than
the right side. These differences provide further clues.

Differences, whatever the type, provide important clues to the VIPs.
These clues help narrow the field. They often lead directly to a VIP.
However, just as often the VIP remains elusive. This is not, however,
the end of the road. These same differences provide a second opportunity to run experiments that can search out the VIP. Three methods of
doing this—component swapping studies, setup/assembly studies, and
unit comparisons—are the topic of Chap. 11.

8.2   Time Differences

Control charts look for changes in the process over time. Figure 8.1
shows an example of a control chart. Any point outside the control
limits indicates a change has taken place. Control charts are covered

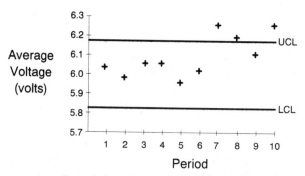

Figure 8.1   Control chart for average: sudden shift.

in detail in Chap. 9. Control charts not only detect the presence of time differences, they provide clues to the cause of the difference through the timing of the change and the pattern of points.

The control chart in Fig. 8.1 indicates that the voltage shifted upward between periods 6 and 7. The time of the jump is an important clue. If a new lot of material was introduced at the same time as the jump, the control chart provides strong evidence that one of the material properties is the cause of the jump and is, at least temporarily, acting as a VIP. Control charts can also identify a point in time where the amount of variation changes. Figure 8.2 shows a sudden increase in the voltage variation. Again the time of the change is an important clue.

Sudden shifts, however, are not the only changes that can be identified by control charts. Many telltale patterns can also develop that provide important clues. With patterns it is the shape of the pattern that provides the clue and not the timing. Figure 8.3 shows several telltale patterns. The gradual downward trend is indicative of tool wear. Cycling may be the result of an on/off-type temperature controller repeatedly raising the temperature and then allowing a period of cool down. The length of the cycle is an important clue. Stratification indicates multiple streams of product or multiple lots of components that differ.

In some cases there may be both timing and pattern clues. Figure 8.4 shows a gradual downward trend interrupted by occasional upward shifts. The downward trend coupled with the timing of the upward shifts both provide clues. The upward shifts might correspond to tool changes or compensating adjustments.

Whenever a difference is found, think experimentation. What can be done to help isolate or confirm the VIP? Save material for further

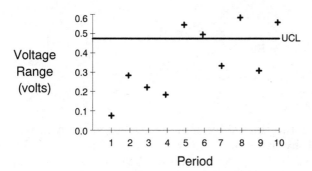

Figure 8.2   Range control chart: increasing variation.

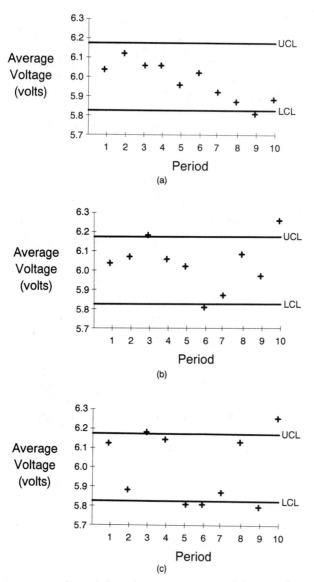

Figure 8.3 Control chart for average: (a) trend downward; (b) cycling; (c) stratification.

testing. Try reversing the change by undoing the suspected cause. If one can trap the VIP by being able to turn the effect on and off, the experiments explained in Chap. 11 can be used to help identify the VIP(s) responsible for the effect. Unstable processes are constantly giving clues. One must learn to watch for these clues. A stable process,

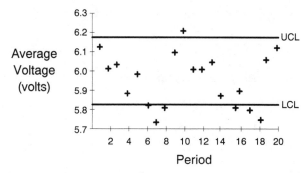

Figure 8.4 Control chart for average: downward trend with shifts up.

however, is more difficult to deal with. First one should look for the other three types of differences. If none are found, further improvement must be accomplished using the second approach: study the input's effects.

8.3 Product Stream Differences

For many processes, the flow of the product is such that different units of product take different paths through the process. Multi-head filling machines, multiple sealing stations, and multiple cavities are all examples of processes that have different paths. These different paths are called *product streams*. When product streams exist, differences may exist between the units coming from the various streams. These differences provide important clues to VIPs. Further, if the difference is consistent over time, a VIP has been trapped and the experiments covered in Chap. 11 can be used to identify the VIP.

Take as an example, a process making enzyme tabs. The enzyme tabs are used by an analyzer to measure the level of certain hormones and drugs in a patient's blood or urine. A tab is shown in Fig. 8.5. The

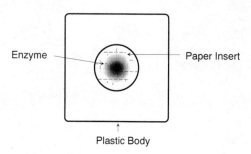

Figure 8.5 Tab.

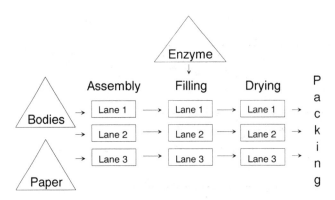

Figure 8.6   Tab process.

tab is the size of and looks similar to a slide. It consists of a plastic tab body which holds a special paper on which the enzyme is coated. The activity level of the enzyme of the tab is the critical characteristic.

The process flowchart is shown in Fig. 8.6. It consists of three steps:

1. Assembly: the paper is cut and assembled into the tab.
2. Filling: the enzyme is placed on the paper.
3. Drying: the tab goes through a drying oven.

There are three assembly stations, three corresponding filling stations, and three lanes through the drying oven.

A Multi-Vari chart was maintained to track the process. Multi-Vari charts will be covered in Chap. 10. On a particular lot of tabs the Multi-Vari chart appeared as in Fig. 8.7. The tabs from lane 1 had consistently higher activity levels than those in the other two lanes. There is a difference. This difference provides a clue to a VIP. How-

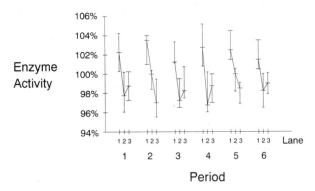

Figure 8.7   Multi-Vari chart of enzyme activity.

ever, there are many candidate inputs that could cause lane differences. Differences in the paper rolls, assembly forces, assembly alignment, fill volume, fill force, fill-head alignment, and lane oven temperatures are but a few of over 30 possibilities that exist.

The existence of a lane difference is not much of a clue. However, because the difference is consistent over time, experimentation is possible to help isolate the VIP. The paper rolls can be reversed to see if the effect stays with the lane or moves with the paper. If the effect stays the same, all inputs associated with the paper are safely eliminated. If the effect reverses itself, paper is the sole cause. If the effect changes, but does not reverse itself, paper is part of the cause but not all of it.

In addition to reversing paper roles, the tabs from lanes 1 and 2 can be switched from one lane to the other between assembly and filling and between filling and the drying oven. This allows a determination of whether the lane difference is due to paper, assembly, filling, drying, or some combination of these. At the end of the study, everything should be returned to its original state to verify that the effect is still present. Such experimentation is called component swapping. It is covered in Chap. 11.

If paper is identified, samples can be sent to the labs. If assembly is different, samples can be saved so that differences can be identified. If filling is identified, further studies are possible to isolate whether it is the pump, the nozzle, the tubing, or the setup. If the drying oven is identified, measurements can be taken to check for temperature differences.

Stream differences offer clues. However, even more important, consistent stream differences allow experimentation that can quickly isolate the VIP.

8.4 Unit Differences

Simply identifying two units of product that perform differently can be useful. The units can then be studied to determine what is different about the units that might cause the difference in performance. If more than two units that are different can be identified, one can look for patterns in order to help identify the VIP. If the units are reusable and consist of multiple parts or assemblies, special studies called component swapping studies and setup/assembly studies can be performed to isolate the VIP.

For example, take two pumps that are performing differently. A diagram of the pump is shown in Fig. 8.8. Assembly consists of placing the base on a flat surface, inserting the piston into the base, laying the cover on top of the base, screwing to the base, and finally screwing in

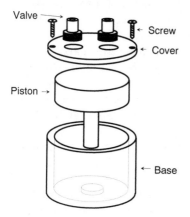

Figure 8.8 Pump schematic.

the two valves. The two pumps have been identified with different flow rates. The first pump has flow rates of 88 to 92 gal/min; the second has 106 to 110 gal/min. To identify the cause of the difference, start by redoing the last assembly step to see if the difference persists. Then redo the last two assembly steps, the last three, and so on, until the whole pump is disassembled and reassembled. If the differences between the two pumps change, the critical assembly operation will be identified.

If the units can be disassembled and reassembled over and over without affecting the difference, the problem is a component problem and not an assembly problem. To identify the critical components, the components can be swapped between the units either one at a time or in combinations. If swapping a component reverses the difference, it is the sole cause of the problem. If swapping a component changes the difference but does not simply reverse it, it is part of the problem. Swapping should continue to identify the other contributing components.

8.5 Within-Unit Differences

There can even be differences within a unit. For example, in making a plastic bag, the strength of the seal may differ between the left and right sides or between the side and bottom seals. Such differences can be identified through concentration diagrams like the one in Fig. 8.9. A *concentration diagram* is simply a picture of the product with marks indicating the location of each defect. Any pattern can be quickly identified. In Fig. 8.9, the largest concentration of defects occurs on the left side near the closure site.

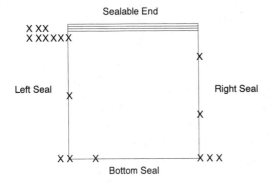

X marks location of defects

Figure 8.9 Concentration diagram of a resealable plastic bag.

Once differences within units are identified they can be dealt with using the same two approaches used to deal with differences between two units: measuring and comparing the attributes of the two parts of the unit, and component swapping studies and setup/assembly studies. Component swapping requires the use of identical parts in both parts of the unit or some sort of symmetry allowing parts to be reversed.

8.6 Summary

The general strategy

The purpose of searching for differences is to provide clues as to the identity of the VIPs. These differences also provide an opportunity to run experiments that can search out the VIP. Differences may exist between periods of time, streams of product, individual units, and within a unit.

Time differences

Control charts are used to identify time differences. Time differences provide clues through the timing of changes and the shape of patterns. When time differences are found, experiments should be used to help identify the VIP. Every attempt should be made to trap the VIP by learning to turn the effect off and on. Then the methods of Chap. 11 can be used to help identify the VIP(s).

For stable processes, the other three types of differences should be searched for first. If none are found, one should proceed to the second approach, studying the input's effects.

Product stream differences

For many processes, the flow of the product is such that different units of product take different paths through the process. These different paths are called product streams. Stream differences offer clues. However, they frequently offer more. Consistent stream differences allow experimentation that can quickly isolate the VIP.

Multi-Vari charts and their derivatives, ANOM and variance components analysis, are useful for identifying stream differences. Component swapping studies, setup/assembly studies, and unit comparisons are powerful tools for isolating the VIP.

Unit differences

The same methods used to identify stream differences can be used to help identify unit differences. Differences between individual units may be exploited by measuring and comparing the attributes of units, and component swapping studies and setup/assembly studies.

Within-unit differences

Concentration diagrams can help to identify differences within a unit. Differences within units may be exploited using the same methods as used with between-unit differences, namely, measuring and comparing the attributes of the parts of the unit, and component swapping studies and setup/assembly studies.

9

Control Charts

9.1 Common Cause and Special Cause Variation

Control charts detect differences over time. If all points remain within the control limits, the process is stable, i.e., no differences exist. When one or more points fall outside the control limits, it is almost certain that differences over time exist. Control charts split the total variation into two components:

1. *Common cause variation.* This is the variation that appears within the control limits.

2. *Special cause variation.* The presence of special causes of variation is indicated by points outside of the control limits.

Take as an example, the effect that line voltage has on sonic sealing of plastics. Electricity provides the energy required to fuse the plastics together. The line voltage is constantly fluctuating by small amounts. This is frequently referred to as noise. These small voltage changes help cause the individual units to differ. It contributes to the variation within the control limits. However, on occasion, line voltage varies by much larger amounts. These conditions are known as brownouts, blackouts, and power surges. They are only temporary, generally lasting from less than a minute to several hours. They result in one group of units being different from the others. In these situations, line voltage is acting as a special cause. It causes points to fall outside the control limits. See Fig. 9.1.

The distinction between common cause and special cause variation is an important one. However, the reason for this distinction is often misunderstood. Common cause and special cause variation are not caused by fundamentally different things. All variation of the output

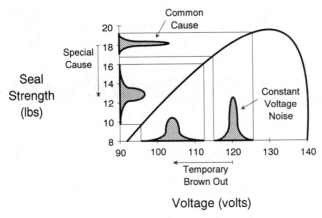

Figure 9.1   Common and special causes.

results from variation of the inputs. In the example above, line voltage acts as both a common cause and a special cause, contributing to both types of variation. Both common cause and special cause variation can be reduced by identifying the key input variables and tightening their control. The distinction between common causes and special causes is one of how to proceed.

The presence of special causes, indicated by points outside the control limits, means that differences exist. In particular, differences over time. These differences should be exploited by using the methods in Part 3. The process is yielding valuable clues that should be listened to. The absence of special causes, indicated by all points within the control limits, means that the process is remaining tight-lipped. If other differences cannot be identified for exploitation, it is time to force the process to talk by purposely changing the inputs and studying their effects. This is the topic of Part 4.

> The distinction between common causes and special causes is one of how to proceed. The presence of special causes means differences exist that should be exploited. The absence of special causes means only that nothing is happening on its own. It is, therefore, time to make something happen.

9.2   Uses of Control Charts

Control charts are used in a wide variety of situations for three different purposes. In order to ensure control charts are properly used, these three uses should be clearly understood. They are

1. *Evaluating processes.*   Control charts are a key part of the capability studies run to evaluate process performance. See Sec. 6.1.

2. *Improving processes.*   Control charts can be used to determine when special causes of variation are present so they may be identified and permanently fixed.

3. *Maintaining processes.*   Control charts can be used to maintain a process by determining when adjustments are required.

Evaluating processes requires special studies. The control chart is only used over a brief period of time. Maintaining processes requires permanent installation of a control chart. Improving processes may require using the control chart for a longer period of time, but not on a permanent basis. Flexibility should be maintained as to the number of samples, the time between samples, and the selection of the samples in order to allow the generation and investigation of important clues.

Sometimes the distinction between improving the process and maintaining the process is missed. Improving the process means identifying special causes and providing permanent fixes. This results in improved understanding of the process and breakthroughs in performance to new levels. Maintaining the process means providing corrections to special causes to return the process to its former level of performance. Over time the performance remains level with occasional blips that are quickly fixed.

Most control charts are being used for maintenance purposes, even when their stated objective is improvement. The telltale indicator is whether the process is improving to new levels. Following improvement efforts, a control chart for maintenance purposes is often required. However, the control chart should first be used as an improvement tool as explained in Sec. 9.6. If the implementation of a control chart is hampered by questions about how many samples should be selected, how frequently they should be selected, whether samples need be taken from all cavities, and so forth, then the up-front improvement activities have not taken place. Use of control charts for improvement first will provide the answers to these questions.

9.3   Average-Standard Deviation Control Charts

This section covers the construction of one type of control chart: the *average-standard deviation control chart.* When constructing a control chart, one must decide on the number of samples per subgroup and the length of time between subgroups. Typically five samples per subgroup are selected. A minimum of two samples per subgroup is required to construct an average-standard deviation control chart. A special control chart, called an individuals control chart, is covered in Sec. 9.5 which requires only one sample per subgroup. Increasing the sample size improves the control chart's ability to detect change. More on this later.

The length of time between subgroups depends on the purpose of the control chart. For evaluating the process as part of a capability study, the time period should be such that the study can be completed in a day. Typically 20 subgroups of five samples are used, so a time period of every half hour would allow the study to be completed in 10 h. For process improvement, the time periods should start small. It might only be every couple of minutes initially. This would allow the identification of cycling or other short-term disturbances that could be missed otherwise. Once confidence is gained in the short-term stability of the process, the time period can be lengthened. Often ½-h or 1-h time periods are used.

For process maintenance, one should already have experience with the process from the improvement phase. The time interval selected will depend on this experience. The time interval should be small when compared to the average length of time between excursions outside of the control limits. Time periods typically range from ½ to 8 h. At other times the time period is allowed to vary. Samples may be taken at the beginning and end of each run. They may also be taken following any temporary shutdown or process adjustment. This maximizes the chances of detecting a change quickly.

After deciding on the number of samples per subgroup and the length of time between subgroups, one needs to determine the control limits. But before control limits can be calculated, some data must be collected. For capability studies, all the data are collected before any calculations are performed. For improvement and maintenance, typically ten subgroups are run before the control limits are calculated. The grand average and the pooled within-subgroup standard deviation of these subgroups are required to compute the control limits. The formulas for control limits are as follows:

$$\text{UCL}_{\overline{X}} = \overline{X} + \frac{3\,s}{\sqrt{n}}$$

$$\text{LCL}_{\overline{X}} = \overline{X} - \frac{3\,s}{\sqrt{n}}$$

$$\text{UCL}_{s} = B_6\, s$$

$$\text{LCL}_{s} = B_5\, s$$

TABLE 9.1   Standard Deviation Control Chart Constants

Sample Size	c_4		$B_5{}'$		B_6	
2	0.7979	(0.6745) *	0.0	(0.0017) *	2.606	(3.205) *
3	0.8862	(0.8326)	0.0	(0.0368)	2.276	(2.571)
4	0.9213	(0.8881)	0.0	(0.0995)	2.088	(2.283)
5	0.9400	(0.9161)	0.0	(0.1626)	1.964	(2.110)
6	0.9515	(0.9329)	0.0289	(0.2182)	1.874	(1.991)
7	0.9594	(0.9441)	0.1129	(0.2656)	1.806	(1.903)
8	0.9650	(0.9521)	0.1786	(0.3062)	1.751	(1.835)
9	0.9693	(0.9581)	0.2318	(0.3411)	1.707	(1.780)
10	0.9727	(0.9628)	0.2759	(0.3714)	1.669	(1.735)
11	0.9754	(0.9665)	0.3134	(0.3980)	1.637	(1.697)
12	0.9776	(0.9696)	0.3456	(0.4215)	1.610	(1.664)
13	0.9794	(0.9721)	0.3737	(0.4425)	1.585	(1.635)
14	0.9810	(0.9743)	0.3985	(0.4614)	1.563	(1.609)
15	0.9823	(0.9761)	0.4206	(0.4785)	1.544	(1.587)
16	0.9835	(0.9777)	0.4405	(0.4941)	1.526	(1.566)
17	0.9845	(0.9791)	0.4585	(0.5084)	1.511	(1.548)
18	0.9854	(0.9803)	0.4748	(0.5215)	1.496	(1.531)
19	0.9862	(0.9814)	0.4898	(0.5336)	1.483	(1.516)
20	0.9869	(0.9824)	0.5036	(0.5449)	1.470	(1.502)
21	0.9876	(0.9833)	0.5163	(0.5554)	1.459	(1.489)
22	0.9882	(0.9841)	0.5281	(0.5651)	1.448	(1.477)
23	0.9887	(0.9848)	0.5391	(0.5743)	1.438	(1.466)
24	0.9892	(0.9855)	0.5493	(0.5829)	1.429	(1.455)
25	0.9896	(0.9861)	0.5589	(0.5910)	1.420	(1.446)

* The values in parentheses guarantee a 1 in 370 chance of being outside the control limits.
† Use of lower control limits is not recommended for most situations.

where n is the number of samples per subgroup, $\overline{X}$ is the grand average, and s is the within-subgroup standard deviation. B_5 and B_6 are constants given in Table 9.1. The other constant in Table 9.1, c_4, is used in the next section. The reason for having two values will be explained shortly. For now, use the second value (in parentheses).

As an example, recall the filling capability study run back in Chap. 6. Control charts were required as part of this study. The data were given in Table 6.1. From these data a grand average of 51.99 ml and a within-subgroup standard deviation of 0.538 were calculated. A control chart of the average is shown in Fig. 6.2. The control limits were calculated as follows:

$$\text{UCL}_{\overline{X}} = 51.99 + \frac{3(0.538)}{\sqrt{5}} = 52.71 \text{ ml}$$

$$\text{LCL}_{\overline{X}} = 51.99 - \frac{3(0.538)}{\sqrt{5}} = 51.27 \text{ ml}$$

The upper control limit for the standard deviation is

$$\text{UCL}_s = 2.110(0.538) = 1.135 \text{ ml}$$

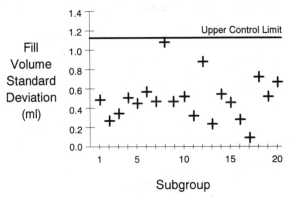

Subgroup

Figure 9.2   Standard deviation control chart.

No lower control limit was calculated based on a warning given later. The standard deviation control chart is shown in Fig. 9.2. As all points are below the upper control limit, the standard deviation control chart indicates that the within-subgroup variation is stable over time.

Now let us look at how control limits work. If σ is the standard deviation of a group of product, then the standard deviation of an average of n units from the same group of product will be

$$\frac{\sigma}{\sqrt{n}}$$

Figure 9.3 shows a histogram of 200 samples from a batch that is uniformly distributed between the values 6 and 14. Also shown are histograms of averages based on two, five, and ten samples from this batch. The larger the sample size, the narrower the histogram will be. The rate of narrowing is given by the equation above. This is true not only for the normal curve, but for any shape histogram.

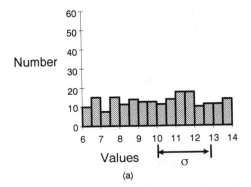

Figure 9.3 (a) Histogram of individual units.

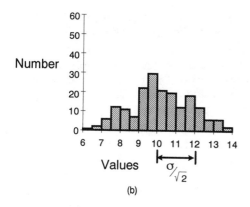

Number

Values $\sigma/\sqrt{2}$

(b)

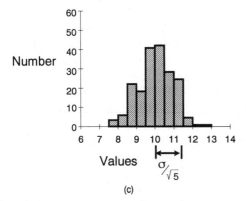

Number

Values $\sigma/\sqrt{5}$

(c)

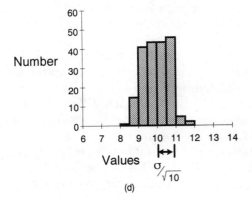

Number

Values $\sigma/\sqrt{10}$

(d)

Figure 9.3 (*Continued*) (*b*) Histogram of averages: N = 2; (*c*) histogram of averages: N = 5; (*d*) histogram of averages: N = 10.

The control limits for the average are the grand average ±3 standard deviations for the subgroup averages. Using the normal curve, the chance of a point being outside the control limits is about 0.3 percent or 1 in 370. The control chart of averages will falsely indicate that the process has changed, when in fact it has not, at a rate of once out of every 370 subgroups. The 1 in 370 chance of a point being outside the limits when no change has taken place means that most times when a point is out, the process has changed. Points within the control limits could occur without any change. However, too many points too close to the control limits or certain patterns might also indicate a change. This is the topic of the next section.

Table 9.1 gives two sets of values for B_5 and B_6 for calculating control limits for the standard deviation. The first set was determined by going ±3 standard deviations from the average. These limits are published in most books and standards dealing with SPC. Because standard deviations do not follow the normal curve, these limits do not ensure the same 1 in 370 rate of false detections. The actual rate varies from 1 in 109 for a sample size of 2 up to 1 in 359 for a sample size of 25.

The second set of values provides the same 1 in 370 false detection rate that the average has. There is an 1 in 740 chance of falsely detecting an increase and an 1 in 740 chance of falsely detecting a decrease. They result in slightly higher upper control limits which help to reduce the rate of false detections commonly experienced on control charts of the standard deviation.

The control limits assume a normal curve. For the averages this is not much of a restriction. Averages tend to follow the normal curve even when the individual units do not. Figure 9.2 shows histograms of the average taken from a batch that is uniformly distributed between 6 and 14. The histograms rapidly approach the normal curve even for sample sizes as small as 5. Therefore, for the average the 1 in 370 false detection rate is ensured for sample sizes of 5 or more, regardless of how the individual units are distributed.

The situation for the standard deviation is much different. The shape of the histogram of standard deviations is sensitive to whether the individual units follow the normal curve. In many situations, standard deviations will be more variable than estimations based on the normal curve would indicate. This is another reason for using the second set of values for B_5 and B_6. They are more conservative.

A second problem associated with control charts of the standard deviation arises because of *round-off error*. Under the assumption of the normal curve, all values are possible including values like 1.2735269185625668696. In practice values are rounded off to values like 1.274, 1.275, and 1.276. Rounding off often reduces the standard deviation. Take the following five values:

1.2735269, 1.2676395, 1.2717901, 1.2742130, and 1.2699812

The standard deviation of these five numbers is 0.0026804. This number could well be above the lower control limit on a standard deviation chart. If these values are first rounded to three significant digits the values become

1.27, 1.27, 1.27, 1.27, and 1.27

The standard deviation is now zero which will certainly fall below the lower control limit. The effect of round off is to increase the incident of estimates of zero for the standard deviation causing an increase in the rate that points fall below the lower control limit. Based on the normal curve, estimates of zero simply will not happen. For this reason it is recommended that lower control limits for the standard deviation not be used unless zero estimates of the standard deviation are rare. Generally, this requires sample sizes greater than 10 and small round-off errors.

How long does it take a control chart to detect a change? This depends on the size of the change as well as the number of samples per subgroup. One measure of the ability of a control chart to detect change is called the *average run length* (ARL). The ARL is the average number of points added to the control chart following a change until that change is detected.

$$\text{Average run length} = \frac{1}{P}$$

where P is the probability that an individual point falls outside the control limits. P depends on the size of the change. When no change has occurred, the ARL is 370. Figure 9.4 shows the ARL curve for a sample size of 5.

For a sample size of 5, shifts in the average of $\sigma/2$ or less are not detected in a reasonable period of time. Shifts of 1σ are typically detected 4.5 periods later. One can produce a large amount of product before a 1σ shift is detected. A shift of 1.5σ is much better. The change is picked up by the first point added to the control chart following the change 64 percent of the time. An average of 1.57 periods is required to detect the change. Odds improve further for a 2σ shift. It will be detected 93 percent of the time by the first point added. This is the reason that a $\pm 1.5\sigma$ operating window should be allowed for as part of

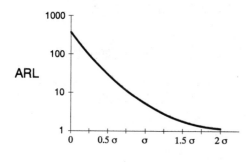

Amount That Average Shifted

Figure 9.4 Average run length curve: sample size = 5.

a capability study. Values of *P* and ARL for a variety of sample sizes are given in Tables 9.2 and 9.3.

9.4 Special Patterns

Patterns other than a point outside the control limits may also indicate that the process has changed. Too many points too close to the

TABLE 9.2 Average Run Lengths (ARL) (Control Chart for Averages)

Sample Size	Amount that the Average Changed					
	0	σ/4	σ/2	σ	1.5 σ	2 σ
2	370.4	223.9	90.65	17.73	5.27	2.32
3	370.4	184.2	60.69	9.76	2.91	1.47
4	370.4	155.2	43.89	6.30	2.00	1.19
5	370.4	133.2	33.40	4.50	1.57	1.08
6	370.4	115.9	26.36	3.44	1.33	1.03
7	370.4	102.0	21.38	2.77	1.20	1.01
8	370.4	90.6	17.73	2.32	1.12	1.00
9	370.4	81.2	14.97	2.00	1.07	1.00
10	370.4	73.3	12.83	1.77	1.04	1.00
11	370.4	66.5	11.13	1.60	1.02	1.00
12	370.4	60.7	9.76	1.47	1.01	1.00
13	370.4	55.6	8.65	1.37	1.01	1.00
14	370.4	51.2	7.73	1.30	1.00	1.00
15	370.4	47.3	6.96	1.24	1.00	1.00
16	370.4	43.9	6.30	1.19	1.00	1.00
17	370.4	40.8	5.75	1.15	1.00	1.00
18	370.4	38.1	5.27	1.12	1.00	1.00
19	370.4	35.6	4.86	1.10	1.00	1.00
20	370.4	33.4	4.50	1.08	1.00	1.00
21	370.4	31.4	4.18	1.06	1.00	1.00
22	370.4	29.6	3.90	1.05	1.00	1.00
23	370.4	27.9	3.66	1.04	1.00	1.00
24	370.4	26.4	3.44	1.03	1.00	1.00
25	370.4	25.0	3.24	1.02	1.00	1.00

TABLE 9.3   Probability of Point Out of Limits (Control Chart for Averages)

Sample Size	Amount that the Average Changed					
	0	σ/4	σ/2	σ	1.5 σ	2 σ
2	0.0027	0.0045	0.0110	0.0564	0.1898	0.4319
3	0.0027	0.0054	0.0165	0.1024	0.3439	0.6787
4	0.0027	0.0064	0.0228	0.1587	0.5000	0.8413
5	0.0027	0.0075	0.0299	0.2225	0.6384	0.9295
6	0.0027	0.0086	0.0379	0.2910	0.7499	0.9712
7	0.0027	0.0098	0.0468	0.3616	0.8336	0.9890
8	0.0027	0.0110	0.0564	0.4319	0.8930	0.9961
9	0.0027	0.0123	0.0668	0.5000	0.9332	0.9987
10	0.0027	0.0136	0.0780	0.5645	0.9594	0.9996
11	0.0027	0.0150	0.0899	0.6242	0.9759	0.9999
12	0.0027	0.0165	0.1024	0.6787	0.9860	1.0000
13	0.0027	0.0180	0.1156	0.7276	0.9920	1.0000
14	0.0027	0.0195	0.1294	0.7709	0.9955	1.0000
15	0.0027	0.0211	0.1438	0.8087	0.9975	1.0000
16	0.0027	0.0228	0.1587	0.8413	0.9987	1.0000
17	0.0027	0.0245	0.1740	0.8693	0.9993	1.0000
18	0.0027	0.0263	0.1898	0.8930	0.9996	1.0000
19	0.0027	0.0281	0.2060	0.9129	0.9998	1.0000
20	0.0027	0.0299	0.2225	0.9295	0.9999	1.0000
21	0.0027	0.0319	0.2393	0.9432	0.9999	1.0000
22	0.0027	0.0338	0.2563	0.9545	1.0000	1.0000
23	0.0027	0.0359	0.2736	0.9637	1.0000	1.0000
24	0.0027	0.0379	0.2910	0.9712	1.0000	1.0000
25	0.0027	0.0401	0.3085	0.9772	1.0000	1.0000

control limits and all the points grouped close to the center are both patterns that should be watched for.

To aid in the interpretation of control charts, Fig. 9.5 breaks the region between the control limits into zones. These zones are constructed by first drawing the centerline. In the case of averages, the centerline is the grand average or target. For standard deviation con-

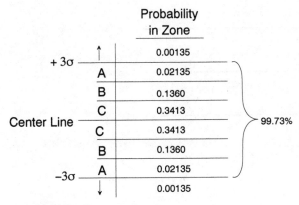

Figure 9.5   Zones for run tests.

trol charts, the centerline, using c_4 from Table 9.1, is calculated as follows:

$$\text{Centerline} = c_4\, s$$

Once the centerline has been drawn, the region between the centerline and specification limits is divided into three equal size regions and labelled A, B, and C as shown. Figure 9.5 shows how many units should fall into each zone. A normal control chart can be characterized by a majority of points (68 percent) falling close to center (zone C) but also a small number of points (4.3 percent) falling close to the control limits (zone A). The absence of either of these conditions is of importance.

Figure 9.6 shows a pattern known as "stratification" or "hugging the centerline." It is characterized by a lack of points close to the control limits. It results from multiple sources of product which differ and are sampled in a stratified fashion. For example, five injection molded parts might be selected every half hour, one from each of the five mold cavities. Selection of one sample from each cavity is stratified sampling. If there are consistent cavity-to-cavity differences, the control chart will look like the one in Fig. 9.6. Stratification indicates stream-to-stream differences exist. The 15 consecutive points in the C zones confirm this pattern.

A second pattern is shown in Fig. 9.7. This one is called "mixture" or "hugging the control limits." It is characterized by a lack of product near the center (C zone). The mixture pattern results from multiple streams that are consistently different. Each group of samples comes from one stream or the other. A mixture pattern indicates stream-to-stream differences exist. It is confirmed by six consecutive points outside the C zones.

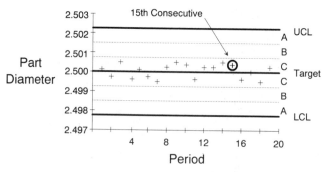

Figure 9.6 Control chart showing stratification (hugging the centerline).

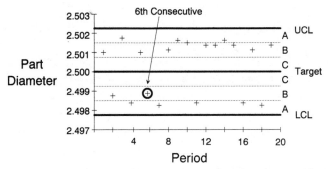

Figure 9.7 Control chart showing mixture (hugging the control limits).

There are a large number of special zone tests to help detect shifting or trending more quickly. The *Western Electric Handbook* gives three additional rules to be used in combination with the standard first rule:

- Any point falling outside the control limits

- Two out of the last three points fall in the same *A* zone

- Four out of the last five points fall in the *A* and *B* zones on the same side of the centerline

- Eight points in a row fall on the same side of the centerline

Each of these tests is a good indicator of change. Their use considerably reduces the time required to detect a change. However, their use also considerably increases the rate of false detections. Using these four rules simultaneously results in one false detection every 65 points. This can result in a lot of unnecessary investigations. By comparison, rule 1 by itself results in only one false detection every 370 points.

Figure 9.8 shows the ARL curves for rule 1 alone and rules 1 to 4 together. A third ARL curve is also shown. This ARL curve is for a control chart using rule 1 only but with the control limits calculated as

$$CL_{\bar{X}}'s = \bar{X} \pm \frac{2.42\,s}{\sqrt{n}}$$

This third procedure's ARL curve is nearly identical to that of rules 1 to 4 with 3σ control limits. The bottom line is that rules 2 to 4 are unnecessarily complex. If one wants to detect a change quicker, one should either increase the sample size or tighten the control limits.

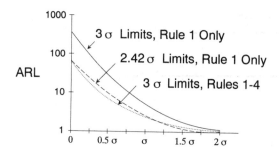

Amount That Average Shifted

Figure 9.8 Average run length curves: sample size = 5.

Tightening the control limits increases the rate of false detections whereas increasing the sample size does not.

9.5   Other Control Charts

Median-range control charts

An alternative to the average-standard deviation control chart is the *median-range control chart*. Use of the median and range instead of the average and standard deviation results in a slight loss of efficiency. However, the loss is minor for smaller sample sizes (10 or less). On the other hand, the median-range chart provides a very powerful graphical presentation. Further, it can be maintained without tedious calculations. Median charts require the sample size per period be odd (3, 5,...). A median-range chart constructed from the fill-volume capability-study data (Table 6.1) is shown in Fig. 9.9.

For each subgroup the values of all five samples are plotted. The middle one is circled. This is the median. The subgroup medians are compared to the upper and lower control limits. The median chart in Fig. 9.9 indicates a stable process. The five values from each subgroup are connected with a vertical bar. The length of this bar is the range. These bars are compared to the template on the right of the chart. The height of the template is equal to the distance from zero to the upper control limit for the range. Bars that are longer than the template should be circled indicating that they are above the upper control limit for the range. In this case all bars fit within the template indicating that the within-subgroup variation is not changing. The template is normally printed separately on clear film so it can be slid around on the chart.

The ranges can also be plotted on a separate control chart as in Fig.

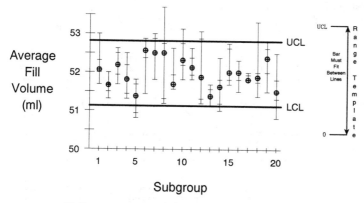

Figure 9.9   Median-range control chart.

6.3. The median-range chart above offers the advantage of making it readily apparent whether an unusually large range is the result of a single abnormal result or the result of an overall increase in the variation. To calculate the control limits (UCL and LCL) and centerline (CL) for the median and range, first determine the average of the subgroup medians and the average of the subgroup ranges. Then calculate the limits as follows:

$$UCL_m = \text{average median} + A_6 \text{ (average range)}$$

$$CL_m = \text{average median}$$

$$LCL_m = \text{average median} - A_6 \text{ (average range)}$$

$$UCL_r = D_4 \text{ (average range)}$$

$$CL_r = d_4 \text{ (average range)}$$

$$LCL_r = D_3 \text{ (average range)}$$

The constants A_6, D_3, D_4, and d_4 are given in Tables 9.4 and 9.5.

Median control charts incorrectly place approximately 1 in 340 points outside the control limits when in fact no change has taken place. This is close to the 1 in 370 for the average control chart. For the range control chart, two sets of values are given for the constants. The first set gives widely published approximations. When no change has taken place these constants result in false detections from 1 in 109 for a sample size of 2 on up to 1 in 230 for larger sample sizes. The second set of values assures a 1 in 370 chance of improperly placing a point outside the control limits. The use of the second set of values is recommended. As with the standard deviation control chart, lower

TABLE 9.4   Range: Control Chart Constants

Sample Size	d_4		$D_3{}'$		D_4	
2	1.0000	(0.8453)*	0.0	(0.0021)*	3.267	(4.017)*
3	1.0000	(0.9381)	0.0	(0.0414)	2.575	(2.924)
4	1.0000	(0.9609)	0.0	(0.1071)	2.282	(2.526)
5	1.0000	(0.9703)	0.0	(0.1705)	2.114	(2.312)
6	1.0000	(0.9752)	0.0	(0.2245)	2.004	(2.176)
7	1.0000	(0.9782)	0.076	(0.2695)	1.924	(2.081)
8	1.0000	(0.9802)	0.136	(0.3071)	1.864	(2.009)
9	1.0000	(0.9816)	0.184	(0.3389)	1.816	(1.954)
10	1.0000	(0.9827)	0.223	(0.3660)	1.777	(1.909)
11	1.0000	(0.9835)	0.256	(0.3895)	1.744	(1.871)
12	1.0000	(0.9842)	0.283	(0.4100)	1.717	(1.840)
13	1.0000	(0.9847)	0.307	(0.4281)	1.693	(1.813)
14	1.0000	(0.9852)	0.328	(0.4442)	1.672	(1.789)
15	1.0000	(0.9855)	0.347	(0.4587)	1.653	(1.768)
16	1.0000	(0.9859)	0.363	(0.4717)	1.637	(1.750)
17	1.0000	(0.9862)	0.378	(0.4836)	1.622	(1.733)
18	1.0000	(0.9864)	0.391	(0.4944)	1.609	(1.718)
19	1.0000	(0.9867)	0.404	(0.5044)	1.596	(1.704)
20	1.0000	(0.9869)	0.415	(0.5135)	1.585	(1.692)
21	1.0000	(0.9871)	0.425	(0.5220)	1.575	(1.680)
22	1.0000	(0.9872)	0.435	(0.5299)	1.565	(1.669)
23	1.0000	(0.9874)	0.443	(0.5373)	1.557	(1.659)
24	1.0000	(0.9875)	0.452	(0.5442)	1.548	(1.650)
25	1.0000	(0.9877)	0.459	(0.5506)	1.541	(1.642)

* The values in parentheses guarantee a 1 in 370 chance of being outside the control limits.
† Use of lower control limits is not recommended for most situations.

TABLE 9.5   Median: Control Chart Constants

Sample Size	A_6
3	1.187
5	0.691
7	0.509
9	0.412
11	0.350
13	0.307
15	0.276
17	0.251
19	0.231
21	0.215
23	0.201
25	0.190

control limits for the range are not recommended for sample sizes of 10 or less.

For the fill-volume capability study, the subgroup medians are 52.1, 51.7, 52.2, 51.8, 51.4, 52.6, 52.5, 52.5, 51.7, 52.3, 52.1, 51.9, 51.4, 51.6, 52.0, 52.0, 51.8, 51.9, 52.4, and 51.5. The average is 51.97. The average range is 1.22. Based on a sample size of 5, A_6 = 0.691, D_4 = 2.312, and d_4 = 0.9703. The control limits are as follows:

$$UCL_m = 51.97 + 0.691(1.22) = 52.81$$

$$CL_m = 51.97$$

$$LCL_m = 51.97 - 0.691(1.22) = 51.13$$

$$UCL_r = 2.312(1.22) = 2.82$$

$$CL_r = 0.9703(1.22) = 1.18$$

Average-range control charts

One can also use other combinations of the average, median, range, and standard deviation control charts. Commonly used are *average-range charts*. This combination was favored historically because of the ease of calculating the range compared to the standard deviation. However, many calculators now have standard deviation keys. Once the data are entered, one key is pressed to get the average and a second key is pressed to get the standard deviation. Using such a calculator, once the data have been entered for calculating the average, calculating the standard deviation is easier than calculating the range. The standard deviation chart is also slightly more powerful. The average-range chart may still be preferred if the users are already trained and comfortable in its use.

The formulas for control limits for the average were based on the within-subgroup standard deviation. When used with a range chart, the following formulas may be used instead:

$$UCL_{\overline{X}} = \overline{X} + A_2 \text{ (average range)}$$

$$= \overline{X} + 3 \frac{\text{(average range)}/d_2}{\sqrt{n}}$$

$$LCL_{\overline{X}} = \overline{X} - A_2 \text{ (average range)}$$

$$= \overline{X} - 3 \frac{\text{(average range)}/d_2}{\sqrt{n}}$$

where n is the number of samples per subgroup. The second set of formulas is the same as the formula based on s with (average range)/d_2 substituted for s. In general, whenever an estimate of σ is required, the average range divided by d_2 may be substituted. Values of d_2 and A_2 are given in Table 9.6.

TABLE 9.6 Average: Control Chart Constants

Sample Size	d_2	A_2
2	1.128	1.880
3	1.693	1.023
4	2.059	0.729
5	2.326	0.577
6	2.534	0.483
7	2.704	0.419
8	2.847	0.373
9	2.970	0.337
10	3.078	0.308
11	3.173	0.285
12	3.258	0.266
13	3.336	0.249
14	3.407	0.235
15	3.472	0.223
16	3.532	0.212
17	3.588	0.203
18	3.640	0.194
19	3.689	0.187
20	3.735	0.180
21	3.778	0.173
22	3.819	0.167
23	3.858	0.162
24	3.895	0.157
25	3.931	0.153

Control charts for individuals

What if there is only one sample per period? One might be mixing batches of chemicals and interested in viscosity. As lots are homogeneous, only one measurement is taken per lot. The individual values are plotted. One would like to be able to add control limits. The procedure for doing this is called an *individuals control chart*. An example is given in Fig. 9.10. The data used to construct this chart are given in Table 9.7.

The control limits were calculated by first taking the difference between consecutive points and then averaging these differences. The average difference for the viscosity data is 0.181. With 20 points, there are 19 differences that go into the average difference. The differences are control charted in Fig. 9.11. The upper control limit for the differences is calculated using the following formula:

$$UCL_D = 3.267 \text{ (average difference)}$$

The value 3.267 is D_4 from Table 9.6 for ranges based on samples of size 2. The upper control limit for the viscosity data is as follows:

$$UCL_D = 3.267(0.181) = 0.591$$

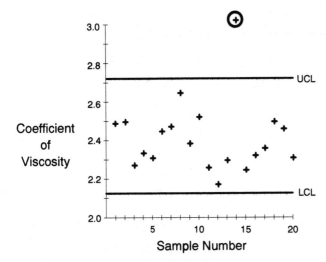

Figure 9.10 Control chart for individuals.

TABLE 9.7 Viscosity Data

Sample Number	Viscosity	Difference
1	2.49	0.01
2	2.50	0.22
3	2.28	0.06
4	2.34	0.02
5	2.32	0.12
6	2.44	0.04
7	2.48	0.16
8	2.64	0.25
9	2.39	0.13
10	2.52	0.26
11	2.26	0.08
12	2.18	0.12
13	2.30	0.73
14	3.03	0.79
15	2.24	0.08
16	2.32	0.04
17	2.36	0.14
18	2.50	0.04
19	2.46	0.15
20	2.31	
	2.418	0.181
	Grand Average	Average Difference

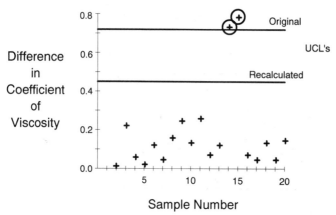

Figure 9.11 Differences chart.

The fourteenth and fifteenth differences fall above this control limit. The differences are affected by the within-subgroup variation as well as differences between subgroups. To help obtain an estimate of the within-subgroup variation that is as little affected by subgroup differences as possible, differences that fall above the upper control limits should be eliminated and the average difference recalculated. For the viscosity data, elimination of the two differences results in a new average difference of 0.113 and a new upper control limit of 0.454. This process is repeated until all remaining points fall below the control limit.

The final average difference is then used to calculate the control limits for the individual points as follows:

$$UCL_X = \overline{X} + 2.66 \text{ (average difference)}$$

$$LCL_X = \overline{X} - 2.66 \text{ (average difference)}$$

For the individuals control chart using the viscosity data:

$$UCL_X = 2.418 + 2.66(0.113) = 2.72$$

$$LCL_X = 2.418 - 2.66(0.113) = 2.12$$

Control charts for individuals track the process average. There is nothing equivalent to the standard deviation or range charts. The difference chart is affected as much by shifting of the average as changes in the variation. It cannot reliably detect changes in the within-subgroup variation.

9.6   Using Control Charts for Process Improvement

Using control charts for evaluating processes was covered in Sec. 6.1. This section covers the use of control charts in process improvement. The next section covers the third use of control charts for process maintenance.

Control charts help to identify key input variables and VIPs. Control charts detect differences over time. These differences are the result of changes in key input variables. Further, because the change is detected by a control chart, the magnitude of these differences is large compared to other sources of variation. The key input variable causing the differences is, at least temporarily, acting as a VIP. Once a key input variable has been identified, improvement requires permanent changes to prevent future problems from reoccurring. The proof of improvement is steadily improving quality.

It is important to be flexible in implementing control charts for improvement. The sampling frequency and sample size should be changed to look at the process in a variety of different ways. Feedback from the control charts should be timely. It is often necessary to track different inputs. Finally, one must be careful to not slip into the maintenance mode.

Beware, there are many difficulties in identifying the key input variables causing differences over time:

Delayed detection.   The input may actually have changed several periods earlier. Control charts do not always detect changes on the first point following the change.

Multiple key inputs causing shifts.   Just when you think you have identified the key input variable causing the process to shift and are waiting for the next process shift in order to verify it, the process may shift due to a second key input.

Lack of feedback on key inputs.   An operator keeping a control chart may be able to see shifting of the output, but not be able to relate it to anything going on. The operator may not have any feedback on the key input causing the shifting. Suppose the shifts are due to oil temperature in the machine. If the operator has no feedback on oil temperature, the cause of the shifting can go undetected. It may be necessary to temporarily implement on-line measurement of different candidate input variables in order to identify the causes of the output shifting.

Control charts can be used to optimize the average as well as reduce variation. They help optimize the average by assuring already identified key input variables are set so the average is on target. Further, control charts can help identify new key input variables that can be set to drive the average even closer to target.

Control charts help reduce variation by identifying VIPs which require tighter controls. As a result, the process can be made more stable. These same VIPs may be contributing to the common cause variation so tighter controls may also make the process more capable. Control charts also track the common cause variation using the standard deviation and range control charts. These charts may help identify a key input variable that is causing the common cause variation to increase or decrease.

While it is possible to detect changes in the common cause variation using the standard deviation and range control charts, these charts are not very sensitive. For a sample size of 5, the upper control limit for the standard deviation is 2.110 times the standard deviation. It is recommended that no lower control limit be used. Changes of 20 to 30 percent in the variation can easily go undetected. Larger sample sizes can help but are expensive.

What can be done to reduce the common cause variation when the standard deviation or range control charts appear stable? This is not the end of the road. However, other approaches must be used such as searching for other types of differences and studying the inputs' effects.

9.7   Using Control Charts for Process Maintenance

The third use of control charts is for process maintenance. During process maintenance, the objective is to maintain the process at its current level. Worsening of the process should be quickly detected. Two mistakes can be made when maintaining the process. The first one is to fail to adjust the process when an adjustment is required. This is called *failure to adjust*. This mistake results in poorer quality. The second mistake is to adjust the process when it does not require adjustment. This is called *overcontrol*. Again, the result is poorer quality. Table 9.8 summarizes these possibilities.

Overcontrol can cause a 50 percent increase in the process variation. The left side of Fig. 9.12 shows a stable process. No adjustments are needed. The right side shows what would happen if adjustments were made every period based on differences between inspection results and the target. The result is a 50 percent increase in the total variation.

One can minimize the chance of making the first error, failure to adjust, by always adjusting. This result is overcontrol resulting in

TABLE 9.8   Two Possible Errors When Making Adjustment Decisions

		Decision	
		Adjust Process	Do Not Adjust Process
Truth	Process Needs Adjustment	Correct	**Failure to Adjust**
	Process Does Not Need Adjustment	**Over Control**	Correct

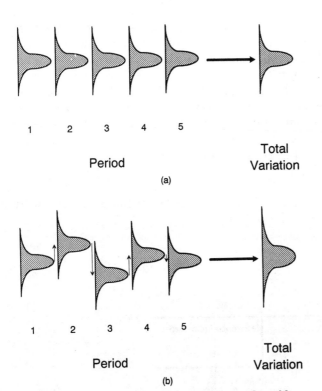

(a)

(b)

Figure 9.12   (a) Stable process: no adjustments; (b) stable process: with unnecessary adjustments.

worsening quality. One can minimize the chance of making the second error, overcontrol, by never adjusting. The result is deviations from target go uncorrected resulting in worsening quality. Adjusting the process only when a point falls outside the control limits minimizes the combined economic loss resulting from both types of error.

When evaluating or improving the process, the control limits for the average are centered around the grand average. These charts then detect any change in the average. For maintaining the process, the control limits should be centered around the target instead. These charts then detect any deviation from target. The formulas for the upper and lower control limits are

$$\mathrm{UCL}_{\bar{x}} = target + \frac{3\,s}{\sqrt{n}}$$

$$\mathrm{LCL}_{\bar{x}} = target - \frac{3\,s}{\sqrt{n}}$$

Control charts decide when adjustments are needed. But once the need for an adjustment is identified, one must also decide on the size of the adjustment. The size of the adjustment should not generally be equal to the amount that the point is off target. Figure 9.13 shows what can happen. The process in Fig. 9.13 is originally centered 1σ above target. Most points fall within the control limits. However, after several points one falls above the upper control limit. If one adjusted by an amount equal to the distance between this point and the target, one would end up with the process 1.3σ below target and be in even worse shape.

As general guidelines:

- For points barely outside the control limits (within $\pm 4\sigma$), adjust by 50 percent of the amount off target.

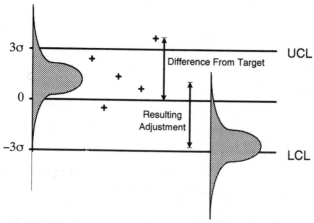

Figure 9.13 Adjusting an amount equal to the distance from target frequently overcorrects.

- For points further out but not too far out (from $\pm 4\sigma$ to $\pm 6\sigma$), adjust by 75 percent of the amount off target.

- For points far outside of the control limits (more than $\pm 6\sigma$), adjust by the full amount off target.

The σ in these adjustment rules refers to the standard deviation of the averages, i.e., the process standard deviation divided by the square root of the sample size (Fig. 9.14).

When maintaining the process, a standard deviation or range chart should also be maintained. When this chart goes out, instead of adjusting the process, the process must be fixed. If the standard deviation chart and the average chart go out simultaneously, do not adjust the process. When the variation increases, the control limits for the average are no longer valid. Reduce the variation first. Then take a new set of samples to determine if the process needs adjustment.

Other control charts are available for maintaining the process including moving average charts, cumulative sum (CUSUM) charts, and exponentially weighted moving average charts. These charts, while more complicated to maintain, can detect smaller changes more quickly.

A simple and easy-to-implement maintenance procedure is *precontrol*. Due to the simplicity of precontrol, valuable information is lost that is important to improvement efforts. Precontrol is only appropriate for maintaining processes with a C_p of 1.5 or greater. Because the focus of this book is improvement, these maintenance procedures are not covered.

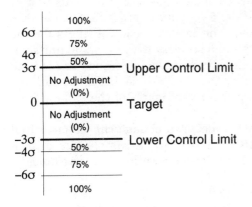

Figure 9.14 Percent of difference to adjust.

9.8 Summary

Common cause and special cause variation

Control charts split the variation into two components:

1. Common cause variation: the variation appearing within the control limits.
2. Special cause variation: variation exceeding the control limits.

Both common cause and special cause variation result from changes in the inputs. A single input can contribute to both the common cause and special cause variation. The distinction between common causes and special causes is one of how to proceed. The presence of special causes means differences exist that should be exploited.

Uses of control charts

Control charts have three uses: (1) evaluating processes, (2) improving processes, and (3) maintaining processes. Improving processes requires permanent fixes preventing problems from reoccurring. The result is breakthroughs to new levels of performance. Maintaining processes means corrective actions to restore performance to normal level. The result is maintenance of the existing level of performance.

Average-standard deviation control charts

Regardless of how the individual units are distributed, averages tend to the normal curve. The standard deviation of the averages gets smaller as the sample size increases at a rate of one over the square root of the sample size.

The control limits for the average assure only 1 in 370 points falls outside the control limits when no change has occurred. This protection is provided for sample sizes of 5 and above regardless of how the individual units are distributed. The modified control limits for the standard deviation provide this same protection if individual units follow the normal curve. The classical limits have increased rates of false detection. Lower control limits for the standard deviation are not recommended unless the incidence of zero estimates of the standard deviation is rare.

The ability of a control chart to detect a change can be measured using average run length (ARL) curves. For a sample size of 5, a $\pm 1.5\sigma$ operating window should be allowed. Smaller changes cannot be reliably detected.

Special patterns

As well as points outside the control limits, one should also inspect for patterns. Two patterns to pay special attention to are hugging the centerline and hugging the control limits. Both patterns indicate the presence of stream-to-stream differences.

The use of special rules in order to reduce the time required to detect a change also increases the rate of false detections and are unnecessarily complex. Their use is not recommended. Instead one should either tighten the control limits or increase the sample size.

Other control charts

Median-range control charts are an alternative to average-standard deviation control charts. They are easy to maintain. Average-range control charts have been popular historically. While calculators and computers have negated their advantages, they continue to be widely used. Individuals charts can be used when only one observation per subgroup is available. Individuals charts track only the average.

Using control charts for process improvement

Control charts identify differences over time resulting from changes in the key input variables. Identification of these key input variables along with permanent changes to prevent future problems leads to improvement. For improvement purposes, control charts should be flexible and timely.

Difficulties in identifying the key input variables causing the time differences arise because of delays in detecting changes, multiple inputs changing, and lack of feedback on key inputs.

A stable process does not signal the end of improvement. However, further improvement requires a change in approach. One must start searching for other types of differences and study the inputs' effects.

Using control charts for process maintenance

When maintaining the process, two errors are possible: failure to adjust and overcontrol. Adjusting only when a point falls outside the control limits minimizes the combined economic loss of these two types of error.

When adjusting the process based on a point outside the control limits, do not adjust by the full distance between this point and the target. For points barely outside the control limits, use only half of this distance. Do not adjust the average when the standard deviation or range chart is also outside the control limits. Reduce the variation first and then resample.

Variation Decomposition

Differences can exist between streams of product, between units, and within units, as well as between time periods. Key to the searching for differences approach is the ability to find differences of all types. Another important factor is the ability to rank these differences so efforts can be concentrated on the largest difference. Three methods are presented in this section for identifying and ranking differences: Multi-Vari charts, ANOM, and variance components analysis (VarComp).

10.1 Multi-Vari Charts

Multi-Vari charts allow the total variation to be decomposed into components including the variation due to time differences, stream-to-stream differences, part-to-part differences, and within-part differences. Using Multi-Vari charts, the component making the largest contribution to the variation can be easily identified. Table 10.1 shows a set of data collected from an injection-molding process making plastic connectors. These connectors are cylindrical in shape. Two parts were selected from each of four mold cavities every hour for 3 h. The outside diameter was measured at each end as well as at the middle of each part. These data were used to construct the Multi-Vari chart shown in Fig. 10.1.

The first step in constructing the Multi-Vari chart is to plot the three outside diameters for each part, one next to the other, and connect them with a heavy line. The top end is shown first, followed by the middle and bottom ends. Figure 10.2 shows the order the outside diameters are plotted in and how to interpret the different patterns that might result. For an individual part any one of these patterns might result from noise. However, if the same pattern keeps repeating itself over and over, then within-part differences are contributing to the overall variation. It is also conceivable that each cavity has a con-

TABLE 10.1 Injection-Molding Data

		Time											
		1				2				3			
		Cavity				Cavity				Cavity			
Part	Location	1	2	3	4	1	2	3	4	1	2	3	4
1	Top	.2522	.2501	.2510	.2489	.2518	.2498	.2516	.2494	.2524	.2488	.2511	.2490
	Middle	.2523	.2497	.2507	.2481	.2512	.2484	.2496	.2485	.2518	.2486	.2504	.2479
	Bottom	.2518	.2501	.2516	.2485	.2501	.2492	.2507	.2492	.2512	.2497	.2503	.2488
	Unit Average	.25210	.24997	.25110	.24850	.25103	.24913	.25063	.24903	.25180	.24903	.25060	.24857
2	Top	.2514	.2501	.2508	.2485	.2520	.2499	.2503	.2483	.2517	.2496	.2503	.2485
	Middle	.2513	.2494	.2495	.2478	.2514	.2495	.2501	.2482	.2509	.2487	.2497	.2483
	Bottom	.2505	.2495	.2507	.2484	.2513	.2501	.2504	.2491	.2513	.2500	.2492	.2495
	Unit Average	.25107	.24967	.25033	.24823	.25157	.24983	.25027	.24853	.25130	.24943	.24973	.24877
Cavity Average		.25158	.24982	.25072	.24837	.25130	.24948	.25045	.24878	.25155	.24923	.25017	.24867
Time Average		.25012				.25000				.24990			
Grand Average		.25001											

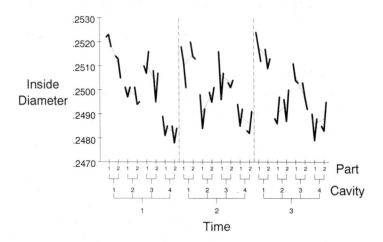

Figure 10.1 Multi-Vari chart: injection molding.

sistent pattern but that the patterns be different for the different cavities.

The second step in constructing the Multi-Vari chart is to calculate the average for each part. The averages for parts coming from the same cavity and time period are connected using dotted lines. The final step is to divide the chart into three sections corresponding to the three time periods.

Now take a look at Fig. 10.1. See if you can identify the largest

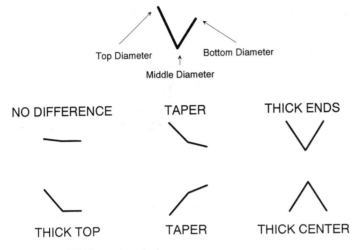

Figure 10.2 Within-part variation.

source of variation. It might be time-to-time differences, cavity-to-cavity differences, part-to-part differences, or within-part differences. Also look to see if you can find any other differences that are contributing to the variation.

The three time periods do not appear different. However, there are consistent differences among the cavities within each time period. Cavity 1 consistently has the largest diameters and cavity 4 consistently has the smallest diameters. These cavity-to-cavity differences are the largest source of variation for this process. The cavity differences are easier to see if the data are plotted in a different order as in Fig. 10.3. A second pattern is that the parts from cavities 2, 3, and 4 appear to have thicker ends. The "V" pattern is exhibited in 16 of 18 parts from these cavities. The parts from cavity 1 may be slightly tapered. Four of six parts exhibit the "\" pattern. The magnitude of these within-part differences is smaller than the cavity-to-cavity differences. Figure 10.4 shows three other patterns that might have occurred and their interpretation. Take some time to make sure you come up with the same interpretations.

A second example of a Multi-Vari chart is given in Fig. 10.5. This Multi-Vari chart is for a sheeting extrusion operation. Twenty consecutive samples 1 in apart were selected every hour for 4 h. This chart demonstrates that the majority of the variation is the result of short-term drifting of the process, probably the result of cycling.

Two control charts of this same process are shown in Fig. 10.6. The first is based on samples of five consecutive parts. This control chart indicates the process is unstable. The second control chart is based on

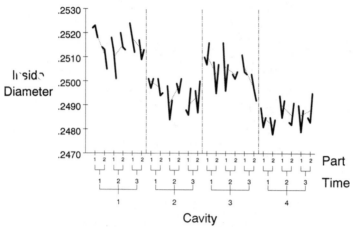

Figure 10.3 Multi-Vari chart: injection molding.

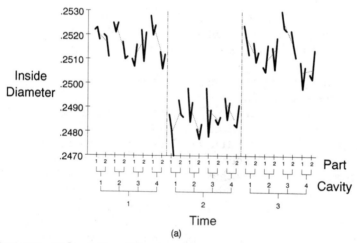

Figure 10.4 (a) Large time differences.

random samples of the process. Each sample of five parts is selected randomly from a tub of several hundred parts. This chart indicates the process is stable. The difference between these two charts is that, because of the way the samples are selected, the short-term drifting is included in the between-subgroup effect of the first chart and in the within-subgroup effect of the second chart.

This example illustrates the importance of collecting and plotting data in a variety of ways to identify differences. Most companies implementing SPC would simply implement a control chart of the second

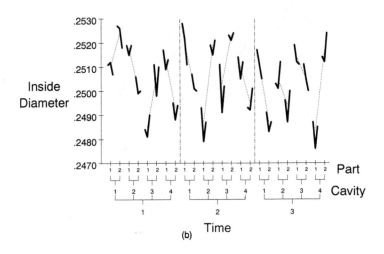

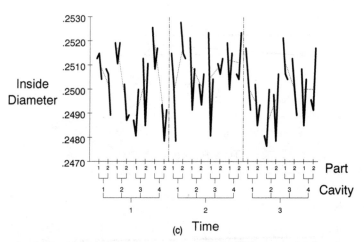

Figure 10.4 (*Continued*) (*b*) Large part-to-part differences; (*c*) large within-part differences.

type and fail to identify the cycling. In this case, because the cycling was identified, further studies were run to measure the period of the cycling. The period was found to be 36 in which happened to be the circumference of the roller bar. This bar was found to be misaligned. Fixing the problem resulted in a 90 percent reduction of the variation.

Multi-Vari charts provide a snapshot of how the process is performing. The single largest source of variation at that time can be clearly identified. A second study some time later may give different results. For example, a sudden shift in the process during one study might

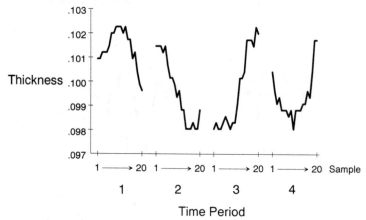

Figure 10.5   Multi-Vari chart of sheeting extrusion.

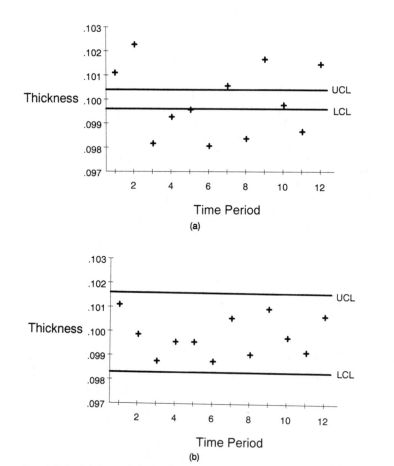

Figure 10.6   (*a*) Control chart of averages: five consecutive samples; (*b*) control chart of averages: five random samples.

cause time-to-time differences to dominate that study. However, such shifts might be rare and might not occur during other studies. On the other studies cavity differences might dominate. For this reason, one may want to repeat Multi-Vari studies several times. One should also try to identify the second largest difference. It might really be the most important difference.

Multi-Vari charts are very effective at identifying the largest source of variation, when one exists. These charts contain enormous amounts of information although extracting this information may require considerable effort. Plotting the data in different orders may help. Yet, despite their usefulness, Multi-Vari charts have three shortcomings:

1. *Lack of method for deciding which differences exist.* The differences are compared with each other to find the largest. When one is clearly larger than the others, Multi-Vari charts will identify it. But a method is needed to decide for each possible difference whether the resulting pattern indicates that real differences exist or if the pattern could result from noise alone. ANOM in the next section provides this method.

2. *Difficult to discern complex relationships including interactions.* Interactions are covered in the next section. When interactions are present, they are important to detect. They are hard to detect using Multi-Vari charts. The ANOM procedure in the next section allows interactions to be detected.

3. *Lack of method for measuring relative contributions of identified differences.* Ideally, once all the differences have been properly identified, one would like to know how much each difference is contributing to the overall variation. From this, the benefits of different improvements can be estimated. VarComp provides the needed tool.

10.2 Analysis of Means (ANOM)

ANOM provides a method for determining which differences exist and for detecting interactions. Some new terminology is required. The possible differences are called *factors*. In the injection-molding study, the factors are time differences, cavity differences, part differences, and within-part differences. The different settings of each factor are called levels. The levels in the injection-molding study are

- time periods: 1, 2, and 3
- cavities: 1, 2, 3, and 4
- parts: 1 and 2 (within each time period and cavity)
- within parts: top, middle, and bottom

Confusion often arises as to the difference between factors and candidate input variables. A factor is the combined effect of one or more input variables. For example, cavity differences might result from dimensional differences in the mold cavities, from differences between the locations of the different cavities on the mold, or from a host of other candidate input variables. Further, some input variables might contribute to more than one factor. Insufficient packing pressure may result in cavity-to-cavity differences as well as within-cavity differences. For each input variable, it is generally easy to decide to which factor or factors it might contribute. Therefore, identifying important factors helps to focus attention on a reduced set of candidate input variables.

For all studies in this chapter, the data must contain results for all possible combinations of the factor levels. Applying ANOM to such data sets is fairly straightforward. ANOM is applied to each factor separately. The first step is to calculate the average for each of the factor levels. These averages are then plotted as in Figs. 10.7 and 10.8.

The last step is to calculate and plot the decision lines. If one or more of the factor-level averages fall outside the decision lines, differences exist between the factor levels. This is the case with cavity differences. If all the factor-level averages fall within the decision lines, any differences that might exist between the factor levels are small compared to the noise. This is the case for time differences.

The most difficult part of ANOM is determining the decision lines. Methods are given for determining the decision lines beginning with the simplest case.

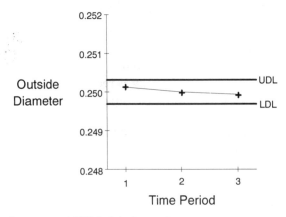

Figure 10.7 ANOM of time periods.

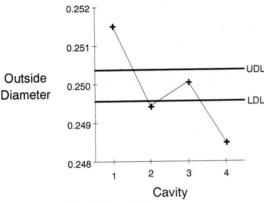

Figure 10.8 ANOM of cavities.

One-factor ANOM

An example of a *one-factor ANOM* is the operator-reproducibility study in Sec. 7.1. The data are reproduced in Table 10.2. The one factor is operators. It has five levels corresponding to five different operators. Each operator measured the reference standard five times. The average reading for each operator is plotted in Fig. 10.9.

Also plotted are the decision lines. The formulas for the decision lines are

$$\text{UDL} = \overline{X} + sh_\alpha\sqrt{\frac{k-1}{kn}}$$

$$\text{LDL} = \overline{X} - sh_\alpha\sqrt{\frac{k-1}{kn}}$$

where $\overline{X}$ = grand average
   s = within-subgroup standard deviation
   k = number of factor levels
   n = number of observations per level
   h_α = constant from Tables 10.3 to 10.5

The constant h_α depends on the desired level of confidence (α), the number of factor levels (k), and the degrees of freedom (df), associated with the within-subgroup standard deviation (s). For the one-factor ANOM:

$$\text{df} = k(n-1)$$

TABLE 10.2   Operator Reproducibility Data

Operators					
1	2	3	4	5	
0.2513	0.2483	0.2429	0.2482	0.2567	
0.2482	0.2508	0.2492	0.2499	0.2573	
0.2491	0.2505	0.2455	0.2507	0.2534	
0.2499	0.2511	0.2464	0.2498	0.2541	Grand
0.2489	0.2503	0.2468	0.2484	0.2564	Average ↓
Average 0.24948	0.25020	0.24616	0.24940	0.25558	0.25016
Std. Dev. 0.0012	0.0011	0.0023	0.0011	0.0017	0.0016 ↑

Within Subgroup
Standard Deviation

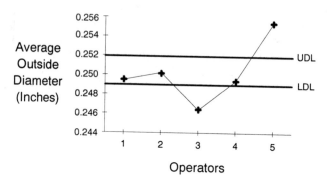

Figure 10.9   ANOM for operators.

TABLE 10.3   Constant h_α for ANOM: $\alpha = 0.10$

DF	Number of Factor Levels (k)																		
	2	3	4	5	6	7	8	9	10	15	20	30	40	60	100	200	300	500	1000
k	2.92	3.16	3.09	3.05	3.03	3.02	3.02	3.01	3.02	3.04	3.07	3.13	3.18	3.25	3.36	3.52	3.61	3.73	3.89
2 k	2.13	2.52	2.59	2.64	2.67	2.70	2.73	2.75	2.78	2.86	2.93	3.02	3.09	3.19	3.32	3.49	3.59	3.72	3.89
3 k	1.94	2.34	2.45	2.51	2.57	2.61	2.64	2.67	2.70	2.81	2.88	2.99	3.06	3.17	3.30	3.48	3.59	3.71	3.88
4 k	1.86	2.27	2.38	2.45	2.51	2.56	2.60	2.63	2.66	2.78	2.86	2.97	3.05	3.16	3.30	3.48	3.58	3.71	3.88
5 k	1.81	2.22	2.34	2.42	2.48	2.53	2.57	2.61	2.64	2.76	2.84	2.96	3.04	3.15	3.29	3.48	3.58	3.71	3.88
6 k	1.78	2.19	2.31	2.40	2.46	2.51	2.56	2.59	2.63	2.75	2.84	2.95	3.04	3.15	3.29	3.48	3.58	3.71	3.88
7 k	1.76	2.17	2.30	2.38	2.45	2.50	2.54	2.58	2.62	2.74	2.83	2.95	3.03	3.15	3.29	3.47	3.58	3.71	3.88
8 k	1.75	2.15	2.28	2.37	2.44	2.49	2.54	2.57	2.61	2.74	2.82	2.94	3.03	3.14	3.29	3.47	3.58	3.71	3.88
9 k	1.73	2.14	2.27	2.36	2.43	2.48	2.53	2.57	2.60	2.73	2.82	2.94	3.03	3.14	3.29	3.47	3.58	3.71	3.88
10 k	1.72	2.13	2.27	2.35	2.42	2.48	2.52	2.56	2.60	2.73	2.82	2.94	3.02	3.14	3.28	3.47	3.58	3.71	3.88
INF	1.65	2.05	2.19	2.29	2.36	2.42	2.47	2.52	2.55	2.69	2.79	2.92	3.01	3.13	3.28	3.47	3.57	3.71	3.88

TABLE 10.4   Constant h_α for ANOM: $\alpha = 0.05$

DF	Number of Factor Levels (k)																		
	2	3	4	5	6	7	8	9	10	15	20	30	40	60	100	200	300	500	1000
k	4.30	4.18	3.89	3.72	3.62	3.56	3.51	3.48	3.45	3.40	3.40	3.41	3.44	3.50	3.58	3.72	3.80	3.91	4.07
2 k	2.78	3.07	3.07	3.07	3.07	3.08	3.09	3.10	3.11	3.16	3.20	3.27	3.33	3.42	3.53	3.69	3.78	3.90	4.06
3 k	2.45	2.79	2.85	2.88	2.91	2.94	2.96	2.98	3.00	3.08	3.14	3.23	3.29	3.39	3.51	3.68	3.77	3.89	4.06
4 k	2.31	2.67	2.74	2.79	2.83	2.87	2.90	2.92	2.95	3.04	3.11	3.20	3.27	3.37	3.50	3.67	3.77	3.89	4.05
5 k	2.23	2.60	2.68	2.74	2.79	2.83	2.86	2.89	2.92	3.02	3.09	3.19	3.26	3.37	3.50	3.67	3.77	3.89	4.05
6 k	2.18	2.55	2.65	2.71	2.76	2.80	2.84	2.87	2.89	3.00	3.08	3.18	3.26	3.36	3.49	3.67	3.77	3.89	4.05
7 k	2.14	2.52	2.62	2.69	2.74	2.78	2.82	2.85	2.88	2.99	3.07	3.18	3.25	3.36	3.49	3.66	3.76	3.89	4.05
8 k	2.12	2.50	2.60	2.67	2.72	2.77	2.81	2.84	2.87	2.98	3.06	3.17	3.25	3.35	3.49	3.66	3.76	3.89	4.05
9 k	2.10	2.48	2.59	2.66	2.71	2.76	2.80	2.83	2.86	2.98	3.06	3.17	3.24	3.35	3.49	3.66	3.76	3.89	4.05
10 k	2.09	2.47	2.57	2.65	2.70	2.75	2.79	2.82	2.85	2.97	3.05	3.16	3.24	3.35	3.48	3.66	3.76	3.89	4.05
INF	1.96	2.34	2.47	2.55	2.62	2.68	2.72	2.76	2.80	2.93	3.02	3.14	3.22	3.33	3.47	3.66	3.76	3.88	4.05

TABLE 10.5   Constant h_α for ANOM: $\alpha = 0.01$

DF	Number of Factor Levels (k)																		
	2	3	4	5	6	7	8	9	10	15	20	30	40	60	100	200	300	500	1000
k	9.92	7.52	6.21	5.55	5.15	4.90	4.72	4.59	4.49	4.23	4.12	4.03	4.01	4.01	4.05	4.14	4.21	4.30	4.44
2 k	4.60	4.48	4.22	4.07	3.98	3.92	3.87	3.85	3.83	3.78	3.78	3.80	3.83	3.88	3.97	4.10	4.18	4.28	4.43
3 k	3.71	3.84	3.75	3.69	3.66	3.65	3.64	3.63	3.63	3.65	3.67	3.73	3.77	3.84	3.94	4.08	4.17	4.28	4.42
4 k	3.36	3.57	3.54	3.53	3.52	3.52	3.53	3.53	3.54	3.58	3.62	3.69	3.74	3.82	3.93	4.08	4.16	4.27	4.42
5 k	3.17	3.42	3.42	3.43	3.44	3.45	3.46	3.48	3.49	3.55	3.59	3.67	3.73	3.81	3.92	4.07	4.16	4.27	4.42
6 k	3.05	3.33	3.35	3.37	3.39	3.40	3.42	3.44	3.45	3.52	3.58	3.66	3.72	3.80	3.92	4.07	4.16	4.27	4.42
7 k	2.98	3.26	3.30	3.32	3.35	3.37	3.39	3.41	3.43	3.50	3.56	3.65	3.71	3.80	3.91	4.07	4.16	4.27	4.42
8 k	2.92	3.21	3.26	3.29	3.32	3.35	3.37	3.39	3.41	3.49	3.55	3.64	3.70	3.79	3.91	4.07	4.16	4.27	4.42
9 k	2.88	3.18	3.23	3.27	3.30	3.33	3.35	3.38	3.40	3.48	3.54	3.63	3.70	3.79	3.91	4.06	4.16	4.27	4.42
10 k	2.85	3.15	3.21	3.25	3.28	3.31	3.34	3.36	3.39	3.47	3.54	3.63	3.69	3.79	3.90	4.06	4.15	4.27	4.42
INF	2.58	2.91	3.01	3.08	3.14	3.19	3.22	3.26	3.29	3.40	3.48	3.59	3.66	3.76	3.89	4.05	4.15	4.26	4.42

The within-subgroup standard deviation is calculated by first determining the standard deviation of the five measurements for each operator. For the operator reproducibility study, these standard deviations are 0.0012, 0.0011, 0.0023, 0.0011, and 0.0017, respectively. The within-subgroup standard deviation is then calculated as follows:

$$s = \sqrt{\frac{(0.0012)^2 + (0.0011)^2 + \cdots + (0.0017)^2}{5}} = 0.0016$$

For the operator reproducibility study:

$$\overline{X} = 0.25016$$
$$s = 0.0016$$
$$k = 5$$
$$n = 5$$
$$\mathrm{df} = 5\,(5 - 1) = 20$$
$$h_{0.05} = 2.79$$

Therefore,

$$UDL = 0.25016 + 0.0016 \ (2.79) \ \sqrt{\frac{5-1}{5 \times 5}} = 0.2519$$

$$LDL = 0.25016 - 0.0016 \ (2.79) \ \sqrt{\frac{5-1}{5 \times 5}} = 0.2484$$

Based on these decision lines, operator differences exist. Operator 3 is below the norm and operator 5 is above the norm.

Two-factor ANOM

The instrument bias study in Sec. 7.4 is an example of a *two-factor ANOM*. The data for this study are given in Table 10.6. The two factors are snap gauges and tubes. In this study, the snap-gauge factor is of primary interest. It is also possible, however, to determine whether differences exist between the tubes. Using these data, the gauge and tube averages were calculated and plotted in separate ANOM plots. The gauge ANOM is shown in Fig. 10.10 and the tube ANOM is shown in Fig. 10.11. The gauge ANOM indicates that gauge 4 is inconsistent with the other four gauges. The tube ANOM indicates that the tubes are significantly different. This is as expected since the tubes were selected to be representative of the full range of production.

The first step in determining the decision lines is to estimate the within-subgroup standard deviation. In this case there are 25 subgroups corresponding to all possible syringe-position combinations. Each subgroup consists of two observations. The standard deviation

TABLE 10.6   Instrument Bias Data

		Snap Gage					Tube Average
		1	2	3	4	5	
Tube	1	0.2515 0.2470	0.2508 0.2502	0.2508 0.2552	0.2591 0.2611	0.2496 0.2492	0.25245
	2	0.2540 0.2531	0.2507 0.2512	0.2545 0.2513	0.2621 0.2606	0.2507 0.2518	0.25400
	3	0.2419 0.2511	0.2451 0.2467	0.2444 0.2472	0.2525 0.2561	0.2441 0.2459	0.24750
	4	0.2566 0.2546	0.2554 0.2565	0.2559 0.2586	0.2659 0.2637	0.2576 0.2576	0.25824
	5	0.2466 0.2486	0.2523 0.2516	0.2480 0.2528	0.2635 0.2589	0.2503 0.2542	0.25268
Gage Average		0.25050	0.25105	0.25187	0.26035	0.25110	0.25297

Grand Average ↑

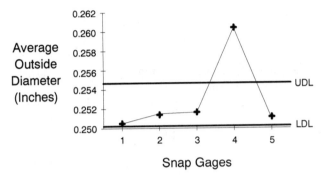

Figure 10.10   ANOM for instrument bias.

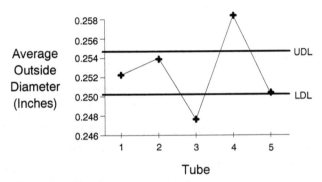

Figure 10.11   ANOM for tube differences.

for each subgroup must be calculated. Then these standard deviations must be combined in the normal fashion:

$$s = \sqrt{\dfrac{s_1^2 + s_2^2 + \cdots + s_{25}^2}{25}}$$

For the above data the within-subgroup standard deviation is

$$s = \sqrt{\dfrac{(0.00318)^2 + (0.00042)^2 + \cdots + (0.00276)^2}{25}} = 0.002242$$

Separate decision limits must be calculated for each factor. The formulas for the decision limits of the ith factor are

$$\mathrm{UDL}_i = \overline{X} + s h_\alpha \sqrt{\dfrac{k_i - 1}{k_1 k_2 n}}$$

$$\text{LDL}_i = \overline{X} - sh_\alpha \sqrt{\frac{k_i - 1}{k_1 \, k_2 \, n}}$$

where $\overline{X}$ = grand average

s = within-subgroup standard deviation

k_i = number of levels for ith factor (i = 1, 2)

n = number of observations in each of the $k_1 \times k_2$ subgroups

df = $k_1 k_2 \, (n - 1)$

h_α = constant from Tables 10.3 to 10.5

The values of k_i and h_α differ for different factors resulting in each factor having its own decision limits.

For the instrument bias study:

$$\overline{X} = 0.25297$$

$$s = 0.002242$$

$$k_1 = k_2 = 5$$

$$n = 2$$

$$\text{df} = (5)(5)(2 - 1) = 25$$

Since $k_1 = k_2$, the values of $h_{0.05}$, UDL, and LDL are the same for both factors. From Table 10.4, $h_{0.05} = 2.74$. The resulting values for UDL and LDL are

$$\text{UDL} = 0.25297 + (0.002242) \, (2.74) \sqrt{\frac{5 - 1}{5 \times 5 \times 2}} = 0.25471$$

$$\text{LDL} = 0.25297 - (0.002242) \, (2.74) \sqrt{\frac{5 - 1}{5 \times 5 \times 2}} = 0.25123$$

Three or more factors

ANOM can be easily extended to more than two factors. Suppose there are m factors with $k_1, k_2, \ldots, k_m$ levels each. Then the decision limits for the ith factor are

$$\text{UDL}_i = \overline{X} + sh_\alpha \sqrt{\frac{k_i - 1}{k_1 \, k_2 \cdots k_m \, n}}$$

$$\text{LDL}_i = \overline{X} - sh_\alpha \sqrt{\frac{k_i - 1}{k_1 \, k_2 \cdots k_m \, n}}$$

where $\overline{X}$ = grand average

s = within-subgroup standard deviation

k_i = number of levels for ith factor (i = 1, 2,..., m)

n = number of observations in each of the $k_1 \times k_2 \times ... \times k_m$ subgroups

df = $k_1 k_2 ... k_m (n - 1)$

h_α = constant from Tables 10.3 to 10.5

The value of s requires calculating the standard deviation of the observations for each of the $k_1 \times k_2 \times ... \times k_m$ combinations of the factor levels. These standard deviations should be combined in the normal fashion.

Interactions

When two or more factors are included in a study, one can also examine *interactions* between the factors. An interaction exists between two factors when certain levels of those factors combine to produce an effect that is either greater than or less than one would predict based on the effect of each factor by itself.

Figure 10.12 shows the effect that compression and temperature has on the pressure inside a hollow ball. Starting with a baseline of no compression at $-20°F$, there is 0.7 atm of pressure inside the ball. If the ball is compressed to half its normal size, the pressure doubles to 1.4 atm (a 0.7-atm increase). If instead, the temperature were raised to 120°F, the pressure increases to 0.92 atm (a 0.22-atm increase). One might predict that changing both compression and temperature might result in a pressure increase of 0.7 + 0.22 = 0.92 atm. This results in

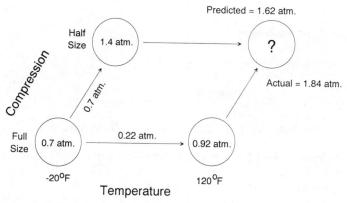

Figure 10.12   Compression*temperature interaction.

a predicted pressure of 1.62 atm when half size is at 120°F. However, the actual pressure under these conditions turns out to be 1.84 atm. Compression and temperature interact to produce a higher pressure than one would predict based on the effect of each factor by itself.

Interactions can result in larger-than-predicted or smaller-than-predicted results. An interaction between two variables means that the effect of the first variable is dependent on where the second variable is set. Optimization requires that both variables be optimized simultaneously. If variables do not interact, their effects are additive. Optimization can be performed on each variable separately.

Interactions are important for two reasons: (1) They are commonplace. Most processes and products have at least one interaction between its key input variables. (2) Failing to identify and take advantage of interactions is a leading reason for suboptimal results. It is especially important to be able to detect whether two factors interact. Each possible interaction must be checked separately. The procedure for determining whether an interaction exists will be demonstrated using the instrument bias study. This study consists of two factors: gauges and parts. ANOMs were done for each of these two factors previously. One of the results was that gauge 4 is inconsistent with the other four gauges. The existence of an interaction between gauge and part can be tested. If such an interaction exists, it means the bias between gauge 4 and the other gauges varies depending on the part. The bias may even result from a single erroneous value. If no interaction exists, the bias is consistent for all parts.

The first step is to calculate the averages for each gauge-tube combination. These are the top set of values in Table 10.7. The second step is to calculate the predicted values for each gauge-part combination. Let,

$\overline{X}_{..}$ = grand average

$\overline{X}_{i.}$ = average of the ith gauge

$\overline{X}_{.j}$ = average of the jth tube

$\overline{X}_{ij}$ = average of the ith gauge–jth tube combination

Then the predicted result for the ith gauge–jth tube combination is

$$\text{Predicted result} = \overline{X}_{..} + (\overline{X}_{i.} - \overline{X}_{..}) + (\overline{X}_{.j} - \overline{X}_{..})$$

$$= \overline{X}_{i.} + \overline{X}_{.j} - \overline{X}_{..}$$

TABLE 10.7 Prediction Errors for Interaction

		Snap Gage					Tube Average
		1	2	3	4	5	
Tube	1	0.24925 -0.24998 -0.00073	0.25050 -0.25053 -0.00003	0.25300 -0.25135 0.00165	0.26010 -0.25983 0.00027	0.24940 -0.25058 -0.00118	0.25245
	2	0.25355 -0.25153 0.00202	0.25095 -0.25208 -0.00113	0.25290 -0.25290 0.00000	0.26135 -0.26138 -0.00003	0.25125 -0.25213 -0.00088	0.25400
	3	0.24650 -0.24503 0.00147	0.24590 -0.24558 0.00032	0.24580 -0.24640 -0.00060	0.25430 -0.25488 -0.00058	0.24500 -0.24563 -0.00063	0.24750
	4	0.25560 -0.25577 -0.00017	0.25595 -0.25632 -0.00037	0.25725 -0.25714 0.00011	0.26480 -0.26562 -0.00082	0.25760 -0.25637 0.00123	0.25824
	5	0.24760 -0.25021 -0.00261	0.25195 -0.25076 0.00119	0.25040 -0.25158 -0.00118	0.26120 -0.26006 0.00114	0.25225 -0.25081 0.00144	0.25268
Gage Average		0.25050	0.25105	0.25187	0.26035	0.25110	0.25297

Grand Average ↑

For example, the predicted value for the first part using the first gauge is

Predicted result = 0.25050 + 0.25245 − 0.25297 = 0.24998

The predicted results are the middle set of values in Table 10.7.

The third step is to calculate the differences between the actual averages and the predicted values. This is the prediction error:

Prediction error = $\overline{X}_{ij}$ − predicted result

$$= \overline{X}_{ij} - \overline{X}_{i.} - \overline{X}_{j} + \overline{X}_{..}$$

For example, the prediction error for measuring the first part using the first gauge is

Prediction error = 0.24925 − 0.24998 = − 0.00073

The prediction errors are the bottom set of values in Table 10.7.

The fourth step is to plot the prediction errors on an ANOM chart as in Fig. 10.13. If there are m factors with $k_1, k_2, \ldots, k_m$ levels each, the decision lines for the interaction between the ith and jth factors are

$$\text{UDL}_{ij} = sh_\alpha^* \sqrt{\frac{k_i k_j - 1}{k_1 k_2 \ldots k_m\, n}}$$

$$\text{LDL}_{ij} = -\text{UDL}_{ij}$$

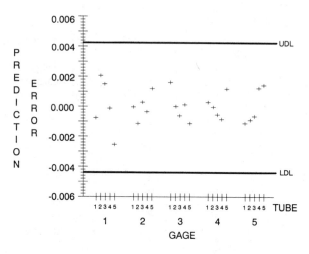

Figure 10.13   ANOM of gauge*tube interaction.

where s = within-subgroup standard deviation
  k_i = number of levels for ith factor (i = 1, 2,..., m)
  n = number of observations in each of the $k_1 \times k_2 \times ... \times k_m$
    subgroups
  df = $k_1 k_2 ... k_m$ (n - 1)
  h_α^* = constant from Tables 10.8 to 10.10

The same estimate of s and associated df are used as before. The above formulas use h_α^* instead of h_α. Values of h_α^* are given in Tables 10.8 to 10.10. When looking up h_α^*, the top of the chart is $k_i \times k_j$ instead of k.

For the gauge*tube interaction, the decision limits are

$$\text{UDL}_{12} = (0.002242)\, 2.78 \sqrt{\frac{5 \times 5 - 1}{5 \times 5 \times 2}} = 0.00432$$

$$\text{LDL}_{12} = -0.00432$$

where s = 0.002242
  $k_1 = k_2 = 5$
  n = 2
  df = (5)(5)(2 - 1) = 25
$h_{0.05}^* = 2.78$

Any point outside the decision line indicates the presence of an interaction. Points above the upper decision line represent factor-level combinations that produce higher-than-predicted results. Points below the lower decision line represent factor-level combinations that pro-

TABLE 10.8   Constant h_α^* for ANOM: $\alpha = 0.10$

DF	Number of Factor Level Combinations ($k=k_i \times k_j$)																		
	2	3	4	5	6	7	8	9	10	15	20	30	40	60	100	200	300	500	1000
k	2.92	3.69	3.45	3.33	3.25	3.21	3.18	3.16	3.14	3.12	3.13	3.17	3.21	3.28	3.37	3.52	3.62	3.73	3.89
2 k	2.13	2.72	2.73	2.74	2.76	2.77	2.79	2.81	2.82	2.90	2.95	3.04	3.11	3.20	3.32	3.50	3.59	3.72	3.89
3 k	1.94	2.49	2.54	2.58	2.62	2.65	2.68	2.71	2.73	2.83	2.90	3.00	3.07	3.18	3.31	3.49	3.59	3.71	3.88
4 k	1.86	2.38	2.45	2.51	2.55	2.59	2.63	2.66	2.69	2.79	2.87	2.98	3.06	3.16	3.30	3.48	3.58	3.71	3.88
5 k	1.81	2.33	2.40	2.47	2.52	2.56	2.60	2.63	2.66	2.77	2.85	2.97	3.05	3.16	3.30	3.48	3.58	3.71	3.88
6 k	1.78	2.29	2.37	2.44	2.49	2.54	2.58	2.61	2.64	2.76	2.84	2.96	3.04	3.15	3.29	3.48	3.58	3.71	3.88
7 k	1.76	2.26	2.35	2.42	2.48	2.52	2.56	2.60	2.63	2.75	2.84	2.95	3.04	3.15	3.29	3.47	3.58	3.71	3.88
8 k	1.75	2.24	2.33	2.41	2.46	2.51	2.55	2.59	2.62	2.74	2.83	2.95	3.03	3.15	3.29	3.47	3.58	3.71	3.88
9 k	1.73	2.23	2.32	2.39	2.45	2.50	2.54	2.58	2.61	2.74	2.83	2.95	3.03	3.14	3.29	3.47	3.58	3.71	3.88
10 k	1.72	2.21	2.31	2.39	2.45	2.50	2.54	2.58	2.61	2.73	2.82	2.94	3.03	3.14	3.29	3.47	3.58	3.71	3.88
INF	1.65	2.11	2.23	2.31	2.38	2.43	2.48	2.52	2.56	2.70	2.79	2.92	3.01	3.13	3.28	3.47	3.57	3.71	3.88

TABLE 10.9   Constant h_α^* for ANOM: $\alpha = 0.05$

DF	Number of Factor Level Combinations ($k=k_i \times k_j$)																		
	2	3	4	5	6	7	8	9	10	15	20	30	40	60	100	200	300	500	1000
k	4.30	4.83	4.29	4.01	3.84	3.74	3.66	3.61	3.57	3.47	3.44	3.45	3.46	3.51	3.59	3.72	3.81	3.92	4.07
2 k	2.78	3.27	3.19	3.16	3.14	3.14	3.14	3.14	3.14	3.18	3.22	3.28	3.34	3.42	3.53	3.69	3.78	3.90	4.06
3 k	2.45	2.92	2.92	2.94	2.95	2.97	2.99	3.00	3.02	3.09	3.15	3.23	3.30	3.39	3.51	3.68	3.77	3.89	4.06
4 k	2.31	2.77	2.80	2.84	2.87	2.89	2.92	2.94	2.96	3.05	3.11	3.21	3.28	3.38	3.50	3.67	3.77	3.89	4.05
5 k	2.23	2.69	2.74	2.78	2.82	2.85	2.88	2.90	2.93	3.02	3.09	3.19	3.27	3.37	3.50	3.67	3.77	3.89	4.05
6 k	2.18	2.63	2.69	2.74	2.78	2.82	2.85	2.88	2.91	3.01	3.08	3.18	3.26	3.36	3.49	3.67	3.77	3.89	4.05
7 k	2.14	2.59	2.66	2.72	2.76	2.80	2.83	2.86	2.89	3.00	3.07	3.18	3.25	3.36	3.49	3.67	3.77	3.89	4.05
8 k	2.12	2.57	2.64	2.70	2.74	2.78	2.82	2.85	2.88	2.99	3.06	3.17	3.25	3.36	3.49	3.66	3.76	3.89	4.05
9 k	2.10	2.55	2.62	2.68	2.73	2.77	2.81	2.84	2.87	2.98	3.06	3.17	3.25	3.35	3.49	3.66	3.76	3.89	4.05
10 k	2.09	2.53	2.61	2.67	2.72	2.76	2.80	2.83	2.86	2.98	3.05	3.17	3.24	3.35	3.49	3.66	3.76	3.89	4.05
INF	1.96	2.39	2.49	2.57	2.63	2.68	2.73	2.77	2.80	2.93	3.02	3.14	3.22	3.33	3.47	3.66	3.76	3.88	4.05

TABLE 10.10   Constant h_α^* for ANOM: $\alpha = 0.01$

DF	Number of Factor Level Combinations ($k=k_i \times k_j$)																		
	2	3	4	5	6	7	8	9	10	15	20	30	40	60	100	200	300	500	1000
k	9.92	8.57	6.75	5.89	5.39	5.08	4.86	4.70	4.58	4.27	4.14	4.05	4.02	4.02	4.05	4.14	4.21	4.31	4.44
2 k	4.60	4.69	4.33	4.14	4.03	3.96	3.91	3.87	3.85	3.79	3.79	3.81	3.83	3.89	3.97	4.10	4.18	4.28	4.43
3 k	3.71	3.95	3.80	3.73	3.69	3.67	3.65	3.65	3.64	3.65	3.68	3.73	3.77	3.84	3.94	4.08	4.17	4.28	4.42
4 k	3.36	3.65	3.58	3.55	3.54	3.54	3.54	3.54	3.55	3.59	3.63	3.69	3.75	3.82	3.93	4.08	4.16	4.27	4.42
5 k	3.17	3.48	3.45	3.45	3.45	3.46	3.47	3.48	3.49	3.55	3.60	3.67	3.73	3.81	3.92	4.07	4.16	4.27	4.42
6 k	3.05	3.38	3.37	3.38	3.40	3.41	3.43	3.44	3.46	3.52	3.58	3.66	3.72	3.80	3.92	4.07	4.16	4.27	4.42
7 k	2.98	3.31	3.32	3.34	3.36	3.38	3.40	3.42	3.43	3.51	3.56	3.65	3.71	3.80	3.91	4.07	4.16	4.27	4.42
8 k	2.92	3.26	3.28	3.31	3.33	3.35	3.38	3.40	3.41	3.49	3.55	3.64	3.70	3.79	3.91	4.07	4.16	4.27	4.42
9 k	2.88	3.22	3.25	3.28	3.31	3.33	3.36	3.38	3.40	3.48	3.54	3.63	3.70	3.79	3.91	4.06	4.16	4.27	4.42
10 k	2.85	3.19	3.23	3.26	3.29	3.32	3.34	3.37	3.39	3.47	3.54	3.63	3.69	3.79	3.91	4.06	4.15	4.27	4.42
INF	2.58	2.93	3.02	3.09	3.14	3.19	3.23	3.26	3.29	3.40	3.48	3.59	3.66	3.76	3.89	4.05	4.15	4.26	4.42

duce lower-than-expected results. Since no points fall outside the decision lines in Fig. 10.13, gauges and tubes do not interact.

Complex studies

The injection-molding data set in Table 10.1 is an example of a *complex study*. It consists of four factors: time period, cavity, part, and lo-

TABLE 10.11   Injection-Molding Data-Part Averages

		Cavity				Time
		1	2	3	4	Average
T i m e	1	0.2521 0.2511	0.2500 0.2497	0.2511 0.2503	0.2485 0.2482	0.2501
	2	0.2510 0.2515	0.2491 0.2498	0.2506 0.2503	0.2490 0.2485	0.2500
	3	0.2518 0.2513	0.2490 0.2494	0.2506 0.2497	0.2486 0.2488	0.2499
Cavity Average		0.2515	0.2495	0.2504	0.2486	0.2500

Grand Average ↑

cation. There is a single data point for each combination of these factor levels. The first difficulty is how to estimate the within-subgroup
variation. The second difficulty is the factor part. It has two levels: 1
and 2. However, there are actually 24 parts, two for each combination
of time and cavity. Levels 1 and 2 refer to the first and second part
within each time-cavity combination. Parts are said to be nested
within time and cavity. The formulas for decision limits in the previous section assume no nested effects.

So what can be done with the injection-molding data? First, time periods and cavities can be analyzed in the normal fashion. The data
have been reorganized in Table 10.11 to help facilitate the analysis.
For each part, the average of the three locations is given. ANOMs for
time periods and cavities were given previously in Figs. 10.7 and 10.8.
These charts indicate the existence of cavity differences. The decision
lines were calculated using the formulas for a two-factor ANOM with

$$\overline{X} = 0.2500$$

$$s = 0.000416$$

$$k_1 = 3(\text{time})$$

$$k_2 = 4(\text{cavity})$$

$$n = 2$$

$$df = 12$$

$$h_{0.05} = 2.67 \ (k = 3) \quad \text{and} \quad 2.85 \ (k = 4)$$

The within-subgroup standard deviation s is based on 12 subgroups of two samples (parts) each. For the time factor, the upper decision limit is

$$\text{UDL} = 0.2500 + (0.000416)(2.67)\sqrt{\frac{3-1}{3 \times 4 \times 2}} = 0.25032$$

An ANOM chart for the time*cavity interaction can also be prepared. The interaction ANOM is given in Fig. 10.14. The predicted values and prediction error required to construct this chart are given in Table 10.12. The decision limits were calculated as follows:

$$s = 0.000416$$
$$k_1 = 3$$
$$k_2 = 4$$
$$n = 2$$
$$df = 12$$
$$h^*_{0.05} = 3.53$$

The value of $h^*_{0.05}$ requires interpolating between 3.57 ($k = 10$, df = 10) and 3.47 ($k = 15$, df = 15) to get 3.53 ($k = 12$, df = 12).

$$\text{UDL}_{12} = (0.000416)3.53\sqrt{\frac{12-1}{24}} = 0.000994$$

$$\text{LDL}_{12} = -0.000994$$

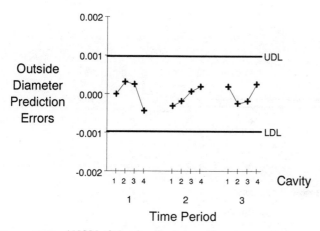

Figure 10.14 ANOM of time*cavity interaction.

TABLE 10.12   Time*Cavity Interaction Prediction Errors

		Cavity				Time Average
		1	2	3	4	
T i m e	1	0.25160 -0.25160 0.00000	0.24985 -0.24960 0.00025	0.25070 -0.25050 0.00020	0.24835 -0.24870 -0.00035	0.2501
	2	0.25125 -0.25150 -0.00025	0.24945 -0.24950 -0.00015	0.25045 -0.25040 0.00005	0.24875 -0.24860 0.00015	0.2500
	3	0.25155 -0.25140 0.00015	0.24920 -0.24940 -0.00020	0.25015 -0.25030 -0.00015	0.24870 -0.24850 0.00020	0.2499
Cavity Average		0.2515	0.2495	0.2504	0.2486	0.2500

Grand Average ↑

The ANOM for time*syringe interaction indicates that no interaction exists.

This takes care of the time and cavity factors. But what about the other two? For location, the averages can be calculated and plotted. If all the plots use the same scale, the size of the differences between locations can be compared to the time and cavity differences in order to compare relative sizes. A plot of the location averages is given in Fig. 10.15. Comparing this plot with Figs. 10.7 and 10.8 indicates that location differences are larger than the time differences but smaller than the cavity differences. Calculation of decision limits for this plot is beyond the scope of this book.

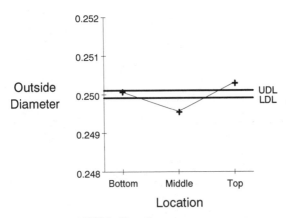

Figure 10.15   ANOM of location averages.

The part factor is a little more difficult. Recall that there are 24 parts. A simple plot of the part averages would be misleading. Since different parts come from different times and cavities, this plot would include the effect of time and cavity differences as well as part differences. An approach similar to the one taken for interactions is required where one first predicts the value for a part based on the time and cavity effects and then subtracts this value from the actual value. This difference represents the part effect.

$$\text{Predicted value} = \text{average of time-cavity combination}$$

$$\text{Prediction error} = \text{part average} - \text{predicted average}$$

For the first part:

$$\text{Predicted value} = 0.2516$$

$$\text{Prediction error} = 0.2521 - 0.2516 = 0.0005$$

The predicted values and prediction errors are given in Table 10.13. A plot of the prediction errors is given in Fig. 10.16. The plot represents the part differences. Since it is of the same scale, it can be compared to the other plots. The ANOM for parts indicates the existence of part-to-part differences. The size of the part-to-part differences is small compared to the cavity differences. The calculation of decision limits for this plot is beyond the scope of this book.

Also of interest is the cavity*location interaction. The prediction errors for each of the cavity-location combinations are plotted in Fig. 10.17. The prediction errors were calculated in Table 10.14. The interaction ANOM indicates that cavity*location interaction exists. The calculation of the decision limits is beyond the scope of this book.

Cavity, location, and cavity*location interaction effects were all found. The combined effect of these three factors is best summarized by the cavity*location interaction plot in Fig. 10.18. This plot differs

TABLE 10.13   Prediction Errors for the Factor Part

Part	Time											
	1				2				3			
	Cavity				Cavity				Cavity			
	1	2	3	4	1	2	3	4	1	2	3	4
1	.25210	.24997	.25110	.24850	.25103	.24913	.25063	.24903	.25180	.24903	.25060	.24857
	-.25158	-.24982	-.25072	-.24837	-.25130	-.24948	-.25045	-.24878	-.25155	-.24923	-.25017	-.24867
	.00052	.00015	.00038	.00013	-.00027	-.00035	.00018	.00025	.00025	-.00020	.00043	-.00010
2	.25107	.24967	.25033	.24823	.25157	.24983	.25027	.24853	.25130	.24943	.24973	.24877
	-.25158	-.24982	-.25072	-.24837	-.25130	-.24948	-.25045	-.24878	-.25155	-.24923	-.25017	-.24867
	-.00051	-.00015	-.00039	-.00014	.00027	.00035	-.00018	-.00025	-.00025	.00020	-.00044	.00010
Average	.25158	.24982	.25072	.24837	.25130	.24948	.25045	.24878	.25155	.24923	.25017	.24867

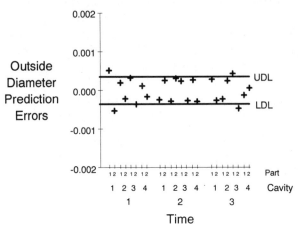

Figure 10.16   ANOM of part prediction errors.

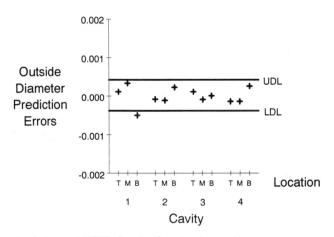

Figure 10.17   ANOM of cavity*location interaction.

from the interaction ANOM in that averages are plotted instead of prediction errors. The same decision limits can be applied as before. However, these decision limits now test for whether any of these three effects exist. This chart shows that cavity 1 exhibits a different pattern than cavities 2 through 4. Cavity 1 exhibits a taper and the other three cavities exhibit thick ends.

In summary, four effects were found: cavity, location, cavity*location interaction, and parts.

TABLE 10.14   Cavity*Location Interaction Prediction Errors

		Cavity				Location Average
		1	2	3	4	
L O C .	Top	0.25192 -0.25178 0.00014	0.24972 -0.24981 -0.00009	0.25085 -0.25074 0.00011	0.24877 -0.24891 -0.00014	0.25031
	Middle	0.25148 -0.25114 0.00034	0.24905 -0.24917 -0.00012	0.25000 -0.25010 -0.00010	0.24813 -0.24827 -0.00014	0.24967
	Bottom	0.25103 -0.25152 -0.00049	0.24977 -0.24955 0.00022	0.25048 -0.25048 0.00000	0.24892 -0.24865 0.00027	0.25005
	Cavity Average	0.25148	0.24951	0.25044	0.24861	0.25001

Grand Average ↑

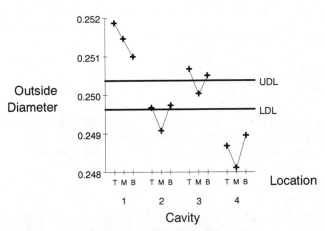

Figure 10.18   Cavity*location interaction plot.

10.3   Variance Components Analysis (VarComp)

Multi-Vari charts allowed the factor contributing the most to the variation to be identified. ANOM allowed all factors contributing to the variation to be identified. A third method exists for determining the relative contribution of each of the factors. This method is called *variance components analysis* or VarComp. A VarComp generally requires a computer for the analysis. The method of analysis is beyond the

TABLE 10.15   Variance Components Analysis for Injection-Molding Data

Factor	Standard Deviation	Percent Reduction Due To Eliminating
Time	0.00000	
Cavity	0.00123 **	52.1%
Part	0.00036 **	3.4%
Location	0.00032 **	2.6%
Time*Cavity	0.00000	
Time*Location	0.00000	
Cavity*Location	0.00024 *	1.5%
Remaining	0.00040	4.2%

* Significant at 0.05 level (less than 1 in 20 odds due to chance)
** Significant at 0.005 level (less than 1 in 200 odds due to chance)

scope of this book. However, a simple example will be given to illustrate what can be done.

Table 10.15 gives the result of a VarComp for the injection-molding study. Estimates of the standard deviation are given for each factor and three interactions. The final row labeled *remaining* includes the effects of other sources of variation including measurement.

The standard deviations are useful for ranking the factors. The factor cavity is clearly associated with the VIP. This agrees with the Multi-Vari chart. In addition, each factor is tested to see if it contributes to the variation. Those factors that contribute are marked with asterisks. Four factors are identified as contributing to the variation: cavity, part, location, and cavity*location interaction. These results agree with the ANOM plots.

Generally ANOM plots and VarComp will agree. However, there may be differences on occasion. ANOM plots are slightly more sensitive to a single factor level differing from the rest. VarComp is slightly more sensitive to a general scattering. While both methods indicate factors affecting the variation, the ANOM plots offer the advantage of indicating how the factor levels differ. The ANOM plots indicate that cavity 1 is highest and cavity 4 lowest. They also indicate that the location effect is the result of the thicker ends and the cavity*location interaction is the result of cavity 1 parts being tapered rather than having thicker ends.

The last column in the VarComp, labeled *percent reduction due to eliminating,* estimates how much the total variation will be reduced if the standard deviation of this factor is reduced to zero. This column helps to estimate the effect of possible improvements. This column clearly indicates that if one wants to be effective, one must concentrate on the VIP associated with cavity-to-cavity differences.

Standard deviations are not additive. Therefore the total standard deviation is not the simple sum of the individual standard deviations, and the percent reductions are not simple to calculate. This also accounts for the fact that the percent reductions do not sum to 100 percent. However, for any possible strategy for reducing the factor standard deviations, the resulting reduction in the output standard deviation can be determined. Table 10.16 shows the reductions in variation resulting from three possible improvements. Strategy 1 assumes a 100 percent reduction in the cavity standard deviation. This results in a 52.1 percent reduction in the total variation. This value is the value used in Table 10.15.

Generally, it is not possible to totally eliminate a factor. What if the standard deviation of the cavity can only be reduced by 80 percent? As indicated under strategy 2, this results in a 49.0 percent reduction in the total variation. This is almost as good as reducing the standard deviation to zero. After the standard deviation of the cavity factor has been reduced by 80 percent, it is no longer a VIP. Other factors have taken over. Therefore, further reductions in the standard deviation of the cavity factor result in little additional improvement. Achieving an 80 percent reduction in the cavity-to-cavity variation requires rework of the mold. At the same time the tapering of cavity 1 and thick ends of cavities 2 to 4 can be reduced by around 50 percent. Under strategy 3, the resulting reduction in output variation is 55.4 percent. VarComp adds to the arsenal a tool for accurately predicting the ef-

TABLE 10.16 **Percent Reduction of Variation for Different Strategies**

Factor	Strategy 1 Percent Reductions in Factor Standard Deviations	Strategy 2 Percent Reductions in Factor Standard Deviations	Strategy 3 Percent Reductions in Factor Standard Deviations
Cavity	100.0%	80.0%	80.0%
Part	0.0%	0.0%	0.0%
Location	0.0%	0.0%	50.0%
Cavity*Location	0.0%	0.0%	50.0%
Remaining	0.0%	0.0%	0.0%
Percent Reduction In Output Variation	52.1%	49.0%	55.4%

fects of improvements. This can prove valuable in cost justifying investments.

Multi-Vari charts, ANOM plots, and VarComp all identify the important factors. These factors are not, however, key input variables and VIPs. More than one key input variable may be associated with each factor. Identifying important factors does not pinpoint the key input variable(s) causing the differences. It does, however, considerably reduce the number of candidate input variables. Like control charts, further investigation is required. This is the topic of the next chapter.

10.4 Summary

Multi-Vari charts

Multi-Vari charts can be used to search for differences between streams of product, between units, within units, as well as between time periods. Multi-Vari charts provide a snapshot of how the process is performing. The single largest source of variation at that time can be clearly identified.

Multi-Vari charts have several shortcomings: lack of method for deciding which differences exist, difficult to discern complex relationships including interactions, and lack of method for measuring relative contributions of identified differences.

Analysis of means (ANOM)

ANOM provides a method for deciding which differences exist. The possible differences are referred to as factors. The different settings for each factor are called levels.

A factor represents the combined effect of one or more key inputs. Some inputs may contribute to more than one factor. Identifying important factors helps to narrow down the list of candidate inputs.

An interaction exists between two factors when the effect of changing the two factors in combination differs from what one would predict based on varying the factors separately. Interactions are important because they are commonplace and play a key role in reducing variation. ANOM provides a method for detecting interactions.

Variance components analysis (VarComp)

VarComp provides estimates of the standard deviation for each factor including interactions which can be used to estimate the effects of different improvement strategies.

Determining Causes
of Differences

11.1 General Approach

Differences may be detected using control charts, Multi-Vari charts, ANOM plots, VarComp, and concentration diagrams. However, detecting the difference is not enough. The cause of the difference must be determined. In some cases this is simple. However, many times considerable testing and experimentation are required to isolate and confirm the cause. This chapter deals with the approaches and tools for determining the causes of differences.

The first step is to ask, "What is known to be different between the two time periods, streams of product, units, or parts of the unit?" These differences are the most likely candidates. Then ask, "What is known to be the same?" These items can be eliminated. Other items may exist which might be different but for which it is not known for sure. An attempt should be made to determine if they are different.

In order to help determine what is different, samples should be saved. If the difference is over time, samples of units and materials should be saved from before and after the change. If the change is over streams of product, samples of units and materials should be saved from each stream of product. If unit-to-unit differences or within-unit differences are found, samples of the units should be saved. In addition, production records should be saved, operators interviewed, and so on. It is important to act fast so vital information is not lost.

Time differences

Control charts not only detect time differences, they help to pinpoint the exact time that the change took place. The time of the change is

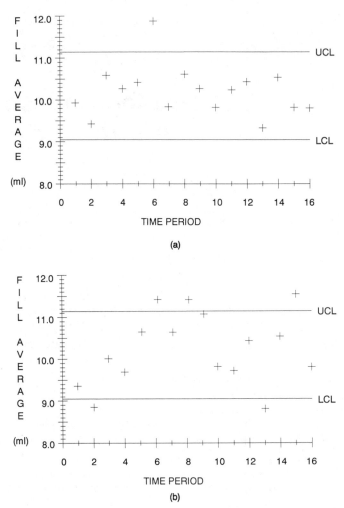

Figure 11.1 (a) One-time change; (b) series of changes.

often the most important clue. It is important to recognize the difference between two commonly occurring situations: the *one-time
change* and a *series of changes*. The one-time change, as in Fig.
11.1a, is a change that occurs once, and for some considerable time
thereafter no further changes occur. The one-time change is the result of an unusual situation. It more often arises from a violation of
normal procedure than not. In this case, saving samples and immediate questioning of all personnel as to whether anything out of the
ordinary occurred are critical. You only have one opportunity to determine the cause.

A series of changes is quite different. The series of changes may take the form of an upward trend, jumps every day after lunch, cycling, or just wandering up and down (see the right part of Fig. 11.2). The cause of the differences is acting on the process all the time. The changes generally result while following normal procedures rather than from violations of those procedures. With a series of change, one has many opportunities to determine the cause and the ability to collect a variety of data in order to help isolate the cause.

Two types of special data are often useful: data to better pinpoint the time of the change and data to determine what is different before and after the change. To better pinpoint the time of the change, the control chart may be temporarily updated on a more frequent basis. Or alternatively samples could be set aside on a more frequent basis for testing once a difference has been detected. If the control chart is updated every 2 h, samples might be set aside every 15 min. Then when a change occurs, these samples can be tested to better determine when and how the process changed.

To help determine what is different before and after the change, suspected inputs should be tracked and correlated to the changes. Many inputs are probably already being tracked. However, there are frequently inputs that are not. On one injection-molding process, downwards shifts were noticed each day following lunch. None of the parameters normally monitored, including mold temperature, indicated any changes. Someone suggested that the machine must be cooling off during lunch and affecting the process in some unknown way. It was decided to monitor the oil temperature of the machine. To

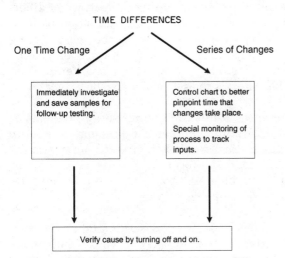

Figure 11.2 Identifying the cause of time differences.

everyone's surprise, the oil temperature dropped during lunch. Procedural changes eliminated the shifts during lunch.

Some inputs can be difficult to measure or track. One might prefer to purposely vary these inputs in designed experiments in order to determine their effect. This topic is covered in Part 4.

The identified cause should always be confirmed. This should be accomplished by purposely varying the cause to turn the effect on and off. The overall approach for time differences is summarized in Fig. 11.2.

Stream differences

Like time differences, stream differences can either be a one-time difference or a series of differences. A one-time difference is one that exists for a short period of time and then disappears for a considerable period of time. It generally results from a violation of normal procedures. Again, immediate investigation and taking of samples are important. One only has one opportunity to determine the cause.

When differences are frequently occurring, the differences between the streams can either be consistent over time or be constantly changing over time. When the size and direction of the differences are constantly changing over time, as in Fig. 11.3a, each stream of product is changing over time. Separate control charts should be established for each stream of product and the methods recommended in the previous section used to isolate the cause.

Stream differences that are consistent over time, as in Fig. 11.3b, are the easiest to work with. Start by examining the pattern of differences. For example it might be determined that the units coming from the two outside lanes of a drying oven differ from the those coming from the two inside lanes. Temperature gradients in the oven are the most likely culprit. Another possibility is that lane 6 is different from all the others. The probable cause is the setup of lane 6 or a component in lane 6.

Consistent stream differences result from either setup problems or component problems. To determine whether the problem is a setup problem and to identify the critical setup step or steps, an assembly/setup study from Sec. 11.3 can be performed. To determine whether the problem is a component problem and to isolate the problem component or components, run a component swapping study as in Sec. 11.2.

Component swapping studies and assembly/setup studies not only help identify the cause of the differences, they serve to confirm the cause. In all other cases, it is important to confirm the identified cause

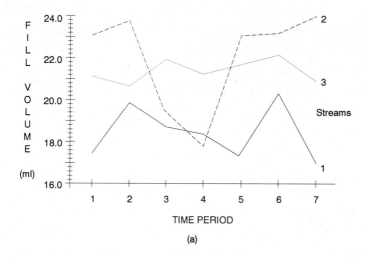

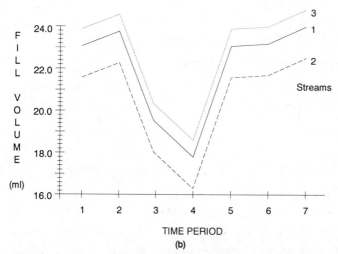

Figure 11.3   (a) Changing stream differences; (b) consistent stream differences.

by purposely varying the cause to turn the effect on and off. The overall approach for stream differences is summarized in Fig. 11.4.

Between- and within-unit differences

When dealing with unit differences and within-unit differences the first step is to determine whether the unit can be repeatedly disassembled and reassembled. If so, the assembly/setup study in Sec.

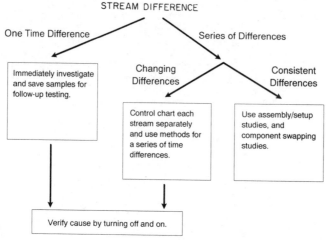

Figure 11.4   Identifying the cause of stream differences.

11.3 and the component swapping study in Sec. 11.2 should be performed to isolate the critical assembly/setup step or the critical component.

If repeated disassembly and reassembly is not possible, unit comparisons as in Sec. 11.4 should be performed. Following the identification of the cause, the cause should be confirmed by turning the effect on and off. Figure 11.5 summarizes the procedure for between- and within-unit differences.

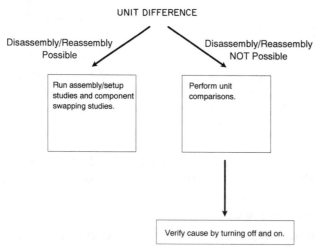

Figure 11.5   Identifying the cause of between- and within-unit differences.

11.2   Component Swapping Studies

Component swapping studies isolate the components responsible for the difference between two units of product. They can also be used to identify the process components (hardware) responsible for the difference between two streams of product. Use of a component swapping study requires

- Identification of units of product or streams of product with consistent differences

- Units that can be repeatedly disassembled and reassembled or process streams that can be repeatedly torn down and set back up

Under these two conditions, the cause of the consistent difference can either be an assembly/setup problem or a component problem.

The first step of a component swapping study is to verify that the difference does exist and is primarily due to components. Once the required conditions are verified, components are exchanged in order to isolate the component or components responsible for the difference.

The basic procedure

The basic procedure is as follows:

I. *Verify difference.* Passing this test verifies that the two units or streams are in fact different and that the primary problem is a component problem and not an assembly/setup problem.
  A. *Collect data.*
   1. Take measurements from both units or streams. For a unit of product, generally one or two measurements are sufficient. For process streams, typically 5 to 100 units are measured. If multiple measurements are taken, average these measurements and record the average.
   2. Disassemble both units and reassemble them or tear down both process streams and set them back up.
   3. Take a second set of measurements from both units or streams.
   4. For a second time, disassemble both units and reassemble them or tear down both process streams and set them back up.
   5. Take a third set of measurements from both units or streams.
  B. *Analyze data.*
   1. Put the results in a table as shown in Table 11.1.

TABLE 11.1 Data for Verification Study

		REPETITIONS			Unit Avg.	Unit Std. Dev.
		1	2	3		
UNITS	1	X_{11}	X_{12}	X_{13}	$\overline{X}_1$	s_1
	2	X_{21}	X_{22}	X_{23}	$\overline{X}_2$	s_2
					$\overline{X}$	s

Grand Average ↑   ↑ Within Unit Standard Deviation

2. Calculate:

$$\overline{X}_1 = \frac{X_{11} + X_{12} + X_{13}}{3}$$

$$\overline{X}_2 = \frac{X_{21} + X_{22} + X_{23}}{3}$$

$$s_1 = \sqrt{\frac{(X_{11} - \overline{X}_1)^2 + (X_{12} - \overline{X}_1)^2 + (X_{13} - \overline{X}_1)^2}{2}}$$

$$s_2 = \sqrt{\frac{(X_{21} - \overline{X}_2)^2 + (X_{22} - \overline{X}_2)^2 + (X_{23} - \overline{X}_2)^2}{2}}$$

$$s = \sqrt{\frac{s_1^2 + s_2^2}{2}}$$

3. Passing this test requires that:

$$\frac{|\overline{X}_1 - \overline{X}_2|}{s} \geq 10$$

II. *Swap components.* Following confirmation of the difference, swap components to identify the components causing the difference.
A. *Prepare plot.*

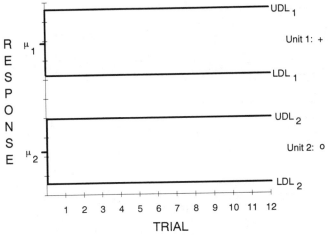

Figure 11.6 Plot for component swapping.

1. Calculate decision limits for both units or streams:

$$UDL_1 = \overline{X}_1 + 5s$$
$$LDL_1 = \overline{X}_1 - 5s$$
$$UDL_2 = \overline{X}_2 + 5s$$
$$LDL_2 = \overline{X}_2 - 5s$$

2. Plot decision lines as in Fig. 11.6.

B. *Perform swaps.*

1. Repeatedly disassemble both units or streams, swap components, and reassemble.

2. Each time take the same number of measurements from both units or streams as before. Record the averages.

3. Plot the averages as in Fig. 11.7 using a "+" for unit 1 and a "0" for unit 2. Either a "+" or "0" outside their respective decision limits indicates that one of the components just swapped is contributing to the cause.

An example of unit differences

Take as an example, a situation where two watches, supposedly identical, gain and lose time at different rates. While the watches could be adjusted, the objective is to make the watches so that time-consuming adjustments are not necessary. Two watches were selected representing the extremes of production. It was decided to measure the time lost or gained over a 24-h period of time. The difference verification data

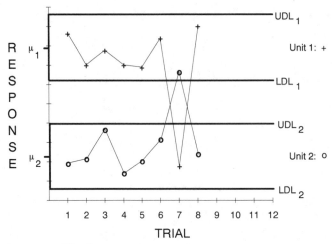

Figure 11.7   Plot for component swapping.

were collected by measuring each of the two watches over three different 24-h time periods. Between each 24-h time period, both watches were completely disassembled and reassembled. The results are shown in Table 11.2.

Verifying the difference requires calculating,

$$\frac{|\overline{X}_1 - \overline{X}_2|}{s} = \frac{|0.673 - -0.620|}{0.075} = 17.24 \geq 10$$

TABLE 11.2   Verification Study for Watches

		REPETITIONS			Watch Avg.	Watch Std. Dev.
		1	2	3		
WATCHES	1	0.59	0.64	0.79	0.673	0.104
	2	-0.62	-0.60	-0.64	-0.620	0.020
					0.027	0.075

Grand Average ↑   ↑ Within Watch Standard Deviation

Since this quantity is greater than 10, the difference is confirmed to exist and be primarily due to components. Based on the above results, the decision limits are as follows:

$$UDL_1 = 0.673 + 5\,(0.075) = 1.048$$

$$LDL_1 = 0.673 - 5\,(0.075) = 0.298$$

$$UDL_2 = -0.620 + 5\,(0.075) = -0.245$$

$$LDL_2 = -0.620 - 5\,(0.075) = -0.995$$

The watches consisted of over 30 parts. Instead of switching each of the 30 components one at a time, the components were grouped into four subassemblies: battery, crystal-electronics, gears, and motor. The study begins by swapping these subassemblies. The results are plotted in Fig. 11.8. The first subassembly swapped is the battery. There is no effect. On the second swap, the batteries were returned to their original watches and the crystal-electronics swapped instead. The crystal-electronics also has no effect. However, when gears are swapped, both points go outside their watch's decision limits. Gears contribute to the problem. The fact that the points fall within the other watch's decision limits indicates that swapping gears completely reverses the difference. Gears are probably the only contributor to the problem.

Just to be on the safe side, the gears are replaced in their original watches and the motors are swapped on the fourth run. As expected, the points indicate that swapping motors has no effect. As confirma-

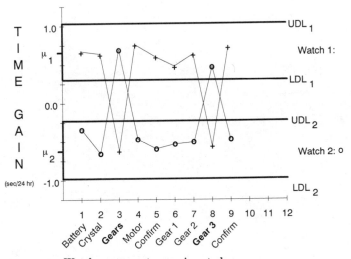

Figure 11.8 Watch component swapping study.

tion that no parts were damaged, and so forth, on trial 5 the motors are placed back in their original watches so that the watches contain exactly the subassemblies they started with. Trial 5 indicates that the watches are still performing the same as they started out. Therefore, the only component or components contributing to the difference are in the gear subassembly.

There are five gears, numbered 1 through 5. On trial 6, gear 1 is swapped and on trial 7 gear 2 is swapped. Neither has any effect. But on trial 8, when gear 3 is swapped, the difference again reverses itself. Gear 3 is the culprit. It is decided to go no further, so a final confirmation trial is performed. On trial 9 all components are returned to their original watches. The points fall back within the decision limits indicating nothing else happened which might have caused the previous points to exceed the decision limits. Gear 3 from both watches were sent to the laboratory for examination to determine how they differed. One of the differences identified was gear diameter. Further tests verified that the diameter of gear 3 was causing the differences. The specifications for the diameter of gear 3 were tightened resulting in a dramatic improvement in watch accuracy.

An example of process stream differences

A second example involves a process for making plastic bags. There are four stations for making the bottom seal. The Multi-Vari chart in Fig. 11.9 clearly indicates that these stations are performing differently. Station 3 is different from the other three. The data for the

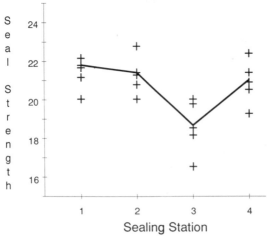

Figure 11.9 Heat sealer Multi-Vari chart.

TABLE 11.3   Heat Sealer Multi-Vari Data

Sealing Station					
1	2	3	4		
22.0	23.0	20.3	21.7		
21.3	21.0	16.8	20.8		
20.2	21.6	18.6	21.1		
21.9	20.3	18.4	22.6		Grand
22.4	21.6	20.0	19.5		↓ Average
Average	21.56	21.50	18.82	21.14	20.76
Standard Deviation	0.86	0.99	1.40	1.15	1.12

↑ Within
  Station
  Standard
  Deviation

Multi-Vari chart are given in Table 11.3. In order to identify why station 3 was different from the other three stations, it was decided to run a component swapping study. The third and fourth stations were selected for the study.

The number of samples to be measured from each station for each setup can be determined using the formula below:

$$n > \frac{100\sigma^2}{(\mu_2 - \mu_1)^2}$$

where n is the required sample size, σ is the process within subgroup variation, μ_1 is the average of the first stream, and μ_2 is the average of the second stream. The above formula assumes σ, μ_1, and μ_2 are known. Using the data from the Multi-Vari chart gives

$$n > \frac{100\,(1.12)^2}{(21.14 - 18.82)^2} = 23$$

Because estimates of σ, μ_1, and μ_2 were used, a larger sample size of 50 was selected.

The results of the difference verification study are given in Table 11.4. Between each setup, the two stations where completely torn apart, cleaned, and reassembled. In addition a new roll of sheeting was placed on the machine. Because

$$\frac{|\overline{X}_1 - \overline{X}_2|}{s} = \frac{|21.45 - 18.62|}{0.187} = 15.13 \geq 10$$

TABLE 11.4 Verification Study for Heat Sealers

		SETUPS			Avg.	Std. Dev.
		1	2	3		
HEAT SEALER	3	18.33	18.69	18.84	18.62	0.262
	4	21.46	21.49	21.41	21.45	0.040
					20.04	0.187

Grand Average ↑   ↑ Setup Standard Deviation

the station difference is verified and determined to be primarily the result of component differences rather than setup differences including material differences. Based on the above results, the decision limits for the third and fourth streams are as follows:

$$UDL_3 = 18.62 + 5 (0.187) = 19.56$$

$$LDL_3 = 18.62 - 5 (0.187) = 17.69$$

$$UDL_4 = 21.45 + 5 (0.187) = 22.39$$

$$LDL_4 = 21.45 - 5 (0.187) = 20.51$$

The heat seal is formed by pressing two sheets of plastic between two bars, the top of which is heated. The heat and force bond the two sheets together. The bottom bar of each station is stationary, being mounted to a common base. The top bars of the four stations are mounted to a common arm that moves all four top bars up and down together. The components are divided into the following categories: bottom bar, top bar, mounting brackets, heater element, and electronics. The results of the component swapping study are given in Fig. 11.10.

Swapping the bottom bar had no effect. Swapping the top bar did have an effect. However, swapping the top bar did not reverse the previous difference. Therefore, the top bar is responsible for part of the difference, but not the whole difference. Swapping the mounting brackets also has an effect. Again it is responsible for part of the difference, but not the whole difference. Neither heater element nor elec-

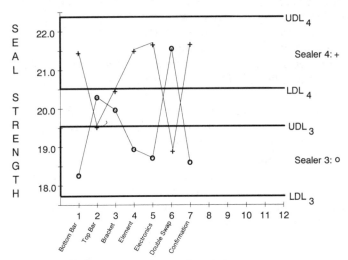

Figure 11.10 Sealer component swapping study.

tronics has an effect. Therefore, the difference is the result of the top bar and the mounting brackets.

To confirm this, two more setups were performed. The first consisted of simultaneously swapping the top bar and mounting bracket. This change reversed the difference. On the final setup, all components are returned to their original station. The original difference remains signifying nothing changed or was damaged during the study that might adversely affect the study results.

Some comments

An important part of performing component swapping studies on units or processes consisting of hundreds and even thousands of components is grouping the components into two to five subassemblies, isolating the key subassemblies, and then further subdividing these subassemblies. Following this strategy, the key components can be isolated from more than a thousand parts in less than 25 swaps.

For an experiment, the chance that one or more points incorrectly fall outside the decision limits ranges from 4 percent for 5 swaps up to 10 percent for 25 swaps. The chance of such an error is reasonably small in itself. However, the real concern is the chance of missing a key component. The chance of making this mistake is considerably smaller. When a point incorrectly falls outside the decision limits, it will fall on the side furthest from the other unit as often as it falls on the side closest to the other unit. When it does fall on the side closest to the other unit, it will most often fall outside the other unit's decision limits. Neither of these situations will result in a key component being missed. In practice, the component swapping procedure given in this section rarely misses key components.

The price to be paid for such a low chance of missing a key component is the verification criterion that the difference be at least 10 standard deviations. This criterion causes few problems for unit differences. In this case the standard deviation is largely measurement error. So long as the process variation is considerably larger than the measurement error, it should be possible to find units that meet this criterion even for stable processes.

The 10 standard deviations criterion causes more problems when dealing with stream differences. In this case, averages of n samples must be used. The standard deviation in question is the standard deviation of these averages which is

$$\frac{\sigma}{\sqrt{n}}$$

where σ is the process standard deviation. Stream differences can be detected that are no more large than 1σ. This can result in sample sizes as large as 100 units per each stream for each swap. The required sample size can be determined using the formula given previously.

11.3   Assembly/Setup Studies

Unit-to-unit differences and stream-to-stream differences can result from either *assembly/setup differences* or *component differences*. The previous section covers the handling of component differences. This section concentrates on assembly/setup differences. Assembly/setup studies can only be performed under the same conditions required for component swapping: there must be consistent unit-to-unit differences or stream-to-stream differences, and the unit or process can be repeatedly disassembled and reassembled.

Assembly/setup differences are of two types:

- Assembly/setup error
- Assembly/setup step that is not controlled tightly enough

An assembly/setup error results in a unit or stream that is outside the norm. If the assembly/setup were repeated, the error would not be expected to reoccur. To determine the assembly/setup step responsible for the error, a slight variation of the component swapping study can be performed. This procedure differs in two ways:

1. The two units/streams are not disassembled and reassembled between the first three trials used to verify the difference. As a result, σ does not include the effect of any setup variation.

2. Once the difference verification test is passed, the first trial represents the result of redoing the last assembly/setup step. The second trial represents the result of redoing the last two assembly/setup steps, and so on, until the unit/stream is completely disassembled and reassembled.

As an example, consider a telephone assembly operation. This operation normally runs free of defects. However, on one particular day, several defective phones were found. In order to determine the cause, an assembly/setup study was performed. For this study, two units were selected, one good and one bad. The characteristic being measured was sound clarity. The study begins by taking three measurements from each phone. These results are recorded in Table 11.5. Using these results the difference verification test is passed as follows:

$$\frac{|\overline{X}_1 - \overline{X}_2|}{s} = \frac{|7.73 - 1.63|}{0.573} = 10.65 \geq 10$$

Then begins the disassemble/reassemble stage of the experiment. There are 12 assembly steps. On the first trial only the twelfth step is redone. On the second trial, both the eleventh and twelfth steps are redone. The results are plotted in Fig. 11.11.

Following the redoing of the fifth step, the bad phone suddenly starts performing like a good phone. The unit differences are in fact due to an assembly problem with the fifth assembly step being the cul-

TABLE 11.5   Verification Study for Phones

		REPETITIONS			Phone Avg.	Phone Std. Dev.
		1	2	3		
PHONES	Good	8.6	7.6	7.0	7.73	0.808
	Bad	1.7	1.6	1.6	1.63	0.058
					4.73	0.573

Grand Average ↑   ↑ Within Phone Standard Deviation

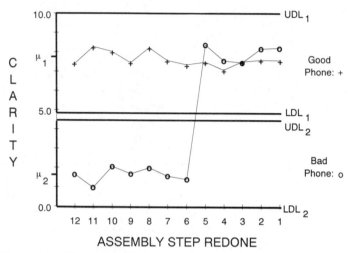

ASSEMBLY STEP REDONE

Figure 11.11   Phone assembly/setup study.

prit. While performing the study the technician noticed that the speaker in the bad unit appeared to be seated slightly off center. The seating of the speaker was done in the fifth step. Examining other bad phones identified the same misaligned speaker. The problem was traced back to a warped guide bar that was replaced.

Performing this type of study when the observed difference is the result of an assembly/setup error generally results in the difference magically disappearing once the assembly/setup step that was done incorrectly is redone. As one disassembles the units/streams, one should be careful to measure and observe differences in how the units/streams were previously assembled or set up. Once the critical step is identified, these differences provide clues to the key input variable causing the problem. Identifying the key input variable responsible is important in preventing the problem from reoccurring. If additional bad units are available, these can help to isolate and confirm the key input variable responsible for the problem.

The second type of cause of assembly/setup differences is an assembly/setup step that is not controlled tightly enough. The result is that each time the unit/stream is assembled or set up, some key input variable is set slightly differently resulting in slightly different results. For unit differences, the differences appear random. No unit is noticeably outside the norm. Figure 11.12 shows a Multi-Vari chart of the results of repeatedly reassembling a unit that has an assembly step that is not controlled tightly enough.

For stream differences, the result of an assembly step that is not

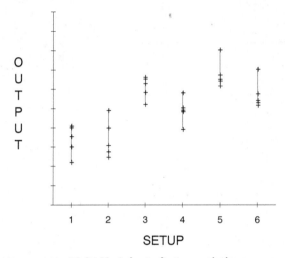

Figure 11.12   Multi-Vari chart of setup variation.

controlled tightly enough, is stream differences that remain consistent until a new setup is performed. Following a new setup the differences all change. A Multi-Vari chart showing what happens to the resulting stream-to-stream differences is given in Fig. 11.13. In the case of an assembly step that is not controlled tightly enough, the same study can be performed as before. The difference is in the telltale pattern. Once the critical assembly/setup step is redone, the points start jump-

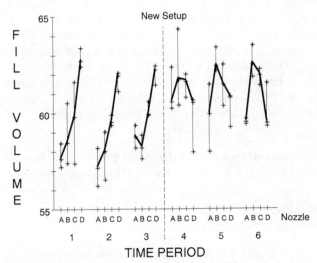

Figure 11.13   Multi-Vari chart of four-station filler.

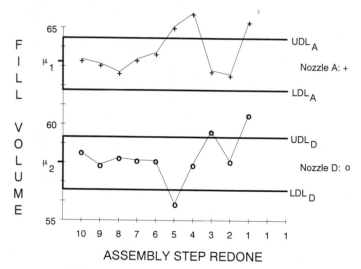

ASSEMBLY STEP REDONE

Figure 11.14   Filler assembly/setup study.

ing all over the place. An example is given in Fig. 11.14. The points become more erratic when the fifth assembly step is redone. The critical step is generally the fist step where a point falls out. It can happen, however, that the critical assembly/setup step actually occurred one or two steps earlier. As a result, if no pattern is evident at the end of the study, it is a good idea to completely disassemble and reassemble the unit/stream a couple of extra times.

If no assembly/setup problem is evident, then the chart will look like Fig. 11.15. The unit/stream differences are not due to assembly/setup. The difference must therefore result from component differences. A component swapping study from the previous section can be performed to identify the critical component(s). In the last three assemblies in Fig. 11.15, both filler streams were completely torn down and set back up. These three assemblies can be used for the difference verification study required for the component swapping study.

One has a choice:

- Start with the component swapping difference verification test. It the difference verification test fails, then perform an assembly/setup study.

- Perform the assembly/setup study first. If nothing is found, then perform the component swapping study.

Generally the first approach is more efficient. It does, however, have one major drawback. If the difference is the result of an assembly/

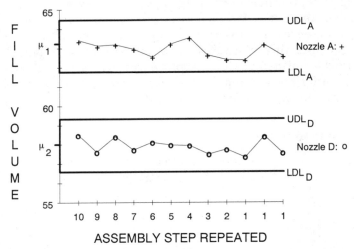

Figure 11.15 Filler assembly/setup study.

setup error, the difference is likely to disappear while performing the component swapping difference verification test. One will have lost the opportunity to identify the critical assembly/setup step. Therefore, the second approach should be used whenever an assembly/setup error is the possible culprit and one does not have further units or streams to run an assembly/setup study should the difference between the two units or streams selected for the component swapping study suddenly disappear.

11.4 Unit Comparisons

When units cannot be disassembled, a different tack must be taken to identify the cause of the unit differences. In this case the attributes of the units can be compared in an attempt to find one or more attributes that differ. *Unit comparisons* work best if there are more than two units to compare.

In one case, the strength of the side seal of a certain potato chip bag was highly variable. The problem resulted in some bags breaking. Samples of good and bad bags are identified and sent to the laboratory. Their material thickness, seal thickness, and various material properties were measured. The laboratory determined that there were higher concentrations of lubricants on the surface of the poorer seals. As a result, a film-washing operation was added that eliminated the problem.

When comparing units, more than one difference may be identified.

Designed experiments where each of the inputs is varied may be necessary to isolate the cause. In other cases, one might not be able to observe any differences. The difference might result from differences in processing temperature or some other parameter that is not readily observable in the finished product. Again purposely varying the inputs might identify the key input. Designed experiments where the inputs are purposely varied are the topic of Part 4.

11.5 Conclusion to Part 3

Part 3 concentrates on identifying differences and determining the underlying cause. Four types of differences are possible:

1. Time differences

2. Stream differences

3. Between-unit differences

4. Within-unit differences

A summary of the procedures for identifying and determining the underlying cause of these differences is given in Table 11.6.

The searching for differences approach is capable of making dramatic improvements quickly. The results are often spectacular, especially at reducing variation. The approach concentrates on the VIPs. However, any time a VIP is identified, it can also be used to better optimize the average.

The alternate approach is studying the inputs' effects. This approach is often more tedious although some methods may be applied

TABLE 11.6 Methods for Searching for Differences

Type of Difference	Methods For Detection	Methods For Isolating Cause
Time Differences	Control Charts Multi-Vari Charts ANOM VarComp	Investigate Instances, Test Samples Control Chart to Pinpoint Times Monitoring of Inputs
Stream Differences	Multi-Vari Charts ANOM VarComp	Investigate Instances, Test Samples Control Chart by Stream Assembly/Setup Studies Component Swapping Studies
Between Unit Differences	Multi-Vari Charts ANOM VarComp	Assembly/Setup Studies Component Swapping Studies Unit Comparisons
Within Unit Differences	Concentration Diagrams Multi-Vari Charts ANOM VarComp	Assembly/Setup Studies Component Swapping Studies Unit Comparisons

quickly. Results may be slower in coming. However, the approach is more cautious, searching for all key inputs, not just VIPs. Studying the inputs' effects is capable of reducing variation even when no differences can be found. Further, it is much better at optimizing the average. This second approach is the topic of the next section.

11.6 Summary

General approach

Identifying differences is not enough. The cause of the difference must be determined. This can require considerable additional testing and experimentation. One should immediately investigate any difference so that important information is not lost. This investigation should determine what is and what is not different between the two time periods, streams, units, or parts of a unit.

In investigating time differences and stream differences, one should distinguish between a one-time change and a series of changes. One should also determine whether the differences are changing over time or are consistent over time.

Component swapping studies and assembly/disassembly studies can be used to isolate the cause of unit differences or consistent stream differences. For units, it is required that the unit can be repeatedly disassembled and reassembled.

Component swapping studies

Component swapping studies require identification of units of product or streams of product with consistent differences, and units that can be repeatedly disassembled and reassembled or process streams that can be repeatedly torn down and set back up. Under these conditions the difference can result from either assembly/setup differences or component differences.

A component swapping study first confirms the existence of the difference and that the difference is due to component differences. It then isolates the component or components causing the difference. Component swapping studies can identify the key component from among more than a thousand components in less than 25 swaps.

Assembly/setup studies

Assembly/setup studies require the same conditions as component swapping studies. An assembly/setup study identifies the assembly or setup step responsible for the difference. If no step is identified, the unit or stream difference must instead be the result of component differences.

Assembly/setup studies are generally run if the component swapping difference verification test fails. However, assembly/setup studies can also be run before the component swapping study. In the case of a possible assembly/setup error, the assembly/setup study should always be run first.

Unit comparisons

For units of product that cannot be disassembled, the product attributes should be compared to identify differences.

Conclusion to Part 3

The searching for differences approach can lead to dramatic improvements quickly. It is especially effective at reducing variation since it concentrates on the VIPs.

The alternate approach is studying the inputs' effects. This approach, while often more tedious, can reduce variation even when no differences are found. Further, it looks for all key input variables resulting in better optimization of the average.

Studying the Inputs' Effects

12

Optimizing
the Average

12.1 Studying the Inputs' Effects

Studying the inputs' effects is the second of the two approaches for identifying key input variables and VIPs. It requires that the candidate input variables be varied in order to study their effect on the outputs. The inputs must be observed as well as the outputs. This is in contrast to the searching for differences approach, where the concentration was primarily on the outputs and the patterns and differences they exhibited.

When studying the inputs' effects, one wants to identify the key input variables, understand their effects on the average, and use this understanding to optimize the average. This chapter deals exclusively with this topic. However, one also wants to study the inputs' effects in order to reduce variation. There are two different approaches for accomplishing this task:

Direct observation. The effect that changes of the inputs have on the variation of the output is observed directly. This requires varying the inputs and measuring the resulting variation of the output. Chapter 14 deals with this topic.

Transmission of variation. The variation transmitted by the inputs to the output can be calculated based on the relationship between the inputs and the output. This requires estimates of the variations of the individual inputs. Chapter 13 deals with this topic.

The rest of this chapter deals exclusively with the problem of optimizing the average. This requires identifying the key input variables, understanding the relationship between these key inputs and the outputs, and using this understanding to target the inputs to optimize the average.

12.2   Identifying Key Input Variables

The first step must be to identify the key input variables. Some key inputs may already have been identified using the search for differences strategy. However, not all key inputs can be so identified. The search for differences approach only identifies those key inputs that, at least temporarily, act as VIPs. Key input variables may also be identified through existing engineering and scientific knowledge. Such knowledge includes lists of important factors, theoretical equations, and simulations. The knowledge may be imprecise, representing an ideal such as the ideal gas law. It is frequently incomplete, modeling only a portion of the total system. Engineering and scientific knowledge must often be supplemented with observational and experimental data.

The search for differences approach uses passive observation of the process to identify key inputs. Another method of identifying key inputs through passive observation is the *scatter diagram*. This method is the topic of the next section. Passive observation, including the search for differences approach and scatter diagrams, will not identify all key inputs. Certain key input variables may not be varying. For such a variable, the only way to detect its effect is to intervene and purposely vary it. Other key inputs may be varying but their effect is too small to be detected in the presence of the VIPs.

Detecting the presence of key input variables (Table 12.1) that are not VIPs requires active experimentation. The primary tool for doing this is called a screening experiment. This is the topic of Sec. 12.4. Response surface studies, covered in Sec. 12.6, can also be used.

TABLE 12.1   Identifying Key Inputs

APPROACH	METHODS
Existing Knowledge	Engineering Knowledge Scientific Knowledge
Passive Observation	Search for Differences Scatter Diagrams
Active Experimentation	Screening Experiments Response Surface Studies

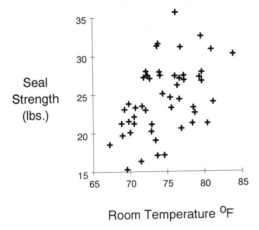

Figure 12.1   Seal-strength scatter diagram.

12.3   Scatter Diagrams

Scatter diagrams look for relationships between inputs and output. An example of a scatter diagram is given in Fig. 12.1. This scatter diagram shows a relationship between seal strength of a heat-sealing operation (the output) and room temperature (the input). At 50 points in time, readings were recorded for room temperature and seal strength. Scatter diagrams can take on any of the shapes shown in Fig. 12.2.

A circular scatter indicates that there is not a relationship between the input and the output. Both the positive correlation and negative correlation patterns indicate a relationship exists. Sometimes the correlation is strong. In this case the points all fall close to a diagonal

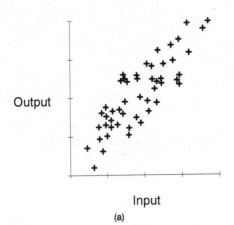

Figure 12.2   (a) Strong positive correlation.

(a)

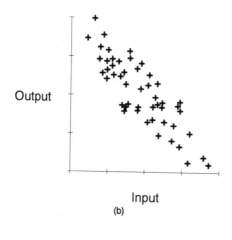

(b)

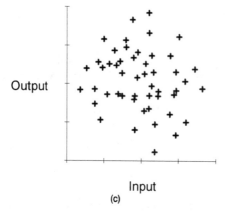

(c)

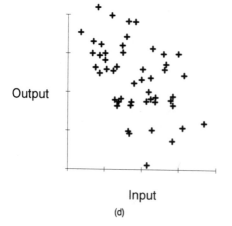

Input

(d)

Figure 12.2 (*Continued*) (*b*)
Strong negative correlation; (*c*)
no correlation; (*d*) weak negative correlation.

line. At other times the correlation is weak. In this case a diagonal line indicating best fit can be drawn, but the scatter around this line is large.

In some cases it may be questionable whether a relationship exists or where to draw the best-fit line. In these cases the following procedure can be used.

I. Procedure for estimating best-fit line
  A. Label the output values $Y_1, Y_2, ..., Y_n$. Label the corresponding inputs $X_1, X_2, ..., X_n$. Here n represents the number of X-Y pairs in the data set.
  B. Calculate the sums below.

$$S_y = Y_1 + Y_2 + ... + Y_n$$

$$S_{yy} = Y_1^2 + Y_2^2 + ... + Y_n^2$$

$$S_x = X_1 + X_2 + ... + X_n$$

$$S_{xx} = X_1^2 + X_2^2 + ... + X_n^2$$

$$S_{xy} = X_1Y_1 + X_2Y_2 + ... + X_nY_n$$

  C. Calculate the intercept a and slope b:

$$b = \frac{S_{xy} - (S_xS_y/n)}{S_{xx} - (S_x^2/n)}$$

$$a = (S_y/n) - b(S_x/n)$$

  D. The best-fit line is given by $y = a + bx$.
II. Procedure for determining whether correlation exists
  A. Calculate the correlation coefficient r:

$$r = \frac{S_{xy} - (S_xS_y/n)}{\sqrt{(S_{xx} - S_x^2/n)(S_{yy} - S_y^2/n)}}$$

  B. If the absolute value of r is greater than the critical value in Table 12.2, then the input and output are correlated.

Many calculators have functions for calculating S_y, S_x, S_{yy}, S_{xx}, S_{xy}, a, b, and r. The correlation coefficient r varies between -1 and 1. Values near 1 indicate a strong positive correlation. Values near -1 indicate a strong negative correlation. Values near zero indicate no correlation exists.

The data set used to draw the scatter diagram in Fig. 12.1 is given in Table 12.3. Using this table:

TABLE 12.2   Correlation Coefficient Critical Values

Sample Size	Confidence Level		
	90%	95%	99%
3	0.9877	0.9969	0.9999
4	0.9000	0.9500	0.9900
5	0.8054	0.8783	0.9587
6	0.7293	0.8114	0.9172
8	0.6215	0.7067	0.8343
10	0.5494	0.6319	0.7646
15	0.4409	0.5140	0.6411
20	0.3783	0.4438	0.5614
25	0.3365	0.3961	0.5052
30	0.3061	0.3610	0.4629
40	0.2638	0.3120	0.4026
50	0.2353	0.2787	0.3610
60	0.2144	0.2542	0.3301
70	0.1982	0.2352	0.3060
80	0.1852	0.2199	0.2864
90	0.1745	0.2072	0.2702
100	0.1654	0.1966	0.2565
150	0.1348	0.1603	0.2097
200	0.1166	0.1388	0.1818
250	0.1043	0.1241	0.1626
300	0.0951	0.1133	0.1485
500	0.0736	0.0877	0.1151
1000	0.0520	0.0620	0.0814

$$S_y = 1226.6$$

$$S_{yy} = 31109.04$$

$$S_x = 3722.3$$

$$S_{xx} = 277832.5$$

$$S_{xy} = 91707.5$$

$$b = \frac{91707.5 - (3722.3 \times 1226.6/50)}{277832.5 - (3722.3^2/50)} = 0.543$$

$$a = (1226.6/50) - 0.543\,(3722.3/50) = -15.9$$

$$r = \frac{91707.5 - (3722.3 \times 1226.6/50)}{\sqrt{(277832.5 - 3722.3^2/50)\,(31109.04 - 1226.6^2/50)}} = 0.457$$

Since r is greater than the 95 percent confidence critical value of 0.2787, a positive correlation exists between seal strength and room temperature. The equation for the best-fit line is $y = -15.9 + 0.543x$. Figure 12.3 shows the scatter diagram with the line added.

Looking at Table 12.2, a minimum of ten X-Y pairs are required to detect large correlations. At least 50 X-Y pairs are required for

TABLE 12.3   Seal-Strength Data

X	Y	X	Y
80.4	21.1	79.6	26.6
69.9	20.1	73.9	31.5
71.7	27.3	71.2	16.2
79.3	27.9	74.2	27.7
73.6	31.5	77.0	27.6
70.6	21.0	76.9	26.7
73.7	28.0	70.6	22.4
69.5	15.1	73.8	17.0
75.8	27.6	69.7	23.9
69.7	21.7	68.6	21.2
75.5	24.5	76.0	35.9
72.8	20.2	68.9	19.8
72.5	27.5	71.3	23.7
76.6	24.3	74.5	17.3
78.5	23.1	73.1	19.0
70.8	23.4	81.0	24.2
69.2	23.7	79.3	27.2
72.9	21.2	76.2	27.1
72.2	27.9	75.4	23.9
80.8	31.0	79.6	32.6
83.4	30.3	67.1	18.7
76.1	26.5	79.1	23.0
74.2	25.3	72.2	23.0
76.4	31.2	78.2	21.1
72.5	27.5	76.3	20.4

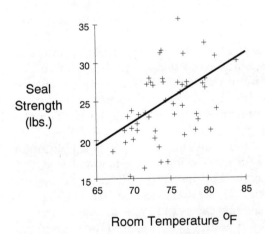

Seal Strength (lbs.)

Room Temperature °F

Figure 12.3   Seal-strength scatter diagram.

smaller correlations. Recommended for most scatter diagrams are 50 to 100 X-Y pairs.

Scatter diagrams can be used to help identify which input is the VIP. If the data are collected as part of normal production, the scatter of the input and output represents their variation during production. As shown in Fig. 12.4, the effect that the input has on the output is

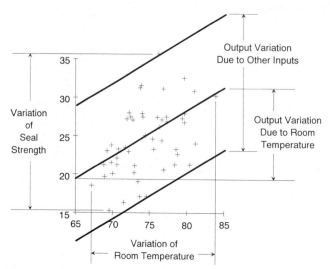

Figure 12.4 Interpreting scatter diagram.

represented by the vertical distance that the best-fit line increases or decreases over the range of the input. The effect that all the other inputs have on the output is represented by the vertical scatter of the points from this line.

In Fig. 12.4, the effect of the other inputs is larger than the effect of room temperature. Therefore, while room temperature is a key input variable, it is not a VIP. Any input that exhibits the strong positive or strong negative pattern is a VIP. The presence of a strong correlation under production conditions indicates the variable is a VIP. The absence of any correlation indicates that the input is not a VIP.

The presence of any correlation indicates the input is a key input variable. However, the lack of a correlation does not mean that the input is not a key input. It may be that the effect that the input has on the output over the range of the scatter diagram is small compared to the effect of other inputs. In extreme cases, the input may not be varying at all and the scatter of input values is the result of measurement errors. To be certain whether a candidate input variable is a key input variable requires purposely varying the inputs over a wide range in order to magnify their effect.

One should also be forewarned that on somewhat rare occasions a scatter diagram can indicate that a correlation exists between an input and output when the input is in fact not a key input variable. The existence of a correlation implies a relationship between the input and the output. But this relationship may not be the direct causal relationship of a key input variable. Changing a key input directly causes the output to change.

In the scatter diagram between room temperature and seal strength a correlation exists. If room temperature is a key input variable, changing the room temperature should change the seal strength. However, there are other possible explanations for the correlation. Consider one possible scenario. The machine is turned on at 8 A.M. each morning and allowed to warm up for a short period of time. However, during most of the morning the machine continues to warm up. As the machine continues to warm up, the seal strengths increase. During the course of the day the room also warms up as a result of the running machines and the increasing outside temperature. Under this scenario, changing the room temperature has no effect on seal strength. However, both room temperature and seal strength are related to time of day. This common relationship to time results in the correlation on the scatter diagram.

Because of the possibility of correlations arising from a relationship other than that of a key input variable, any key inputs identified by scatter diagrams should be verified by purposely varying them. Screening experiments can be used to accomplish this. Scatter diagrams can also be used to help set tolerances on key inputs as shown in Fig. 12.5.

12.4 Screening Experiments

Screening experiments* allow a large number of candidate input variables to be purposely varied to identify the key input variables. The candidate inputs may have been identified from scatter diagrams, searching for differences, or theoretical considerations. Screening experiments are the one sure way of determining whether a candidate input variable is in fact a key input variable. Complete coverage of screening experiments requires more space than possible in this book. There are many books devoted entirely to this subject. Here procedures will be given for designing and analyzing screening experiments containing from 3 to 16 inputs.

Designing a screening experiment consists of selecting the outputs of interest, deciding how each output is to be measured, choosing the inputs to study, and selecting the ranges over which to vary the inputs. Based on this information the trials to be run are determined.

For products, the inputs are design parameters and material properties such as dimensions, elasticity of a spring, electrical output of a

---

*In statistical jargon these are referred to as fractional factorial studies.

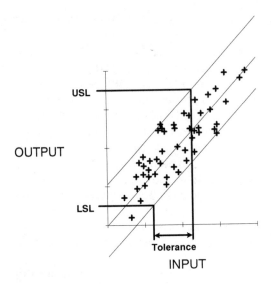

Figure 12.5 Setting tolerances.

component, viscosity, and so forth. Each trial requires that one or more prototypes be produced with a specific combination of these design parameters. Each design parameter will be set to either its high value or low value on a particular trial. The door-hinge case study in Chap. 2 provides an example of the application of screening experiments to product design.

For processes, the inputs are process parameters such as temperature, dwell time, roller speed, pressure, and so on. Each trial requires that the process be set up to the specified conditions and run until it stabilizes. Then the samples may be selected. Each process parameter will be set to either its high value or low value on a particular trial. Anywhere from 1 to 50 samples per setup are typical. The heat-seal case study is an example of the application of screening experiments to process design.

Procedure for designing a screening experiment

The basic procedure for designing a screening experiment is as follows:

Select outputs. Determine which outputs to study. More than one output is typically studied. Include all outputs for which you wish to optimize the average and reduce variation as well as all outputs serving as constraints. If one is trying to optimize part strength, constraints might be part weight and surface finish. Failure to include constraints might result in a recommended design or setup that later proves infeasible due to some other problem.

Decide on measurement methods. For each output, the method used to measure it must be selected. Variable measures should be used whenever possible. If there are several competing measurement methods, they might all be included and the study used to compare these methods. Sometimes considerable effort is required for the development of measurement methods.

Select number of samples per trial. With variable measures, when the cost of producing and testing a unit is high, a single unit per trial is feasible. When testing is nondestructive, multiple measurements should be taken of this unit. However, many times the cost of producing and measuring a single unit is small when compared to the cost of setting up a trial. In these cases ten to 50 samples per trial are recommended. If a pass-fail test is used, 250 samples per trial and up are required. Enough samples should be selected to ensure that at least a dozen failures are observed during the course of the study. In other words, conducting a study in a region that produces around one defect per million requires a total of 12 million samples. If the study has eight trials, 1.5 million samples per trial are required.

Select inputs. All inputs that might affect any of the outputs should be considered. Do not be afraid to include a large number of inputs. Up to 16 inputs can be studied in 32 trials using the designs in this book. In general, the number of trials required will be approximately double the number of inputs.* Inputs can include continuous variables like inside diameter and temperature as well as discrete variables such as machine, operator, and the presence or absence of an additive. To be included in a screening experiment, the input must be capable of being controlled, at least during the experiment. Each trial will specify where each input should be set. This excludes an input like room humidity if one has no means of controlling it. However, often inputs that are difficult or impossible to control in actual production conditions can be controlled for the purpose of the experiment. As an example, consider the outside diameter of a subassembly where the current process is not able to produce parts to the required tolerance. However, for the purpose of experimentation, the parts can be inspected and parts with the desired outside diameter selected. In a second ex-

---

*This is for what statisticians call resolution IV studies.

ample, one might wish to include both material temperature and room temperature as inputs. The objective is to determine whether preheating the material might be of benefit. Normally the material resides in the room and so is at room temperature. For the purpose of experimentation, a tent and space heater can be rented and used to preheat the material. Following the experiment a preheating chamber can be built if warranted by the results.

Select ranges for inputs. Screening experiments require that each input be restricted to just two levels. For continuous inputs like temperature and inside diameter, this requires selecting a high and low value. For discrete inputs like machine, operator, and the presence or absence of an additive, two levels must be selected. In the case of the presence or absence of an additive, there are only two levels. However, for machines and operators there can be more than two levels. In these cases, two of the machines or two of the operators must be selected for inclusion in the experiment. When selecting the two levels to be included, one should consider the ones most likely to be different, that is, the machines with the best and worst history or the most and least experienced operators. The same is true for the high and low levels of continuous inputs. The levels should be selected to magnify the effect. There will be more on this later. When sorting is performed to control an input, the exact levels can be determined later.

Determine trials. The number of trials is determined by the number of input variables as follows:

3 to 4 inputs	8 trials
5 to 8 inputs	16 trials
9 to 16 inputs	32 trials

The next three sections give the specific trials to run for 8-, 16-, and 32-trial experiments.

Screening experiments are most successful when designed by a team. A variety of opinions and knowledge should be considered. If the experiment is costly to run, it is worthwhile to have a statistician or another expert review the design. An expert has access to many more designs than can be presented here.

Screening experiments with eight trials

Table 12.4 provides the information required to determine where to set each input on each of the eight trials. If one has three inputs, the first three columns are used. If one has four inputs, the first four col-

TABLE 12.4   Eight-Trial Screening Experiment

Trial Number	Column						
	A	B	C	D	E	F	G
1	+	-	+	-	-	+	-
2	+	+	-	-	+	-	-
3	-	-	+	+	+	-	-
4	+	-	-	+	-	-	+
5	-	+	-	+	-	+	-
6	-	+	+	-	-	-	+
7	+	+	+	+	+	+	+
8	-	-	-	-	+	+	+
	1	2	3	4	1*2 3*4	1*3 2*4	2*3 1*4
Input Variables Corresponding to Column							

umns are used. The other columns and their labels will not be used until it is time to perform the analysis. The columns corresponding to the inputs contain pluses and minuses. A plus means to set the input to its high value. A minus means to set the input to its low value. In the case of a discrete input, one level should be arbitrarily assigned to the pluses and the other to the minuses. As an example consider an experiment consisting of the following three inputs:

Temperature (200 to 225°F)

Time (0.35 to 0.45 s)

Die type (design 1 versus design 2)

Temperature is assigned to column 1. A plus represents 225°F and a minus represents 200°F. Time is assigned to column 2. A plus represents 0.45 s and a minus represents 0.35 s. Die type is assigned to column 3. It is decided to let the plus represent design 1 and the minus represent design 2. The resulting design is given in Table 12.5.

Screening experiments with more than eight trials

For five to eight inputs use the 16-trial screening experiment given in Table 12.6. For 9 to 16 inputs, use the 32-trial screening experiment given in Table 12.7. In both cases, assign the inputs to the columns starting with the left-hand column.

The heat-seal case study in Chap. 2 contains eight inputs. The first eight columns of Table 12.6 were used to design the 16-setup study.

TABLE 12.5   Trials for Study with Three Inputs

Trial Number	Input Settings		
	Temperature	Time	Die Type
1	225 °F	0.35 sec	design 1
2	225 °F	0.45 sec	design 2
3	200 °F	0.35 sec	design 1
4	225 °F	0,35 sec	design 2
5	200 °F	0.45 sec	design 2
6	200 °F	0.45 sec	design 1
7	225 °F	0.45 sec	design 1
8	200 °F	0.35 sec	design 2

TABLE 12.6   Sixteen-Trial Screening Experiment

Trial Number	A	B	C	D	E	F	G	H	I	J	K	L	M	N	O
1	+	-	-	-	+	+	-	+	-	-	-	+	+	+	-
2	+	+	-	-	-	-	+	+	+	-	-	-	-	+	+
3	+	+	+	-	-	+	-	+	+	+	+	+	-	-	-
4	+	+	+	+	+	+	+	+	+	+	+	+	+	+	+
5	-	+	+	+	-	-	+	-	-	-	-	+	+	+	-
6	+	-	+	+	-	+	-	+	+	-	+	-	+	-	-
7	-	+	-	+	-	+	-	+	-	+	-	-	+	-	+
8	+	-	+	-	+	-	+	-	+	-	+	-	+	-	+
9	+	+	-	+	+	-	-	-	+	-	+	-	+	-	-
10	-	+	+	-	+	-	-	+	-	-	+	+	-	-	+
11	-	-	+	+	+	+	-	-	+	-	-	-	-	+	+
12	+	-	-	+	-	+	+	-	-	-	+	+	-	-	+
13	-	+	-	-	+	+	+	-	-	+	+	-	-	-	+
14	-	-	+	-	-	+	+	+	+	-	+	-	+	-	-
15	-	-	-	+	+	-	+	+	+	+	+	+	+	+	-
16	-	-	-	-	-	-	-	-	+	+	+	+	+	+	+

A	B	C	D	E	F	G	H	I	J	K	L	M	N	O
1	2	3	4	5				1*2	1*3	1*4	2*3	2*4	3*4	
					6			4*5	2*5		1*5		3*5	
						7		3*6	2*6	1*6		5*6	4*6	
							8	5*7	6*7	4*7	3*7	2*7	1*7	
								7*8	4*8	3*8	5*8	6*8	1*8	2*8

Input Variables Corresponding to Column

These correspond to trials 2 through 17. Two additional trials, trials 1 and 18, were also run for purposes described later.

The door-hinge case study in Chap. 2 contains 13 inputs. Therefore, the 32-trial screening experiment was used. The first 13 columns of Table 12.7 were used to generate the design presented in Chap. 2. In this case one additional trial, trial 33, has been added.

Analyzing screening experiments

Analyzing a screening experiment consists of calculating the effect of each parameter, group of interactions, and so on; sorting the effects into order of importance; and deciding which effects are significant. To

TABLE 12.7 Thirty-two-Trial Screening Experiment

Trial Number	Column																														
	A	B	C	D	E	F	G	H	I	J	K	L	M	N	O	P	Q	R	S	T	U	V	W	X	Y	Z	a	b	c	d	e

(The body of the table contains a 32-row matrix of + and − signs indicating the experimental design for trials 1 through 32 across columns A–e.)

Input Variables Corresponding to Column

calculate the effect of a parameter, take the average of the setups corresponding to the pluses and take the average of the setups corresponding to the minuses. Subtract the average of the minuses from the average of the pluses. The resulting value is the effect.

Take as an example the data from the heat-seal case study. The data for trials 2 through 17 are given in Table 12.8. Also given are the corresponding pluses and minuses used to create the design given in Table 2.6. To calculate the effect of the temperature of the hot bar (HB):

$$\text{Average}_+ = \frac{X_2 + X_3 + X_4 + X_5 + X_7 + X_9 + X_{10} + X_{13}}{8}$$

$$= \frac{25.1 + 27.4 + 11.3 + 15.7 + 11.8 + 11.3 + 28.9 + 31.7}{8}$$

$$= 20.40$$

$$\text{Average}_- = \frac{X_6 + X_8 + X_{11} + X_{12} + X_{14} + X_{15} + X_{16} + X_{17}}{8}$$

$$= \frac{24.3 + 11.8 + 16.9 + 20.6 + 12.2 + 18.6 + 15.9 + 10.5}{8}$$

$$= 16.35$$

$$\text{Effect}_{HB} = \text{average}_+ - \text{average}_- = 20.40 - 16.35 = 4.05$$

TABLE 12.8   Analysis for Heat-Seal Data

Trial Number	HB	CB	D	P	C	TH	MT	RT	Int	Int	Int	Int	Int	Int	Int	Average
2	+	-	-	-	+	+	-	+	-	-	-	+	+	+	-	25.1
3	+	+	-	-	-	-	+	+	-	-	-	+	-	+	+	27.4
4	+	+	+	-	-	+	-	-	+	+	-	+	-	-	-	11.3
5	+	+	+	+	+	+	+	+	+	+	+	+	+	+	+	15.7
6	-	+	+	+	-	-	+	-	-	-	+	+	+	+	-	24.3
7	+	-	+	+	-	+	-	+	-	+	+	-	-	+	-	11.8
8	-	+	-	+	-	+	-	+	-	+	-	+	-	-	+	11.8
9	+	-	+	-	+	-	+	-	-	+	-	-	+	-	+	11.3
10	+	+	-	+	+	-	-	-	+	-	+	-	+	-	-	28.9
11	-	+	+	-	+	-	-	+	-	-	+	+	+	-	+	16.9
12	-	-	+	+	+	+	-	+	-	+	-	-	+	+	+	20.6
13	+	-	-	+	-	+	+	-	-	-	+	+	-	-	+	31.7
14	-	+	-	-	+	+	+	-	-	+	+	-	+	-	-	12.2
15	-	-	+	-	-	+	+	+	+	-	+	-	+	-	-	18.6
16	-	-	-	+	+	-	+	+	+	+	-	+	-	-	-	15.9
17	-	-	-	-	-	-	-	-	+	+	+	+	+	+	+	10.5

1	2	3	4					1*2	1*3	1*4	2*3	2*4	3*4	
				5				4*5	2*5		1*5		3*5	
					6			3*6	2*6	1*6		5*6	4*6	
						7		5*7	6*7	4*7	3*7	2*7	1*7	
							8	7*8	4*8	3*8	5*8	6*8	1*8	2*8

Input Variables Corresponding to Column

The effect of 4.05 was reported in Table 2.7. Similarly, the effect of the other seven parameters can be calculated. The individual effects of the eight parameters are referred to as the *main effects*.

In addition, effects can be calculated for the interactions. In the type of screening experiment presented here, the interactions cannot be estimated individually. To do so would greatly increase the number of trials required. Instead, the interactions are grouped together. The combined effect of the interactions in a group can be estimated.

For the 16-trial screening experiment in Table 12.6, columns I through O correspond to the interaction groups. The labels at the bottom of the columns identify the interactions that belong to the group. For example, column I corresponds to the interaction between the parameters assigned to columns 1 and 2, plus the interaction between the parameters assigned to columns 4 and 5, and so forth.

The effects for the interaction groups are calculated the same as for the parameters: the average of the pluses minus the average of the minuses. One cannot distinguish between the interactions confounded within a group using the data collected. However, the existence of an interaction between two parameters is generally accompanied by the existence of both of the parameter's main effects. This fact allows one to rank the interactions as most to least likely. Sometimes the confounding of interactions requires that additional data be collected in order to distinguish between the interactions.

The main effects only estimate the linear effects of the parameters.

These are based on only two points, the high and the low values. Frequently these parameters also have nonlinear effects. While the screening experiment cannot estimate these nonlinear effects, it is possible to determine whether any such nonlinear effects exist. Testing for the presence of nonlinear effects requires adding the center point of the study region to the trial run. It is preferable to run it more than once. In the heat-seal case study, trials 1 and 18 are both run at this center point. The combined effect of all nonlinear terms is calculated as follows:

$$\text{Effect}_{nl} = \text{average design points} - \text{average center points}$$

$$= \frac{25.1 + 27.4 + 11.3 + \dots + 10.5}{16} - \frac{28.5 + 28.2}{2} = -9.98$$

Table 12.9 shows all the effects for the heat-seal case study. The effects have been sorted by the magnitude of the effect. The terms with larger effects are more important.

The estimated effects consist of the true effect of the parameter plus some noise due to variation. If the true effect is large compared to the noise, the estimated effect is a good predictor of the true effect. Repeating the study will get close to the same result. If, however, the true effect is small compared to the noise or even nonexistent, the estimated effect is primarily noise. Repeating the study will result in a different value. How does one determine when the effect is real or just noise? A variety of approaches exist, each with its associated weakness. One will be presented here based on half-normal probability plots.

TABLE 12.9 Effects Table

Ranking	Process Parameters	Effect
1	Int - HB*D, CB*TH, C*MT, P*RT	-11.62
2	nl - Combined Nonlinear Effects	-9.98
3	D - Dwell Time	-4.12
4	HB - Temperature - Hot Bar	4.05
5	P - Pressure	3.42
6	MT - Material Temperature	2.52
7	Int - CB*D, HB*TH, P*MT, C*RT	1.10
8	RT - Room Temperature	-0.95
9	Int - HB*CB, P*C, D*TH, MT*RT	0.48
10	CB - Temperature - Cold Bar	0.38
11	Int - D*C, P*TH, HB*MT, CB*RT	-0.28
12	Int - CB*P, HB*C, D*MT,TH*RT	-0.20
13	Int - HB*P, CB*C, TH*MT, D*RT	-0.17
14	Int - D*P, C*TH, CB*MT, HB*RT	0.15
15	C - Cooling Air Pressure	-0.10
16	TH - Material Thickness	0.00

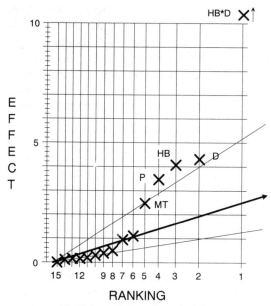

RANKING

Figure 12.6   Half-normal paper for 16-trial screening experiment.

Figure 12.6 shows a half-normal probability plot of the effects for the heat-seal study. The combined effect of the nonlinear terms cannot be included in a half-normal probability plot. The other 15 effects are plotted, starting with the smallest, above the marked locations. The upper limit for the left-hand axis should be only slightly larger than the largest observed effect.

In Fig. 12.6 a line established using the smaller effects has been drawn in. This line should start at the point marked with the small solid circle (more easily seen in Fig. 12.9). Points significantly *above* this line represent parameters with true effects greater than the noise. Lines with twice and half times the slope of this line have also been drawn in. TH*D, TH, D, P, and MT fall above these lines. In addition, the combined nonlinear effect is large compared to these other effects. This resulted in only these six effects being reported as significant in Table 2.7.

If no effects exist, then the points on the plot should ideally fall along a straight line. Four plots without any significant effects are shown in Fig. 12.7. While the ideal is a line, there is variation around this line. The points will become more variable on the right side of the plot, exactly where we have the most interest. Example 1 is as we would like the plots to appear. It clearly indicates no significant ef-

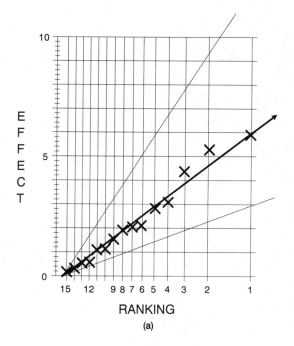

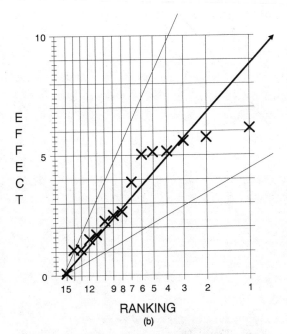

Figure 12.7 (a) Half-normal plot with no effect—Example 1; (b) half-normal plot with no effect—Example 2.

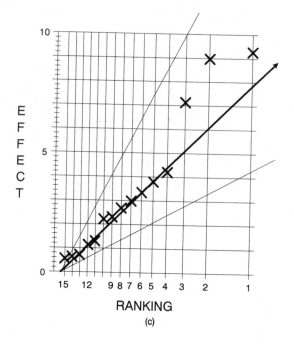

RANKING

(c)

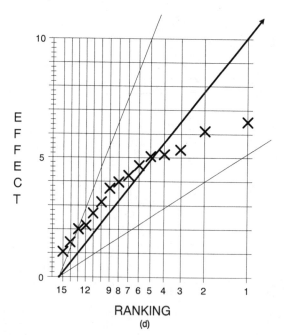

RANKING

(d)

Figure 12.7 (*Continued*) (*c*) Half-normal plot with no effect—Example 3; (*d*) half-normal plot with no effect—Example 4.

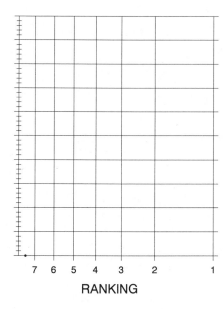

7   6   5   4   3   2   1

RANKING

Figure 12.8 Example of half-normal paper for eight-trial screening experiment.

fects. On Examples 2 and 4, the extreme (right side) effects are below the line signifying these effects are smaller than expected. This causes no problems as we are only looking for effects *above* the line. Example 3, however, is easily misinterpreted and demonstrates the importance of drawing the lines with twice and half times the slope of the line through the smaller effects. These lines indicate that the points in Fig. 12.6 are much further off the line than the points in Example 3. Blank forms for plotting half-normal plots are given in Figs. 12.8 through 12.10. Different forms are required depending on whether 8, 16, or 32 trials were run.

One group of interactions tested significant containing HB*D, CB*TH, C*MT, and P*RT. On what basis was only the HB*D interaction reported in Table 2.7? Interactions tend to occur between main effects that are significant. Also, the larger the main effect, the more likely it is to interact. The four interactions along with the ranks of their main effects are shown in Table 12.10. The HB*D is clearly the most likely. Physics and experience also indicate that temperature and time tend to interact. The conclusion is therefore fairly safe.

The possibility does, however, exist that the wrong interaction was selected or that a second interaction exists in the group. Being certain requires additional data to be collected in order to obtain separate estimates of these four interactions. The process for doing this is called *augmentation* and is described in Sec. 12.6. Augmentation is also required in order to obtain separate estimates of the nonlinear effects.

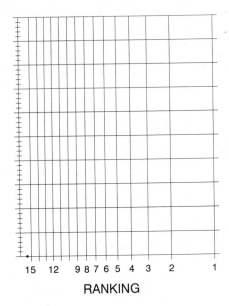

Figure 12.9 Example of half-normal paper for 16-trial screening experiment.

RANKING

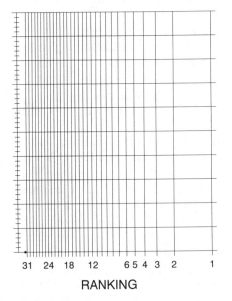

Figure 12.10 Example of half-normal paper for 32-trial screening experiment.

RANKING

TABLE 12.10 Likelihood of Interactions

INTERACTIONS	RANKS OF MAIN EFFECTS	AVERAGE RANK
HB * D	3, 4	3.5
P * RT	5, 8	6.5
C * MT	6, 15	10.5
CB * TH	10, 16	13.0

How screening experiments work

Screening experiments are effective because

- They provide multiple observations at the high and low levels of each input to provide better estimates of the effects of the inputs and to allow the effect to be distinguished from the noise.
- They vary the inputs over wide ranges to magnify the effect of the inputs.
- They search for interactions so key inputs are not missed as a result.
- They group the interactions, allowing models to be developed based on the smallest number of trials possible.
- They provide protection against inadvertent changes to inputs not included in the study.

When varying inputs to see if they affect the output, one must contend with unwanted variation in the results. When identifying key design parameters, two prototypes made to identical specifications will not function identically. The variation between two supposedly identical prototypes can hide the effect due to changing a design parameter. When studying process parameters, process variation can hide the effect of adjusting a process parameter. Minimizing the effect of this unwanted variation requires magnifying effects and multiple observations. Look at Fig. 12.11. What does it tell you? The fact is it tells you almost nothing. The difference between the two points could have resulted from either high variation with no effect or low variation with a large effect as shown in Fig. 12.12. Based on the figure above, it cannot be determined whether temperature has an effect or not.

The approach of varying one variable at a time relies heavily on

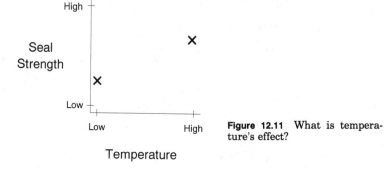

Figure 12.11 What is temperature's effect?

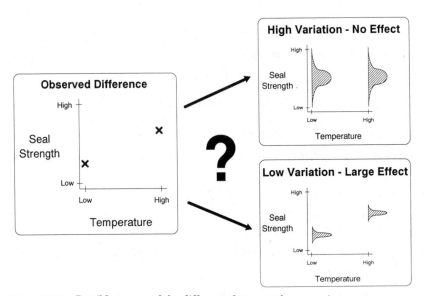

Figure 12.12 Possible causes of the difference between the two points.

these one-versus-one comparisons. Errors are frequently made as a result of the inability to separate effect from noise. Screening experiments have multiple observations at the high and low settings of each parameter. The screening experiments therefore use 4-versus-4 (8 trials), 8-versus-8 (16 trials), and 16-versus-16 (32 trials) comparisons as in Fig. 12.13. Multiple observations allow the effect to be distinguished from the noise. They also offer a second advantage. The more points that are gathered, the more accurate the estimate of the effect will be. Multiple observations allow us to better peer through the noise to see the effects of the key inputs.

The second approach used to help overcome variation is *bold exper-*

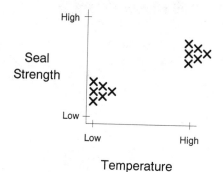

Figure 12.13 With multiple observations temperature's effect is evident.

imentation. As shown in Fig. 12.14, bold experimentation magnifies the effects of the parameters so they are easier to detect. Through bold experimentation, effects can be detected which are never seen as part of everyday operations.

Another important feature of screening experiments is the grouping of interactions together. This allows interactions to be detected without dramatically increasing the number of trials required. The approach of varying one variable at a time cannot detect interactions. The efficient screening of interactions will allow models to be developed based on the minimum number of trials possible. The construction of these models is covered in Sec. 12.6.

One final important feature of screening experiments is that they provide protection against shifting of the process over time adversely

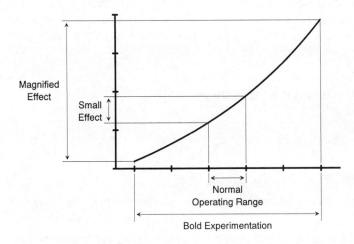

Figure 12.14   Bold experimentation magnifies effects.

TABLE 12.11   Screening Experiments versus Varying One Variable at a Time

Comparison	Screening Experiment	Vary One Variable At a Time
Average Number of Trials	21	45
Percent of Time One of 3 Most Important Variables is Missed	0%	7%
Percent of Time a Non-Key Variable is Classified as Key	11%	83%
Percentage Identifying Pressure as Adjustment Parameter	100%	23%

affecting the results. The trials are such that the estimates of the parameters remain valid even in the presence of shifting. Sorting the trials into a different order will result in this protection being lost. The approach of varying one variable at a time is susceptible to making errors in the presence of shifting.

A simulation of the heat-seal process described in the heat-seal case study has been used in a course on screening experiments for the last 8 years. The students are allowed to play with the process using the approach of varying one variable at a time. Later they run a screening experiment on it. The results of their performance using the two approaches are summarized in Table 12.11. The difference is dramatic. The screening experiment requires half the effort to achieve twice the results. This experience truly convinces the students of the superiority of screening experiments.

12.5   Understanding the Input/Output Relationship

In Sec. 12.1, a three-step process was presented for optimizing the average:

1. Identify the key input variables.
2. Understand the relationship between the key inputs and the outputs.
3. Use this understanding to select targets for the key inputs to optimize the average.

Scatter diagrams and screening experiments provide the tools necessary for accomplishing the first step: identifying the key inputs. The next step is to understand the relationship between the key inputs and the outputs. This understanding should be expressed in the form of an equation giving the effect the inputs have on the output. Polynomial equations are generally used. A polynomial equation is of the form:

$$Y = c_{000} + c_{100}\,X_1 + c_{010}\,X_2 + c_{001}\,X_3 + c_{200}\,X_1^2 + c_{020}\,X_2^2 + c_{002}\,X_3^2$$
$$+ c_{110}\,X_1 X_2 + c_{101}\,X_1 X_3 + c_{011}\,X_2 X_3$$

where Y is the output, X represents the inputs, and c is a constant to be determined based on the data.

Terms like $c_{100}\,X_1$ are called linear terms. Screening experiments concentrate on these terms. *The $c_{200}\,X_1^2$ terms are called quadratic terms. Adding center points to a screening experiment allows one to determine whether any quadratic terms exist. Two-way interactions are represented by terms like $c_{110}\,X_1 X_2$.* Other terms can be added if required including cubic terms, $c_{300}\,X_1^3$, and three-way interaction terms, $c_{111}\,X_1 X_2 X_3$.

Polynomial equations are used because they are extremely flexible, being able to take on a wide variety of shapes. Over the region of study they can be made to approximate the real equation as close as one desires. Generally, the quadratic polynomial above, consisting of linear, quadratic, and two-way interactions, is sufficient. Screening experiments do a good job of preparing to obtain such an equation. They determine the linear terms, determine whether one needs to worry about quadratic terms, and narrow down the list of possible interactions to just a handful. Finishing up the job requires that additional data be collected and used in order to estimate the constants. The tool for doing this is a response surface study. This is the topic of Sec. 12.6.

While the mathematical form of the equation is necessary, it is also difficult to fully understand on its own. Understanding the relationship between the key inputs and outputs is greatly enhanced by plotting the equation. Three types of plots that are particularly useful are shown in Fig. 12.15. The first of these plots, the *line plot*, can be used for inputs that do not interact. For inputs that interact, the *interaction* and *contour plots* should be used instead.

12.6   Response Surface Studies

Response surface studies provide an equation representing the effect of the key inputs on the output. Typically a quadratic polynomial is fit

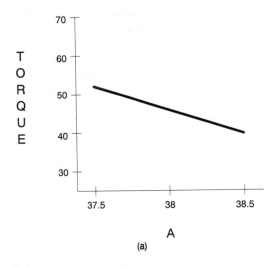

A

(a)

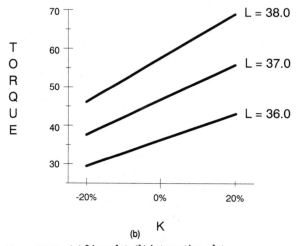

K

(b)

Figure 12.15 (*a*) Line plot; (*b*) interaction plot.

to the data. However, the form of the equation can be varied to match the situation. The design and analysis of response surface studies are beyond the scope of this book. However, a few comments are in order.

While response surface studies can be run from scratch, they are most efficient when run in conjunction with the type of screening experiments covered in Sec. 12.4. Take a simple example. Suppose there are eight candidate input variables. Unknown to the experimenter, five of these inputs are key, two have quadratic effects, and two interactions exist. One has three possible courses of action:

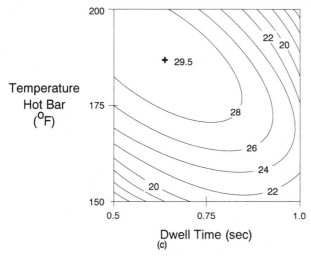

Figure 12.15 (*Continued*) (*c*) Contour plot of seal strength.

1. *Run a response surface on all eight inputs.* This requires a minimum of 55 trials.

2. *Select five inputs and run a response surface.* This reduces the number of trials to 31. However, to be successful, it requires correctly guessing the five key inputs.

3. *Run a screening experiment and augment to get a response surface.* The screening experiment requires 18 trials (including two center points). Augmenting to get the response surface requires an additional 12 setups. This gets to the answer in the fewest number of trials without running the risk of having to guess the correct key inputs.

Two examples of the augmentation process have been provided in the heat-seal case study and the hinge case study. What makes the screening experiment so efficient is the grouping of the interactions. Augmentation requires software to help design and analyze the response surface study. Several packages are available commercially that are capable of augmentation. These all use a method of designing the response surface called *D-optimal designs*.

The use of D-optimal designs is appropriate when variation is present as is the case when actual data are collected. The heat-seal case study is such an example. D-optimal designs is not the most efficient method of augmentation when the data are coming from a simulation where the same answer is always obtained for a specific combination of the inputs. The hinge case study is an example of this situation. In this case specific setups were selected to estimate individual constants in the equation.

12.7 Targeting the Key Input Variables

Once the equation and plots are obtained, finding the targets for the inputs that optimize the average is straightforward. The plots provide the simplest method. Using the plots, the minimum and maximum can be easily identified. When centering on a target, the plots allow one to explore the full range of combinations of the inputs that achieve the desired target.

Setting the key input variables to solely optimize the average may adversely affect the variation as well as other things such as costs and production volume. Variation may be affected because changing the setting of a VAP may increase or decrease the transmitted variation. Therefore, the strategy for optimizing the average must be combined with the strategy for reducing variation to obtain the overall best targets.

Using the strategy of studying the inputs' effects to reduce variation is the topic of Chaps. 13 and 14.

12.8 Summary

Studying the inputs' effects

Optimizing the average requires identifying the key inputs, understanding the effect of the key inputs on the output, and using this understanding to set targets for the inputs that optimize the average. There are two approaches to reducing variation: direct observation and transmission of variation.

Identifying key input variables

Key input variables can be identified through existing knowledge, passive observation (search for differences and scatter diagrams), and active experimentation (screening experiments and response surface studies).

Scatter diagrams

Scatter diagrams look for relationships between the inputs and the outputs. As such, they help identify key input variables. If a strong correlation exists under normal production conditions, the input is a VIP.

Screening experiments

Screening experiments allow a large number of inputs to be purposely varied in order to identify the key input variables. A screening experiment on a product design requires a certain number of prototypes be made with purposeful changes in the design parameters. A screening experiment on a production process requires running a series of setups corresponding to different combinations of the process parameters. For each setup, the process is run until it stabilizes before data are collected.

The critical steps in designing a screening experiment are selection of outputs, measurement methods, inputs, and input ranges. Analyzing a screening experiment requires calculating the effect of each parameter, sorting the effects into order of importance, and deciding which effects are significant.

Screening experiments are far superior to the approach of varying one variable at a time. They also allow models to be developed based upon the smallest number of trials possible. Their effectiveness is the result of multiple observations, bold experimentation, looking for interactions, grouping the interactions, and protection against inadvertent changes.

Understanding the input/output relationship

The relationship between the inputs and output should be expressed in the form of an equation. Typically a quadratic polynomial is adequate. To aid in understanding the equation, one can use line plots, interaction plots, and contour plots.

Response surface studies

Response surface studies provide an equation representing the effect of the key inputs on the output. The strategy of running a screening experiment and then augmenting to get a response surface is extremely efficient. It fits the appropriate model in the fewest number of trials without running the risk of incorrectly guessing the key inputs.

Targeting the key input variables

The plots can be used to target the inputs in order to minimize the variation. Targeting the inputs to optimize the average may adversely affect the variation. Therefore optimizing the average should be combined with the strategy for reducing variation.

13

Variation Transmission Analysis

13.1 Two Approaches to Identifying VIPs

Key to reducing variation is identifying the VAPs and VIPs. There are two different approaches to identifying the VAPs and VIPs:

1. *Direct observation.* The effect that changes of the inputs have on the variation of the output is observed directly.

2. *Variation transmission analysis.* The variation transmitted by the inputs to the output can be calculated based on the relationship between the inputs and the outputs and on estimates of the variations of the individual inputs.

Take a simple example. Figure 13.1 shows a fictional relationship between the input X and the output Y. The equation describing this relationship is $Y = e^X$. Further assume that the variation of X follows the normal curve with a standard deviation of $\sigma_X = 0.1$. As a result of the nonlinear relationship between X and Y, the variation of Y depends on where X is targeted. See Fig. 13.2. Figure 13.3 shows the standard deviation of Y as a function of where X is targeted. The standard deviation of Y is 0.274 when X is targeted at 1 and 0.744 when X is targeted at 2.

If all this information about X and Y were unknown, how might one determine whether X affects the variation of Y? The obvious approach is to select several values of X, adjust X to these values, and measure the resulting variation. Figure 13.4 shows the results of a study where X was set to 1, 1.5, and 2 with ten samples taken at each of these three settings. To estimate the effect of X on the variation of Y, the standard

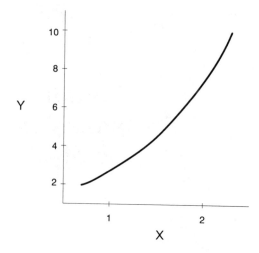

Figure 13.1 The effect of X on Y.

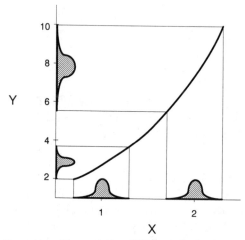

Figure 13.2 The variation of Y depends on where X is targeted.

deviation of Y was calculated for each of these three values of X. These three standard deviations are plotted in Fig. 13.5 along with the best-fit curve. The effect of X on the standard deviation of Y is clearly evident.

An alternate approach is to fit a curve to the points in Fig. 13.4. The equation for this curve is

$$Y = 4.078 - 4.245\,X + 2.902\,X^2$$

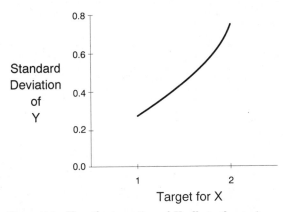

Figure 13.3 How the targeting of X affects the variation of Y.

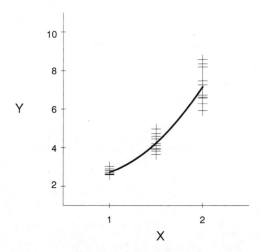

Figure 13.4 Multi-Vari plot of the data.

Then based on this curve, the standard deviation of Y can be calculated as a function of t_X, the target of X, and σ_X, the standard deviation of X:

$$\sigma_Y = \sqrt{(-4.245 + 5.804\, t_X)^2\, \sigma_X^2 + 16.843\, \sigma_X^4}$$

Plugging $\sigma_X = 0.1$ into this equation gives the curve shown in Fig. 13.6. The true curve is also given for comparison. Once again the effect of X on the standard deviation of Y is clearly evident.

Both methods find VAPs and VIPs. Each has its associated advantages and disadvantages. A comparison of the two approaches will be presented in the next chapter. But first, methods for applying each ap-

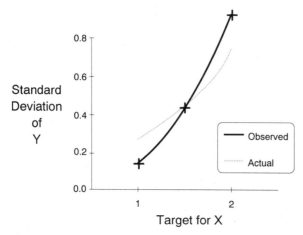

Figure 13.5   Direct observation of X's effect on the variation of Y.

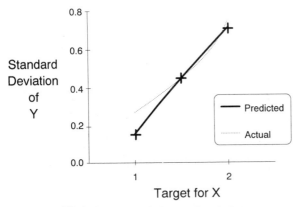

Figure 13.6   Variation transmission analysis' prediction of X's effect on the variation of Y.

proach will be presented. The rest of this chapter is devoted to the transmission of variation approach. Chapter 14 is devoted to the direct-observation approach.

13.2   Variation of a Polynomial

Screening experiments augmented into response surfaces provide equations relating the inputs to the output. Typically these equations take the form of quadratic polynomials, that is, of the form:

$$Y = c_{000} + c_{100}X_1 + c_{010}X_2 + c_{001}X_3 + c_{200}X_1^2 + c_{020}X_2^2 + c_{002}X_3^2$$
$$+ c_{110}X_1X_2 + c_{101}X_1X_3 + c_{011}X_2X_3$$

In this case, the squared standard deviation of Y is

$$\sigma_Y^2 = c_{100}^2\,\sigma_1^2 + c_{010}^2\,\sigma_2^2 + c_{001}^2\,\sigma_3^2 + c_{200}^2(4\,t_1^2\,\sigma_1^2 + 2\,\sigma_1^4) + c_{020}^2$$
$$(4\,t_2^2\,\sigma_2^2 + 2\,\sigma_2^4) + c_{002}^2\,(4\,t_3^2\,\sigma_3^2 + 2\,\sigma_3^4) + c_{110}^2\,(t_1^2\,\sigma_2^2 + t_2^2\,\sigma_1^2 + \sigma_1^2\,\sigma_2^2)$$
$$+ c_{101}^2\,(t_1^2\,\sigma_3^2 + t_3^2\,\sigma_1^2 + \sigma_1^2\,\sigma_3^2) + c_{011}^2\,(t_2^2\,\sigma_3^2 + t_3^2\,\sigma_2^2 + \sigma_2^2\,\sigma_3^2)$$
$$+ 2\,c_{100}\,c_{200}\,(2\,t_1\,\sigma_1^2) + 2\,c_{100}\,c_{110}\,(t_2\,\sigma_1^2) + 2\,c_{100}\,c_{101}\,(t_3\,\sigma_1^2)$$
$$+ 2\,c_{010}\,c_{020}\,(2\,t_2\,\sigma_2^2) + 2\,c_{010}\,c_{110}\,(t_1\,\sigma_2^2) + 2\,c_{010}\,c_{011}\,(t_3\,\sigma_2^2)$$
$$+ 2\,c_{001}\,c_{002}\,(2\,t_3\,\sigma_3^2) + 2\,c_{001}\,c_{101}\,(t_1\,\sigma_3^2) + 2\,c_{001}\,c_{011}\,(t_2\,\sigma_3^2)$$
$$+ 2\,c_{200}\,c_{110}\,(2\,t_1\,t_2\,\sigma_1^2) + 2\,c_{200}\,c_{101}\,(2\,t_1\,t_3\,\sigma_1^2) + 2\,c_{020}\,c_{110}\,(2\,t_1\,t_2\,\sigma_2^2)$$
$$+ 2\,c_{020}\,c_{011}\,(2\,t_2\,t_3\,\sigma_2^2) + 2\,c_{002}\,c_{101}\,(2\,t_1\,t_3\,\sigma_3^2) + 2\,c_{002}\,c_{011}\,(2\,t_2\,t_3\,\sigma_3^2)$$
$$+ 2\,c_{110}\,c_{101}\,(t_2\,t_3\,\sigma_1^2) + 2\,c_{110}\,c_{011}\,(t_1\,t_3\,\sigma_2^2) + 2\,c_{101}\,c_{011}\,(t_1\,t_2\,\sigma_3^2)$$

where t_1, t_2, and t_3 are the input targets and σ_1, σ_2, and σ_3 are the input standard deviations. To get the standard deviation of Y, do not forget to take the square root. This equation is quite lengthy. Not something one would want to use with a calculator. However, these types of equations for the variation can be easily incorporated into programs or entered into mathematics packages for evaluation and plotting.

The above equation is for three inputs only. A procedure will be presented for determining the standard deviation of Y for any number of inputs. Assume Y can be expressed in the form below:

$$Y = c_0 + c_1 f_1(X_1,\ldots,X_n) + c_2 f_2(X_1,\ldots,X_n) + \ldots + c_m f_m(X_1,\ldots,X_n)$$

where the c_is are constants, and the $f_i(\ )$s are functions of the X_is. In the quadratic polynomial the $f_i(\ )$s are restricted to the following forms:

$$f(X_1, X_2,\ldots,X_n) = X_i$$
$$f(X_1, X_2,\ldots,X_n) = X_i^2$$
$$f(X_1, X_2,\ldots,X_n) = X_i X_j \qquad i \neq j$$

Then the squared standard deviation of Y is:

$$\sigma_Y^2 = c_1^2\,\text{VAR}[f_1(X_1, X_2,\ldots,X_n)] + c_2^2\,\text{VAR}[f_2(X_1, X_2,\ldots,X_n)] + \ldots$$
$$+ c_m^2\,\text{VAR}[f_m(X_1, X_2,\ldots,X_n)] + 2\,c_1\,c_2\,\text{COV}[f_1(X_1, X_2,\ldots,X_n),$$
$$f_2(X_1, X_2,\ldots,X_n)] + 2\,c_1\,c_3\,\text{COV}[f_1(X_1, X_2,\ldots,X_n), f_3(X_1, X_2,\ldots,X_n)]$$
$$+ \ldots + 2\,c_{m-1}\,c_m\,\text{COV}[f_{m-1}(X_1, X_2,\ldots,X_n), f_m(X_1, X_2,\ldots,X_n)]$$

This expression consists of two types of terms: variance terms, VAR[ ], and covariance terms, COV[ ]. There is one variance term for each $f_i(\ )$, that is, m variance terms in all. There is one covariance term for each pair of $f_i(\ )$, $f_j(\ )$, $i < j$, that is, $m(m - 1)/2$ covariance terms in all.

The next step is to plug expressions for VAR[$f_i(\ )$] and COV[$f_i(\ )$, $f_j(\ )$] into the equation above. Some required expressions are

$$\text{VAR}[X_i] = \sigma_i^2$$

$$\text{VAR}[X_i^2] = 4\,t_i^2\,\sigma_i^2 + 2\,\sigma_i^4$$

$$\text{VAR}[X_i\,X_j] = t_i^2\,\sigma_j^2 + t_j^2\,\sigma_i^2 + \sigma_i^2\,\sigma_j^2$$

$$\text{COV}[X_i, X_i^2] = 2\,t_i\,\sigma_i^2$$

$$\text{COV}[X_i, X_i\,X_j] = t_j\,\sigma_i^2$$

$$\text{COV}[X_i^2, X_i\,X_j] = 2\,t_i\,t_j\,\sigma_i^2$$

$$\text{COV}[X_i\,X_j, X_i\,X_k] = t_j\,t_k\,\sigma_i^2$$

In the covariance expression, the order of the two terms does not matter, that is,

$$\text{COV}[f_i(\ ), f_j(\ )] = \text{COV}[f_j(\ ), f_i(\ )]$$

In addition:

$$\text{COV}[f_i(\ ), f_j(\ )] = 0$$

if $f_i(\ )$ and $f_j(\ )$ have no X_is in common. This implies,

$$\text{COV}[X_1, X_2] = 0$$

$$\text{COV}[X_1, X_2^2] = 0$$

$$\text{COV}[X_1\,X_2, X_3\,X_4] = 0$$

$$\text{COV}[X_1^2, X_2\,X_3] = 0$$

among other things.

As an example of the procedure for determining the standard deviation of the output Y, assume:

$$Y = 2 + 10\,X_1 + 3\,X_2^2 + 5\,X_1\,X_2$$

There are two inputs ($n = 2$) and three nonconstant terms ($m = 3$). Y can be written in the required form as follows:

$$c_0 = 2$$

$$c_1 = 10 \qquad f_1(X_1, X_2) = X_1$$

$$c_2 = 3 \qquad f_2(X_1, X_2) = X_2^2$$

$$c_3 = 5 \qquad f_3(X_1, X_2) = X_1 X_2$$

The squared standard deviation of Y can then be written as:

$$\sigma_Y^2 = 10^2 \, \text{VAR}[X_1] + 3^2 \, \text{VAR}[X_2^2] + 5^2 \, \text{VAR}[X_1 X_2]$$
$$+ 2 \, (10) \, (3) \, \text{COV}[X_1, X_2^2] + 2 \, (10) \, (5) \, \text{COV}[X_1, X_1 X_2]$$
$$+ 2 \, (3) \, (5) \, \text{COV}[X_2^2, X_1 X_2]$$

The required variance and covariance expressions are

$$\text{VAR}[X_1] = \sigma_1^2$$

$$\text{VAR}[X_2^2] = 4 \, t_2^2 \, \sigma_2^2 + 2 \, \sigma_2^4$$

$$\text{VAR}[X_1 X_2] = t_1^2 \, \sigma_2^2 + t_2^2 \, \sigma_1^2 + \sigma_1^2 \, \sigma_2^2$$

$$\text{COV}[X_1, X_2^2] = 0$$

$$\text{COV}[X_1, X_1 X_2] = t_2 \, \sigma_1^2$$

$$\text{COV}[X_2^2, X_1 X_2] = 2 \, t_1 \, t_2 \, \sigma_2^2$$

Plugging these into the previous expression gives

$$\sigma_Y = \sqrt{\begin{array}{l} 100 \, \sigma_1^2 + 9 \, (4 \, t_2^2 \, \sigma_2^2 + 2 \, \sigma_2^4) + 25 \, (t_1^2 \, \sigma_2^2 + t_2^2 \, \sigma_1^2 + \sigma_1^2 \, \sigma_2^2) \\ + 100 \, (t_2 \, \sigma_1^2) + 30 \, (2 \, t_1 \, t_2 \, \sigma_2^2) \end{array}}$$

In the hinge case study, a screening experiment was augmented into a response surface study to produce the following equation:

$$\text{Torque} = 97.7 - 14.51 \, A - 12.95 \, B - 3.855 \, C + 3.505 \, D + 2.467 \, E$$
$$+ 0.257 \, F - 11.35 \, \text{UC} + 20.56 \, H - 3.42 \, K + 10.54 \, L + 0.105 \, K L$$
$$- 0.0475 \, M + 0.2378 \, P + 75.3 \, f$$

See if you can derive the equation given for the squared standard deviation of torque:

$$\sigma_{\text{torque}}^2 = 210.5 \, \sigma_A^2 + 167.7 \, \sigma_B^2 + 14.86 \, \sigma_C^2 + 12.29 \, \sigma_D^2 + 6.086 \, \sigma_E^2$$
$$+ 0.06631 \, \sigma_F^2 + 128.8 \, \sigma_{\text{UC}}^2 + 422.7 \, \sigma_H^2 + 11.70 \, \sigma_K^2 + 111.1 \, \sigma_L^2$$

$$+ 0.002256 \, \sigma_M^2 + 0.05655 \, \sigma_P^2 + 5670 \, \sigma_f^2 + 2.213 \, \sigma_L^2 t_K - 0.7182 \, \sigma_K^2 t_L$$
$$+ 0.01102 \, (\sigma_K^2 \, \sigma_L^2 + \sigma_L^2 \, t_K^2 + \sigma_K^2 \, t_L^2)$$

As a more difficult exercise, see if you can derive the expression given at the beginning of this section for the standard deviation of a quadratic polynomial with three inputs.

13.3 Approximating the Variation

The approach in the previous section works only for polynomials no more complex than a quadratic. An alternate approach is given here that works for any equation that is *differentiable* (a calculus term). The results, while approximate, are fairly accurate. This approach requires the use of differentiation from calculus. Those not familiar with calculus may skip to the next section.

Suppose Y is a function of $X_1, X_2, \ldots, X_n$. Let this function be written:

$$Y = g(X_1, X_2, \ldots, X_n)$$

The approximation assumes that g is twice differentiable. Let the partial derivatives be denoted:

$g_1(X_1, X_2, \ldots, X_n)$ = first partial with respect to X_1

$g_2(X_1, X_2, \ldots, X_n)$ = first partial with respect to X_2

$\ldots$

$g_n(X_1, X_2, \ldots, X_n)$ = first partial with respect to X_n

$g_{1,1}(X_1, X_2, \ldots, X_n)$ = second partial with respect to X_1

$g_{2,2}(X_1, X_2, \ldots, X_n)$ = second partial with respect to X_2

$\ldots$

$g_{n,n}(X_1, X_2, \ldots, X_n)$ = second partial with respect to X_n

$g_{1,2}(X_1, X_2, \ldots, X_n)$ = second partial with respect to X_1 and X_2

$g_{1,3}(X_1, X_2, \ldots, X_n)$ = second partial with respect to X_1 and X_3

$\ldots$

$g_{n-1,n}(X_1, X_2, \ldots, X_n)$ = second partial with respect to X_{n-1} and X_n

The squared standard deviation of Y is approximately equal to

$$\sigma_Y^2 = g_1(t_1, t_2, \ldots, t_n)^2 \, \sigma_1^2 + g_2(t_1, t_2, \ldots, t_n)^2 \, \sigma_2^2 + \ldots + g_n(t_1, t_2, \ldots, t_n)^2 \, \sigma_n^2$$
$$+ \tfrac{1}{2} \, g_{1,1}(t_1, t_2, \ldots, t_n)^2 \, \sigma_1^4 + \tfrac{1}{2} \, g_{2,2}(t_1, t_2, \ldots, t_n)^2 \, \sigma_2^4$$

$$+ \ldots + \tfrac{1}{2}\, g_{n,n}(t_1, t_2, \ldots, t_n)^2\, \sigma_n^4 + g_{1,2}(t_1, t_2, \ldots, t_n)^2\, \sigma_1^2\, \sigma_2^2$$

$$+ g_{1,3}(t_1, t_2, \ldots, t_n)^2\, \sigma_1^2\, \sigma_3^2 + \ldots + g_{n-1,n}(t_1, t_2, \ldots, t_n)^2\, \sigma_{n-1}^2\, \sigma_n^2$$

This approximation was obtained by taking the second-order Taylor series expansion at $(t_1, t_2, \ldots, t_n)$, rewriting it in terms of $Z_i = X_i - t_i$, and then applying the procedure given in the previous section for determining the standard deviation of a quadratic polynomial.*

As an example, let:

$$Y = 5\, X_1 e^{(-X_2)} = g(X_1, X_2)$$

The partial derivatives are as follows:

$$g_1(X_1, X_2) = 5\, e^{(-X_2)}$$

$$g_2(X_1, X_2) = -5\, X_1\, e^{(-X_2)}$$

$$g_{1,1}(X_1, X_2) = 0$$

$$g_{2,2}(X_1, X_2) = 5\, X_1\, e^{(-X_2)}$$

$$g_{1,2}(X_1, X_2) = -5\, e^{(-X_2)}$$

Plugging these into the formula for σ_Y^2 gives

$$\sigma_Y^2 = 25\, e^{2(-t_2)}\, \sigma_1^2 + 25\, t_1^2\, e^{2(-t_2)}\, \sigma_2^2 + 12.5\, t_1^2\, e^{2(-t_2)}\, \sigma_2^4 + 25\, e^{2(-t_2)}\, \sigma_1^2\, \sigma_2^2$$

As a second example, let us apply this approximation to the first example given in the previous section. There,

$$Y = 2 + 10\, X_1 + 3\, X_2^2 + 5\, X_1 X_2 = g(X_1, X_2)$$

The partial derivatives are

$$g_1(X_1, X_2) = 10 + 5\, X_2$$

$$g_2(X_1, X_2) = 6\, X_2 + 5\, X_1$$

$$g_{1,1}(X_1, X_2) = 0$$

$$g_{2,2}(X_1, X_2) = 6$$

$$g_{1,2}(X_1, X_2) = 5$$

Plugging these into the formula for σ_Y^2 gives

$$\sigma_Y^2 = (10 + 5\, t_2)^2\, \sigma_1^2 + (6\, t_2 + 5\, t_1)^2\, \sigma_2^2 + 18\, \sigma_2^4 + 25\, \sigma_1^2\, \sigma_2^2$$

---

*This is for the curious and is not necessary for learning the methods.

This expression is identical to the one obtained in the previous section. The approximation given for σ_Y^2 is exact for quadratic polynomials. For more complex equations, it retains a high degree of accuracy.

Deriving the formula for the output's variation is straightforward, but tedious. However, once the equation has been derived, there are several important analyses that can be performed. The first of which is parameter design.

13.4   Parameter Design

Recall that during parameter design the targets for the inputs are set. These targets must be chosen to optimize the average, reduce variation, and reduce costs. Frequently tradeoffs must be made. The variation transmission analysis approach to parameter design requires two things: (1) an equation describing the relationship between the inputs and the outputs, and (2) information on the amount that each input varies.

From the equation, a formula for the standard deviation of the output is derived. Either of the two approaches given previously can be used. This equation expresses the standard deviation of the output σ_Y, as a function of the input's targets t_is, and the input's standard deviations σ_is:

$$\sigma_Y = f(t_1, t_2, \ldots, t_n, \sigma_1, \sigma_2, \ldots, \sigma_n)$$

Plugging the values of σ_i into this equation simplifies the equation so that σ_Y is simply a function of the input's targets:

$$\sigma_Y = f(t_1, t_2, \ldots, t_n)$$

This equation can be examined and plotted to determine how targeting of the inputs affects the variation and to identify the targets that minimize the variation. Two examples have been given previously as part of the heat-seal and hinge case studies.

In the heat-seal case study, the following relationship was found between the four key variables and seal strength:

Seal strength $= -431.35 + 3.933\,\text{HB} + 273.9\,D + 0.03803\,P$

$+\ 0.06120\,\text{MT} - 0.008947\,\text{HB}^2 - 75.72\,D^2 - 0.9640\,\text{HB}\,D$

From this equation, the formula for the squared standard deviation of seal strength is

$$\sigma_{SS}^2 = (3.933\ \sigma_{HB})^2 + (273.9\ \sigma_D)^2 + (0.03803\ \sigma_P)^2 + (0.0612\ \sigma_{MT})^2$$
$$+ (-0.008947)^2\ (4\ t_{HB}^2\ \sigma_{HB}^2 + 2\ \sigma_{HB}^4)$$
$$+ (-75.72)^2\ (4\ t_D^2\ \sigma_D^2 + 2\ \sigma_D^4)$$
$$+ (-0.964)^2\ (\sigma_{HB}^2\ \sigma_D^2 + t_{HB}^2\ \sigma_D^2 + t_D^2\ \sigma_{HB}^2)$$
$$+ 4\ (3.933)\ (-0.008947)\ t_{HB}\ \sigma_{HB}^2 + 4\ (273.9)\ (-75.72)\ t_D\ \sigma_D^2$$
$$+ 2\ (3.933)\ (-0.964)\ t_D\ \sigma_{HB}^2 + 2\ (273.9)\ (-0.964)\ t_{HB}\ \sigma_D^2$$
$$+ 4\ (-0.008947)\ (-0.964)\ t_{HB}\ t_D\ \sigma_{HB}^2$$
$$+ 4\ (-75.72)\ (-0.964)\ t_{HB}\ t_D\ \sigma_D^2$$

The inputs' standard deviations were estimated to be

$$\sigma_{HB} = 2°F$$
$$\sigma_D = 0.08\ s$$
$$\sigma_P = 1\ lb$$
$$\sigma_{MT} = 4°F$$

Plugging these into the above equation gives the following expression for seal-strength standard deviation:

$$\sigma_{SS} = \sqrt{\begin{array}{l} 542.57 - 3.9426\ t_{HB} - 561.27\ t_D + 0.0071622\ t_{HB}^2 \\ + 150.50\ t_D^2 + 2.0067\ t_{HB}\ t_D \end{array}}$$

It is this formula that is required for parameter design. It shows that targeting of only two of the key variables, temperature of the hot bar and dwell time, affects the variation. These two key parameters are called *variation-reducing parameters*. The other two key variables, pressure and material temperature, are *target-adjusting variables*.

The contour plot in Fig. 13.7 shows how targeting of temperature of the hot bar and dwell time affects seal strength. Targeting temperature of the hot bar at 186°F and dwell time at 0.625 s minimizes the variation. Why does targeting of temperature of the hot bar and dwell time affect the variation while targeting of pressure and material variation does not? To understand why, one must first determine which of the inputs are VIPs. In the next section, a method is given for doing this. However, for the time being, assume that it is already known that there is just one VIP, namely dwell time.

Figure 13.8 shows a plot of the effect that dwell time has on seal strength. Setting dwell time to 0.625 makes the process less sensitive to the dwell-time variation, reducing the transmitted variation. Tar-

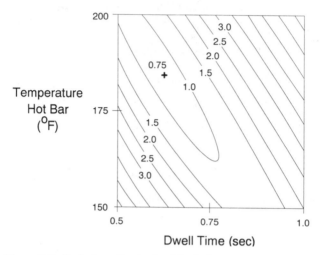

Figure 13.7   Seal-strength standard deviation.

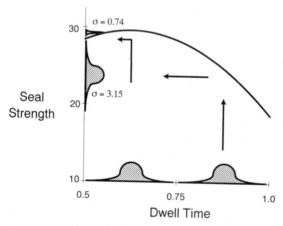

Figure 13.8   Dwell time's effect (HB = 186, P = 100, MT = 90).

geting dwell time affects the variation because of dwell time's quadratic effect. In general, VIPs with nonlinear effects act as VAPs.

Figure 13.9 shows the effect of changing the temperature of the hot bar. Because of the interaction with dwell time, setting the temperature of the hot bar to 186°F makes the process less sensitive to the dwell time, reducing the dwell-time variation transmitted. In general, key input variables that interact with a VIP act as VAPs.

The VAPs are VIPs with nonlinear effects and key input variables

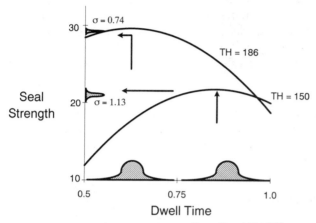

Figure 13.9   Temperature—hot bar's effect (P = 100, MT = 90).

interacting with a VIP. Adjusting the targets of other key input variables will not affect the variation. This is the case with both pressure and material temperature. Both have linear effects so that adjusting their targets does not change the variation that gets transmitted to seal strength. Further, neither interacts with anything else. They, therefore, cannot be used to make the process less sensitive to some other key input variable.

Parameter design identifies the VAPs. It targets them to minimize the variation. Once this has been accomplished, further reductions of the variation require tighter controls on the VIPs. Identifying the VIPs and determining appropriate tolerances is the topic of the next section.

13.5 Tolerance Design

Tolerance design is performed after parameter design. The purpose of tolerance design is to select tolerances for each of the inputs around the targets selected during parameter design. As part of parameter design, an equation for the standard deviation of the output was derived. This equation expresses the standard deviation of the output σ_Y as a function of the input's targets t_is and the input's standard deviations σ_is:

$$\sigma_Y = f(t_1, t_2, \ldots, t_n, \sigma_1, \sigma_2, \ldots, \sigma_n)$$

Plugging the values of t_i into this equation simplifies the equation so that σ_Y is simply a function of the input's standard deviations:

$$\sigma_Y = f(\sigma_1, \sigma_2, \ldots, \sigma_n)$$

This equation can be examined to determine how the standard deviations of the individual inputs contribute to the overall variation. The primary objective is to identify the VIPs and tighten their tolerances in order to reduce variation. However, at the same time tolerances on non-VIPs should be relaxed to reduce costs. Two examples of tolerance design have been given previously as part of the heat-seal and hinge case studies.

The first step in tolerance design is to identify the VIPs. This requires computing the amount of variation in the output contributed by each of the individual inputs. The transmitted contribution of an individual input σ_{ti}, is

$$\sigma_{t1} = \sqrt{f(\sigma_1, \sigma_2, \ldots, \sigma_n)^2 - f(0, \sigma_2, \ldots, \sigma_n)^2}$$

$$\sigma_{t2} = \sqrt{f(\sigma_1, \sigma_2, \ldots, \sigma_n)^2 - f(\sigma_1, 0, \ldots, \sigma_n)^2}$$

$$\ldots$$

$$\sigma_{tn} = \sqrt{f(\sigma_1, \sigma_2, \ldots, \sigma_n)^2 - f(\sigma_1, \sigma_2, \ldots, 0)^2}$$

These standard deviations of the input's transmitted variation can be ranked and plotted in a Pareto chart in order to determine the largest contributions. Those inputs with the largest σ_{ti}s are the VIPs.

As a simple example, assume:

$$Y = -40 + 0.8 X_1 + 8 X_2 - 0.32 X_2^2$$

where initially $\sigma_1 = 0.2$

$\qquad\qquad \sigma_2 = 1.0$

Then the standard deviation of Y is

$$\sigma_Y = \sqrt{0.64 \, \sigma_1^2 + 64 \, \sigma_2^2 + 0.1024 \, (4 \, t_2^2 \, \sigma_2^2 + 2 \, \sigma_2^4) - 10.24 \, t_2 \, \sigma_2^2}$$

Based on the above equation, setting $t_2 = 12.5$ minimizes the standard deviation of Y over the region of study: $10 \le X_1 \le 20$ and $5 \le X_2 \le 15$. X_2 is a VAP. Plugging in 12.5 for t_2 simplifies the previous equation to

$$\sigma_Y = \sqrt{0.64 \, \sigma_1^2 + 0.2048 \, \sigma_2^4}$$

$$= f(\sigma_1, \sigma_2)$$

This is the equation required for tolerance design. Using this equation, the total variation transmitted by the two inputs is $f(0.2, 1.0) = 0.48$. The contributions to this total of each of the inputs are

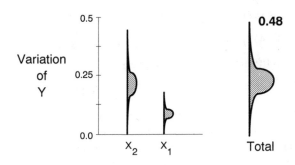

Figure 13.10   Transmitted variation.

$$\sigma_{t1} = \sqrt{f(0.2, 1.0)^2 - f(0, 1.0)^2}$$

$$= 0.16$$

$$\sigma_{t2} = \sqrt{f(0.2, 1.0)^2 - f(0.2, 0)^2}$$

$$= 0.4525$$

A good way of summarizing the results is in a Pareto chart as in Fig. 13.10. Clearly X_2 is causing the majority of the variation. X_2 is the VIP.

How are the transmitted variations of the individual inputs related to the total transmitted variation? In this particular case, the following relationship holds:

$$\sigma_Y = \sqrt{\sigma_{t1}^2 + \sigma_{t2}^2} \qquad \text{or} \qquad \sigma_Y^2 = \sigma_{t1}^2 + \sigma_{t2}^2$$

This equation demonstrates a key point: standard deviations do not add. The total standard deviation is not a simple sum of the individual standard deviations. Instead, the inputs' transmitted standard deviations must be squared before adding and then the square root taken at the end. This serves to magnify the contribution of those inputs with the largest transmitted standard deviations making it doubly important to concentrate on the VIPs. The above relationship only holds when no interactions are present. To look at how interactions complicate matters, let us turn to the heat-seal case study.

Using the equation resulting from the response surface study, the following formula for the standard deviation of seal strength was derived:

$$\sigma_{SS}^2 = (3.933\, \sigma_{HB})^2 + (273.9\, \sigma_D)^2 + (0.03803\, \sigma_P)^2 + (0.0612\, \sigma_{MT})^2$$

$$+ (-0.008947)^2\, (4\, t_{HB}^2\, \sigma_{HB}^2 + 2\, \sigma_{HB}^4)$$

$$+ (-75.72)^2\, (4\, t_D^2\, \sigma_D^2 + 2\, \sigma_D^4)$$

$$+ (-0.964)^2\, (\sigma_{HB}^2\, \sigma_D^2 + t_{HB}^2\, \sigma_D^2 + t_D^2\, \sigma_{HB}^2)$$

$$+ 4\,(3.933)\,(-0.008947)\,t_{HB}\,\sigma_{HB}^2 + 4\,(273.9)\,(-75.72)\,t_D\,\sigma_D^2$$

$$+ 2\,(3.933)\,(-0.964)\,t_D\,\sigma_{HB}^2 + 2\,(273.9)\,(-0.964)\,t_{HB}\,\sigma_D^2$$

$$+ 4\,(-0.008947)\,(-0.964)\,t_{HB}\,t_D\,\sigma_{HB}^2$$

$$+ 4\,(-75.72)\,(-0.964)\,t_{HB}\,t_D\,\sigma_D^2$$

During parameter design, it was determined that targeting of temperature of the hot bar at 186°F and dwell time at 0.625 s minimizes the transmitted variation. Plugging these values into the equation above allows the expression for the standard deviation of seal strength to be reduced to:

$$\sigma_{SS} = \sqrt{\begin{array}{l} 0.000004292\,\sigma_{HB}^2 + 0.003906\,\sigma_D^2 + 0.001446\,\sigma_P^2 \\ + 0.003745\,\sigma_{MT}^2 + 0.0001601\,\sigma_{HB}^4 + 11467\,\sigma_D^4 + 0.9293\,\sigma_{HB}^2\,\sigma_D^2 \end{array}}$$

$$= f\,(\sigma_{HB},\,\sigma_{HB},\,\sigma_{HB},\,\sigma_{HB})$$

The standard deviations of the inputs are

$$\sigma_{HB} = 2°F$$
$$\sigma_D = 0.08\ s$$
$$\sigma_P = 1\ lb$$
$$\sigma_{MT} = 4°F$$

Therefore, the standard deviation of the total transmitted variation is $f(2, 0.08, 1, 4) = 0.75$. The variation transmitted by the individual inputs is

$$\sigma_{tHB} = \sqrt{f\,(2, 0.08, 1, 4)^2 - f\,(0, 0.08, 1, 4)^2}$$

$$= 0.162$$

$$\sigma_{tD} = \sqrt{f\,(2, 0.08, 1, 4)^2 - f\,(2, 0, 1, 4)^2}$$

$$= 0.702$$

$$\sigma_{tP} = \sqrt{f\,(2, 0.08, 1, 4)^2 - f\,(2, 0.08, 0, 4)^2}$$

$$= 0.038$$

$$\sigma_{tMT} = \sqrt{f\,(2, 0.08, 1, 4)^2 - f\,(2, 0.08, 1, 0)^2}$$

$$= 0.245$$

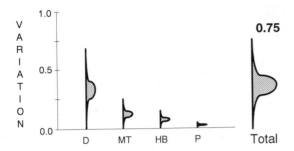

Figure 13.11 Transmitted variation (HB = 186, D = 0.625).

The Pareto chart is given in Fig. 13.11. Clearly dwell time is the largest contributor and thus the VIP. How do the σ_{ti}s relate to σ_{SS}? The equation below gives this relationship:

$$\sigma_{SS} = \sqrt{\sigma_{tHB}^2 + \sigma_{tD}^2 + \sigma_{tP}^2 + \sigma_{tMT}^2 - 0.9293 \, \sigma_{HB}^2 \, \sigma_D^2}$$

The extra term, $-0.9293 \, \sigma_{HB}^2 \, \sigma_D^2$, is small compared to the rest of the expression. Therefore, even though interactions are present, a good approximation for σ_{SS} is

$$\sigma_{SS} \approx \sqrt{\sigma_{tHB}^2 + \sigma_{tD}^2 + \sigma_{tP}^2 + \sigma_{tMT}^2}$$

$$= 0.76$$

Identifying the VIPs is just the first step of tolerance design. The next step is to set tolerances for the key inputs. The VIPs represent the key inputs whose tolerances are critical. These VIP tolerances must be left as they are to obtain the current variation or must be tightened to reduce the variation. One should also consider loosening the tolerances on non-VIPs in order to reduce costs.

For any proposed modifications to the tolerances, new σ_{ti}s can be specified and the resulting change in variation calculated. For example, to determine the effect of cutting the dwell-time tolerance in half requires calculating the resulting transmitted variation:

$$\sigma_{SS} = f(2, 0.04, 1, 4) = 0.32$$

The result is

$$100 \, (0.75 - 0.32)/0.75 = 57\% \text{ reduction in the variation}$$

A Pareto chart of the contributions of the individual inputs can be obtained for this new set of tolerances to determine how to improve even further. The results are shown in Fig. 13.12. Material tempera-

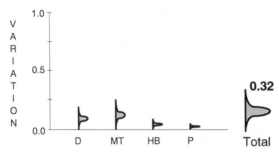

Figure 13.12 Transmitted variation after reducing dwell-time variation.

ture is now the VIP. Further reductions in the variation require reducing the transmitted variation of material temperature. One can explore a variety of different tolerances before selecting one.

13.6 Summary

Two approaches to identifying VIPs

When using the strategy of studying the inputs' effect, there are two approaches to identifying VIPs:

1. *Direct observation.* The effect that changes of the inputs have on the variation of the output is observed directly.

2. *Variation transmission analysis.* The variation transmitted by the inputs to the output can be calculated based on the relationship between the inputs and the outputs and on estimates of the variations of the individual inputs.

Variation of a polynomial

The variation of quadratic polynomials can be derived in a straightforward manner.

Approximating the variation

The variation of any function can be accurately approximated by using the second-order Taylor series expansion approach presented.

Parameter design

During parameter design, targets for each of the inputs are selected. The variation transmission approach to parameter design requires an equation describing the relationship between the inputs and the outputs, and information on the amount that each input varies.

The variation transmission approach to parameter design consists of determining the equation describing the variation of the output in terms of the input's targets and standard deviations, plugging the estimates of the input's standard deviations into this equation, plotting the effects of the input's targets on the output standard deviation, and selecting the targets that minimize the output standard deviation.

Inputs whose targets affect the output variation are called variation adjustment parameters or VAPs. They are either VIPs with nonlinear effects, or key input variables that interact with a VIP.

Tolerance design

During tolerance design, tolerances are determined for each of the inputs. The variation transmission approach to tolerance design consists of plugging the input's targets determined during parameter design into the equation describing the variation of the output in terms of the input's targets and standard deviations, identifying the VIPs by Pareto charting the total variation and the contributions of the individual inputs, tightening tolerances on VIPs in order to reduce variation, and loosening tolerances on non-VIPs to reduce costs.

14

The Direct
Approach

14.1 Measuring Transmitted Variation
Directly

An alternative to the variation transmission approach is to measure the variation directly. In its simplest form, this requires running screening experiments and response surface studies using the standard deviation* as a *response variable*.

Take as an example the heat-seal case study. On each setup, ten samples were measured. The averages of these ten samples were calculated and analyzed in order to determine the key input variables. At the same time the standard deviations of these samples were also calculated and analyzed. Both dwell time and temperature of the hot bar (through the interaction) tested as significant. Adjusting these two variables can change the variation. They are therefore VAPs.

This approach is very appealing, both in the ease of application and the fact that additional data are not required. The analysis involves analyzing the standard deviation just as one would analyze the average. No new method of analysis is required as is the case with variation transmission analysis. Further, nothing is required beyond the data collected in order to analyze the average. One may already have data sets collected to analyze the average. They can simply be reanalyzed looking at the standard deviation. However, despite this appeal, the direct approach has several major drawbacks:

1. The variation observed during the course of the study may not be indicative of the variation present during actual usage or production

---

*Actually, for statistical reasons, the log of the standard deviation should be analyzed.

conditions. Generally, the variation during the course of study is smaller than the full range that will be experienced later. This can result in missing VAPs.

2. The direct approach only identifies VAPs and helps to target them to minimize the variation (parameter design). The direct approach cannot isolate the contributions of individual inputs required for tolerance design.

3. The direct approach is generally limited to detecting VAPs that can be used to obtain 50 percent reductions or greater. VAPs that can effect 20 or 30 percent reductions frequently go undetected.

Despite these limitations, using the direct approach is certainly worthwhile. Certainly, as part of any screening experiment or response surface study, the standard deviation should be analyzed as well as the average. The added information is essentially free, as no additional data are required. Any VAPs that are identified can result in valuable improvements.

However, one should not rely solely on direct observation. It is still worthwhile to perform a variation transmission analysis. Frequently, VAPs are identified that are missed by direct observation. Variation transmission analysis can also be used to predict performance under conditions of variation different from the experimental conditions. Further, the variation transmission analysis can be used to perform tolerance design including identifying the VIPs.

The fact that variation transmission analysis can detect VAPs missed by the direct observation may be somewhat surprising. But time after time, performance of a variation transmission analysis following a response surface study where the standard deviation was analyzed, results in additional VAPs being identified. Let us turn to an example to see why. Suppose that:

$$Y = 8.125 - 0.4\,X + 0.185\,X^2 - 0.006\,X^3$$

A plot of the effect of X on Y is shown in Fig. 14.1. The variation of Y is approximately

$$\sigma_Y = \sqrt{(-0.4 + 0.37\,t_X - 0.018\,t_X^2)^2\,\sigma_X^2 + \frac{(0.37 - 0.036\,t_X)^2\,\sigma_X^4}{2}}$$

Further assume that $\sigma_X = 0.2$. A plot of the effect of t_X on σ_Y is shown in Fig. 14.2. The standard deviation of Y is 0.2001 when $t_X = 5$, 0.2725 when t_X is 7.5, and 0.3000 when $t_X = 10$. Adjusting t_X from 10 down to 5 reduces the standard deviation by 0.0999 or 33 percent. In addition, the effect of t_X on the standard deviation of Y is nonlinear.

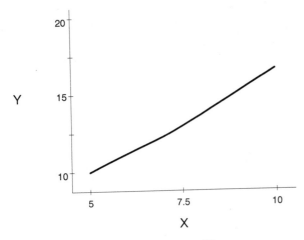

Figure 14.1   Effect of input X on output Y.

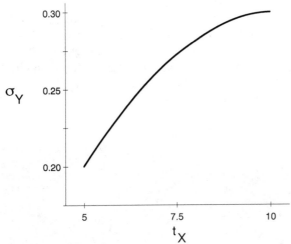

Figure 14.2   Effect of t_X on σ_Y.

The sizes of the true linear and quadratic effects are

$$\text{True linear effect} = 0.3000 - 0.2001 = 0.0999$$

$$\text{True quadratic effect} = 0.2725 - (0.2001 + 0.3000)/2 = 0.02245$$

Now suppose one wanted to estimate the effect of t_X on the variation of Y by direct observation. One way of doing this would be to take ten samples when $t_X = 5$, ten more samples when $t_X = 7.5$, and a final set

TABLE 14.1 Data for Estimating Effect of X on Variation of Y

	Target of X		
	5	7.5	10
Values	10.36	13.40	16.55
	10.07	13.43	16.91
	10.14	13.17	16.92
	10.28	13.28	16.64
	9.71	13.34	16.67
	10.19	13.30	16.55
	10.05	13.08	16.68
	9.98	13.13	17.10
	10.37	12.57	17.04
	9.91	12.78	16.74
Average	10.11	13.15	16.78
Std. Dev.	0.208	0.278	0.199

of ten samples when $t_X = 10$. For each group of ten samples, the standard deviations could be calculated and used to estimate the effect of t_X on σ_Y. One such data set is given in Table 14.1. A plot of the standard deviations is shown in Fig. 14.3 along with the true values. These standard deviations vary widely around the true values. This demonstrates the inaccuracy involved in estimating standard deviations with small sample sizes.

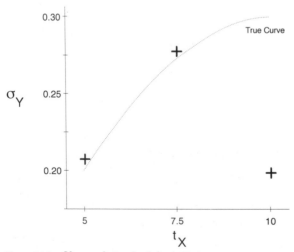

Figure 14.3 Observed standard deviations.

Based on the above data, the observed linear and quadratic effects of adjusting t_X are

$$\text{Observed linear effect} = 0.199 - 0.208 = -0.009$$

$$\text{Observed quadratic effect} = 0.278 - (0.208 + 0.199)/2 = 0.0745$$

Also collected were 99 additional sets of similar data. The 100 estimates of the linear and quadratic effects are shown in the histograms in Fig. 14.4. Both histograms have a wide range overlapping zero. As a result of the poor estimates of the standard deviations, these observed effects are also poor estimates of the true linear and quadratic effects. Using direct observation, the effect of t_X on σ_Y cannot be reliably estimated or even demonstrated to exist.

An alternate approach to estimating the effect of t_X on the standard deviation of Y is to first estimate the relationship between X and Y and then use the variation transmission approach to estimate σ_Y. The best-fit curve to the data in Table 14.1 is

$$Y = 5.7755 + 0.63181X + 0.046859X^2$$

This best-fit curve is shown in Fig. 14.5 along with the true curve. There is some lack of fit due to variation in the data and the fact that the true cubic polynomial is being approximated by a quadratic polynomial.

In addition, an estimate of σ_X is required. So in addition to the data

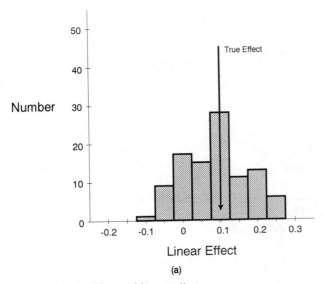

Figure 14.4 (a) Observed linear effects.

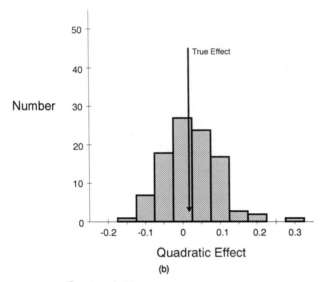

Quadratic Effect

(b)

Figure 14.4 (*Continued*) Observed quadratic effects.

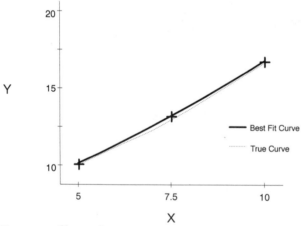

X

Figure 14.5   Observed averages.

collected above, 50 measurements of X were taken and the standard deviation calculated. The resulting estimate of σ_X is 0.1704. Using these results, the standard deviation of Y can be estimated as follows:

$$\sigma_Y = \sqrt{\begin{array}{l}(0.63181)^2\, \sigma_X^2 + (0.046859)^2\,(4\, t_X^2\, \sigma_X^2 + 2\, \sigma_X^4) \\ + 4\,(0.63181)(0.046859)\, t_X\, \sigma_X^2\end{array}}$$

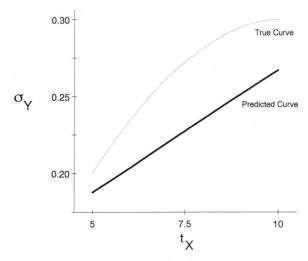

Figure 14.6 Predicted standard deviations.

The predicted effect of t_X on σ_Y is shown in Fig. 14.6. Once again, there is some lack of fit due to variation in the data and the fact that the true cubic polynomial is being approximated by a quadratic polynomial. Evaluating the estimate of σ_Y gives 0.1875 at t_X = 5, 0.2274 at t_X = 7.5, and 0.2674 at t_X = 10. Using these results the predicted linear and quadratic effects can be calculated as follows:

Predicted linear effect = 0.2674 − 0.1875 = 0.0799

Predicted quadratic effect = 0.2274 − (0.1875 + 0.2674)/2 = −0.00005

The same 99 additional sets of data used to construct the histograms in Fig. 14.4 were also analyzed using the variation transmission approach. In addition, new estimates of σ_X were obtained for each data set. The 100 estimates of the linear and quadratic effects are shown in the histograms in Fig. 14.7. Using the variation transmission analysis approach, the spread of the histograms is much narrower. The linear histogram does not overlap zero indicating the linear effect can be reliably detected. This example demonstrates the ability of the variation transmission approach to identify VAPs using the same data where direct observation failed to detect the parameter. It also points out several other considerations.

With sample sizes of 10 per trial, direct observation can only reliably detect VAPs that can be used to reduce the variation by at least 50 percent. Smaller effects can be detected using direct observation if larger samples of 50 to 100 per trial are taken. This will generally allow VAPs to be detected that can reduce the variation by at least 30

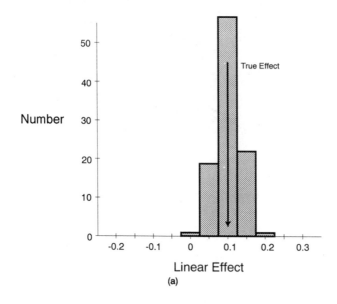

Linear Effect

(a)

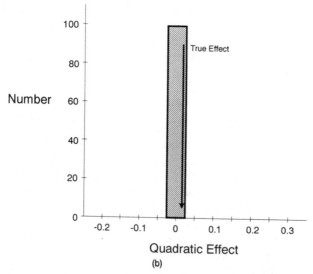

Quadratic Effect

(b)

Figure 14.7   (a) Predicted linear effects; (b) predicted quadratic effects.

percent. However, in both cases, the variation transmission analysis can still detect even smaller effects. The example also points out a weakness of variation transmission analysis. The analysis is only as good as the equation used. It is important to perform lack-of-fit tests during response surface studies to avoid biasing of the estimates. However, despite this biasing, in most cases the biased estimates of the variation transmission analysis will be far better than the unbiased, but more variable estimates obtained by direct observation.

Another weakness of the variation transmission analysis is that it is also dependent upon estimates of the standard deviations of the various inputs. The analysis is only as good as these estimates. However, the variation transmission analysis is no worse off than direct observation. To work best, direct observation requires that the variation during the course of the study be representative of the full range of variation of the inputs. Generally, the variation during the study will be less than this. At least variation transmission analysis allows screening experiments and response surface studies to be run over short periods of time, while the estimates of the standard deviations of the inputs can be collected over a more extended and more representative period of time.

14.2 The Noise-Array Approach

An improvement on the direct-observation approach requires the use of *noise arrays*. Instead of relying on the variation of the inputs during the study to be representative of the full range of actual conditions, a noise array can be used to purposely vary the inputs by an amount proportional to their actual variation. This approach is especially valuable when dealing with usage variation, variation due to deterioration, or faced with the "closer to the target function the better" situation.

Example 1

In designing a copier it is necessary that the copier continue to work well under a variety of usage conditions including varying weights of paper, changing temperatures, and changing humidity. A screening experiment was being designed to explore the effect that the design parameters of a particular component have on copy quality. Rather than include these three usage factors as inputs to be varied during the screening experiment, it was decided to include them in a separate noise array. This noise array is shown in Table 14.2.

The screening experiment, without the three usage factors, requires that 16 prototypes of this component be constructed, each with different combinations of the design parameters. Then each prototype should be tested under all the combinations of the usage factors given in the noise array. For each prototype, the average and standard deviations of the four readings should be calculated. These standard de-

TABLE 14.2 Copier Noise Array

TRIALS	INPUTS		
	Paper Weight	Temperature	Humidity
1	5/16	100	95
2	7/16	50	95
3	7/16	100	30
4	5/16	50	30

viations measure the robustness of the design to the usage factors. Small values are preferred. They should be analyzed as any other output.

Example 2

A pump is being designed that is subject to wear. It is important to design the pump to minimize the effect of wear. To measure wear, the noise array given in Table 14.3 was used. Each prototype design was tested according to the noise array. The difference between the initial performance and final performance measures the robustness of the design to wear. Small values are preferable. These differences can be analyzed just like any other output.

Example 3

Continuing with the pump in Example 2, it is also desirable to make the pump as accurate as possible. Since the pump volume is adjustable by the user, this fits the "closer to the target function the better" situation. A constant bias between the knob setting and the delivered

TABLE 14.3 Pump Wear Noise Array

TRIALS	INPUTS
	Age of Pump
1	0 hours
2	2000 hours

TABLE 14.4   Pump Adjustment Noise Array

TRIALS	INPUTS
	Set Delivery Rate
1	10 ml/min
2	15 ml/min
3	20 ml/min

volume can be easily adjusted through calibration. The main concern is that the relationship between the knob setting and the delivered volume be linear. To measure the linearity of this relationship, the noise matrix shown in Table 14.4 was run. Each prototype was tested according to the noise matrix and the resulting linearity calculated as follows:

$$\text{Linearity measure} = x_{15} - \frac{(x_{10} + x_{20})}{2}$$

Here x_{10} represents the result of trial 1, x_{15} represents the result of trial 2, and x_{20} represents the result of trial 3. Small values of this linearity measure signify a linear relationship. This linearity measure can be analyzed just like any other output.

Noise arrays can be set up in numerous ways and analyzed using a variety of measures of goodness. Taguchi provides a variety of measures of goodness covering a wide variety of situations which he calls *signal-to-noise ratios*. The lesson in these examples is that almost any desired property of the product or process can be measured and thus studied through the construction of noise arrays and measures of goodness. The construction of these noise arrays and measures of goodness is beyond the scope of this book.

Changes in the factors included in the noise array are carefully controlled. Making these changes proportional to the actual variation ensures that the variation of the noise factors is representative of actual conditions. However, even better is to make these changes even larger than the actual variation to magnify the effects one is trying to detect. Further, tolerance design can be performed on the factors included in the noise array. Noise arrays can help overcome many of the problems associated with the direct-observation approach.

There is, however, one very severe restriction on noise arrays. So long as the noise array only includes usage factors, wear over time, and user-adjustable parameters, the noise array is essentially a test array. The number of prototypes or process setups required is determined by the screening experiment or response surface study. If, however, one were to include a design parameter, material property, process parameter, and so on, in the noise array, the noise array would require multiple prototypes or setups for each screening-experiment trial. The total number of prototypes or setups would equal the number of screening-experiment trials times the number of trials in the noise array. These types of studies are generally prohibitively expensive to run. Variation transmission analysis can achieve the same results with only one prototype or setup per screening-experiment trial.

14.3 Summary

Measuring transmitted variation directly

Directly measuring the variation requires that the standard deviation be calculated for each trial and analyzed. Direct measurement of the variation has several drawbacks:

1. The variation observed during the study may not be representative of the full range of variation experienced in actual usage and production conditions. Using the variation transmission approach, estimates of the input's variation can be obtained over extended periods of time. Different values can even be tried to explore different scenarios.

2. The direct approach only identifies VAPs. It can, therefore, only be used for parameter design. The variation transmission approach can also be used to identify VIPs allowing tolerance design to be performed.

3. The direct approach has limited ability to detect VAPs. For ten samples per trial, only VAPs capable of 50 percent reductions in the variation can be detected. Using the same data, the variation transmission analysis can detect other VAPs capable of as small as 25 percent reductions in the variation.

Despite these drawbacks, the standard deviations should always be analyzed in addition to the averages. Any insight gained is essentially free and may result in significant improvements. However, direct observation does not eliminate the need for performing a variation transmission analysis.

The noise-array approach

Many of the drawbacks of the direct-observation approach can be overcome by noise arrays. Inputs are purposely varied in the noise arrays.

These inputs can be varied in proportion to their actual variation or varied over a much wider range in order to magnify the desired effects.

Noise arrays and measures of goodness can be constructed to study almost any desired characteristic of a product or process. They are generally restricted to usage factors, deterioration over time, and user-adjustment factors. The inclusion of design parameters, material properties, process parameters, and so on, dramatically increase the number of prototypes or setups required, making such studies prohibitively expensive to run.

15

Conclusion

15.1 Conclusion to the Book

The goal of this book is to provide the strategies and tools necessary to optimize products and processes. The goal of optimization is:

> Every unit of product performs exactly as required, every time, for all manners and conditions of use.

This requires both optimizing the average and reducing the variation around this average. An important part of the strategies and tools presented is to achieve this objective at reduced costs.

At the heart of the strategies for optimization is the input/output model (Fig. 15.1). The inputs include design parameters, material properties, process parameters, tooling parameters, methods used, operator skills, environmental factors, usage factors, and measurement errors. The outputs are the key quality and performance characteristics. As part of optimization, one needs to select the targets and tolerances for the inputs that come closest to the objective. Selecting these targets and tolerances requires classifying the inputs into the following categories (Fig. 15.2):

Candidate input variables. Those inputs that might affect the system.

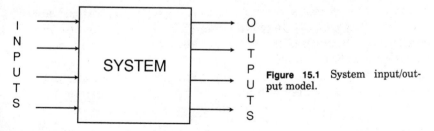

Figure 15.1 System input/output model.

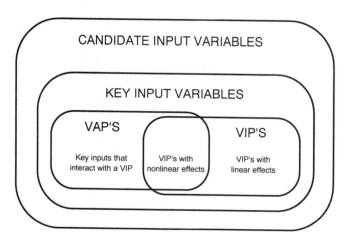

Figure 15.2   Categories of input variables.

Key input variables.   Those inputs that can affect the output, either by affecting the average or by contributing to the variation.

Variation inducing parameters (VIPs).   Those key input variables making significant contributions to the variation of the output.

Variation adjustment parameters (VAPs).   Those key inputs whose targeting affects the transmitted variation.

The input's targets are determined during parameter design. The basic approach is to

- First, set the targets of the VAPs to minimize the variation.
- Next, set the targets of the other key input variables to optimize the average. If more key inputs exist than are required to put the average on target, some may be set to reduce costs. If fewer key inputs exist than are required to put the average on target, compromise targets for the VAPs may be required.
- Finally, set the targets of all other candidate inputs to minimize costs.

Once targets are selected, tolerances around these targets must be determined. This is best accomplished as a separate step called tolerance design. The basic strategy for accomplishing parameter design is to tighten the tolerances of the VIPs to achieve the required reduction in variation and loosen tolerances on non-VIPs to reduce costs.

Making these strategies work requires efficient methods of quickly developing the high degree of understanding required. There are two basic approaches to identifying key input variables, VAPs, and VIPs:

Searching for differences.   Differences over time, streams of products, between units, and within a unit are identified and studied in order to determine the key input responsible for the difference.

Studying the inputs' effects.   Inputs are observed or purposely varied in order to determine their effects on the output.

A summary of the tools used by each of these approaches is given in Table 15.1.

One final tool is in a class of its own: the capability study. After all the other tools have been applied during product design, process development, and manufacturing, the capability study is the one tool that determines whether the objectives have been successfully met. Capability studies measure the quality of the design as well as the quality of the process. Passing the capability study means the process is stable and capable of producing the product. It also means the product has been designed so that it can be produced by the process. Capability studies evaluate the match between product and process.

Optimization requires everyone's cooperation. Targeting and variation are affected by the product design, materials, and process. It requires the different design groups and manufacturing to work together. It also requires the involvement of purchasing and outside suppliers. It even requires the involvement of marketing in determining specification limits and in estimating the amount of variation of the usage factors. As W. Edwards Deming said, "Optimization means cooperation."

TABLE 15.1   The Two Approaches and Their Tools

Searching for Differences	Studying the Inputs' Effects
Control Charts	Scatter Diagrams
Multi-Vari Charts	Screening Experiments
Analysis of Means (ANOM)	Response Surface Studies
Variance Components Analysis	Variation Transmission Analysis
Assembly/Setup Studies	Noise Arrays
Component Swapping Studies	
Unit Comparisons	
Concentration Diagrams	

The benefits of optimization and variation reduction are improved quality, reduced costs, and shorter development times. The methods outlined in this book offer a clear competitive advantage to those that adopt them.

Index

ABOUT THE AUTHOR

Wayne A. Taylor is Director of Quality Technologies for
the IV Systems Division of Baxter Healthcare Corporation
in Round Lake, Illinois, a Fortune 100 leader in its
industry. There he has implemented many of the
innovative techniques and programs described in this book.
His efforts have played an instrumental role in Baxter's
acknowledged reputation for world-class quality. He
received his Ph.D. from Purdue University.